Judi

THE PYTHOUSE RIOTERS

To remind you of Book Club!

Love
Sue

2.12.23

O NCE, ON THIS EARTH, once, on this familiar spot of ground, walked other men and women, as actual as we are today, thinking their own thoughts, swayed by their own passions, but now all gone, one generation vanishing after another, gone as utterly as we ourselves shall shortly be gone like ghosts at cockcrow.

G.M. Trevelyan, An Autobiography and Other Essays

Hold me now	It's a bitter pill	Now kings will rule
Oh hold me now	I swallow here	And the poor will toil
'Til this hour	To be rent	And tear their hands
Has gone around	From one so dear	As they tear the soil
And I'm gone	We fought for justice	But a day will come
On the rising tide	And not for gain	In this dawning age
For to face	But the magistrate	When an honest man
Van Diemen's land	Sent me away	Sees an honest wage

Hold me now
Oh hold me now
'Til this hour
Has gone around
And I'm gone
On the rising tide
For to face
Van Diemen's land

Lyrics from 'Van Diemen's Land' – U2 – from their Album 'Rattle and Hum' 1988
Song writers; Adam Clayton/Dave Evans/Larry Mullen/Paul Hewson

The Pythouse Rioters

from Tisbury to Tasmania

CHRISTINA RICHARD

THE HOBNOB PRESS

First published in the United Kingdom in 2023

by The Hobnob Press,
8 Lock Warehouse, Severn Road, Gloucester GL1 2GA
www.hobnobpress.co.uk

© Christina Richard, 2023

The Author hereby asserts her moral rights to be identified as the Author of the Work.

All rights reserved. No part of this publication may be reproduced, stored in a retrieval system, or transmitted in any form or by any means, electronic, mechanical, photocopying, recording or otherwise, without the prior permission of the publisher and copyright holder.

British Library Cataloguing in Publication Data
A catalogue record for this book is available from the British Library

ISBN 978-1-914407-61-1

Typeset in Minion Pro.
Typesetting and origination by John Chandler

Contents

	With a little help from . . .	vi
	Pythouse Rioters - Who's Who	vii
1	November 1830 (1)	1
2	The Birth of Captain Swing	11
3	More hardships	23
4	'pull down your messhines'	30
5	November 1830 (2)	41
6	The Full Panoply	54
7	The Visitations of Providence	64
8	Setting an Example	75
9	Overspill and the Criminal-Waste-Management System	85
10	Heroes? – the Landlords	98
11	Influencers and bloggers	107
12	An Organiser and a Windbag	114
13	John Benett – Anti-Hero?	126
14	Planned or spontaneous?	139
15	The Garden of Eden?	146
16	'Servants of the crown'	158
17	Roped to the Plough	169
18	Brave boys	177
19	'gallant poachers'	188
20	The Intrepid Jerrards	198
21	Successful Settlers	207
22	Habitat	220
23	Red herrings and loose ends	231
24	Aftermath	241
25	A Changing Society	249
	Notes and References	262
	Bibliography	270
	Index of Names and Places	273

With a little help from . . .

I NEED TO THANK Ray Simpson both for reading the whole text and for providing me with relevant cuttings from all sorts of newspapers and periodicals. Liz Curzen, Nicky Bartlett and Jane Hanbidge also ploughed through the book and suggested little changes - thank you all. Steve Toomer introduced me to the joys of metal detecting, providing me with some of the original musket balls fired at the time of the riot by the Hindon Troop of the Wiltshire yeomanry and insight into the possible firing lines. Ruth Dresman drew the heading for the first chapter – John Benett in his cabriolet - drawing convincing horses being quite beyond my capabilities. Thank you Ruth, and Steve. Tisbury History Archive provided some useful written work by previous local historians, including Dr Mary Dalton's monograph on the riots, which inspired me originally. But most of all I need to acknowledge the work of Jill Chambers compiler of the Wiltshire Machine Breakers Volumes 1 and 11, whose work on the Swing Riots is unsurpassed – my book covers a very small number of the rioters and places involved, but she has researched the whole episode in full. Without her incredible research I could not have written this book.

Finally, a big thank you to Mike, my lovely husband, who sadly didn't live long enough to see it published.

Christina Richard,
September 2023

Pythouse Rioters – Who's Who

ABREE, (Abery, Albury, Abrey) William	Stonemason, working at Wardour
A'COURT, Colonel Charles	Assistant Poor Law Commissioner
ALDERSON, Mr Justice Edward Hall	Special Commissioner
ALFORD, Samuel	Tenant farmer, Withyslade Farm
ANDERSON, William	Surgeon Superintendent, 'Eliza'
ANSTEY, Thomas	Settler, VDL, Anstey Park, Oatlands
ARTHUR, George	Lt. Governor VDL 1824
ARUNDELL, James Everard, 10th Earl of	Landowner, Wardour Estate
AXFORD, Thomas	Settler, VDL, Thorpe Farm, Bothwell
BALL, Thomas	Mr Benett's coachman at Pythouse
BANSTONE (Macey) Samuel	Agricultural Labourer, Fonthill Gifford
BARKER, Thomas	Mill owner, Sydney, NSW
BARRETT, John	Agricultural labourer/mason East Hatch
BARRETT, Samuel	Agricultural labourer, Ansty
BECKFORD, William	Landowner, Fonthill Estate
BENETT, John, MP	Landowner, Pythouse Estate
BENETT, Lucy nee Lambert	Wife of John Benett, Pythouse
Von BIBRA family	Settlers, VDL, Coburg near Cressy
BIRT (Burt, Burke) Thomas	Top Sawyer, Fonthill Gifford
BISDEE, John	Settler VDL Hutton Park: Gov. Hobart Town Gaol
BISHTON, Rev.	Settler VDL, Westbury, Launceston
BLANDFORD, James	Ploughman, Tisbury
BOWEN, John	Commander first VDL settlers
BOYES, G W T	Settler and diarist, VDL
BRADLEY, Michael	Agricultural Labourer, Chilmark
BRADY, Matthew	Bushranger, VDL
BRASHER, John	Mill Owner, Wilton
BRASHER, Samuel	Son of above mill owner, Wilton
BRICKELL, (Brickle) John	Carter for Mr Benett, Pythouse
BRINE, James	Tolpuddle 'martyr'
BRISTOW, Henry	Parish Overseer Wiltshire, Tisbury
BROTHERTON, Col.	Army officer in charge of security for

	Warminster
BROWNE, Rev. Dr	Evangelical Minister, Launceston VDL
BRUMBY family	Settlers, VDL, Cressy
BURTON, John	Agricultural Labourer, Tisbury
BUXTON, Thomas	Settler, VDL at Little Swan Port
CANDY, Mr	Tenant farmer, Fonthill Gifford
CARLILE, Richard	Publisher, and radical thinker, London
CHEVERILL, James	Potter and labourer, Ridge Farm
COBBETT, William	Radical Journalist, MP for Oldham
COCK, Captain Robert	Master, 'Eleanor'
COCKBURN, James	Gardener for Mr Benett at Pythouse
COLLINS, David	First Lt. Gov. VDL
COOMBES, James	Tenant Farmer, Wardour
CUFF, James	Employer of Thomas Rixon
DANIELL, William	Methodist Minister, Warminster
DAVEY, Thomas	Second Lt. Gov. VDL
DIDDAMS, Enoch	Publican and political reformist, Hampshire
DOGGRELL, James	Mr Benett's farm bailiff at Pythouse
DOGGRELL, Noah	Gamekeeper for Mr Benett at Ruddlemoor Farm
DUKE, John	Mr Benett's employee at Pythouse
DUNDAS, Charles	MPO for Newbury, Berkshire
ESTCOURT, T G B	Special Commissioner
EYRES, Samuel	Agricultural Labourer, Tisbury
FARQUHAR, John	Landowner, Fonthill Abbey
FORD, John	Agricultural Labourer at Pythouse East Hatch
FOYLE, James	Edmund White's neighbour, Course Street Tisbury
FRANKLAND, Mr	Surveyor, VDL
GLOVER, John	Settler and artist, VDL
GRAY, William	Agricultural Labourer, Tisbury
GREEN, James	Agricultural Labourer, Tisbury
GREEN, James	Resident of Crown Street, Westminster
GREY, Earl	Whig, Prime Minister
GROVE, Charlotte	Ferne House, Donhead, daughter of Thomas Grove
GROVE, Harriet	Ferne House, Donhead, daughter of Thomas Grove
GROVE, Thomas	Landowner, Ferne House, Donhead
GROVE, Thomas	Son of Thomas Grove, Ferne House
GROVES, Captain John	Ship's Master. 'Eliza'
GUNN, William	Settler, VDL, Old Beach, Sorell and Superintendent, Prison Barracks, Hobart
HAMMETT, James	Tolpuddle 'martyr'
HARDING, John	Agricultural Labourer, East Knoyle
HAWKINS, Lt.	Settler, VDL, Little Swan Port

HONE, William	Satirist
HOWICK, Viscount	Under Secretary of State for War
HUNT, Henry	Radical politician and MP for Preston
JAY, James	Mr Benett's Farm Bailiff, Linley Farm
JAY, John	Tenant farmer, Linley Farm
JAY, Thomas	Farm Bailiff, Fonthill Gifford Farm
JEFFREY, William	Bailiff to Lord Arundell
JENNINGS, John	Labourer, Wilton
JERRARD, Charles, senior	Agricultural Labourer, Tisbury
JERRARD, Charles, junior	Carter, Tisbury
JOLIFFE, Rev.	Curate, Barton Stacey, Hampshire
JUKES, John	Mr Benett's employee at Pythouse
KEMP, Anthony Fenn	Entrepreneur and settler, VDL
KING, Augustine	William Snook's employer
KING, Henry	Landowner, Chilmark
LAMBERT, James	Gentleman, Hatch
LAMPARD, James	Tenant farmer, Lawn
LANSDOWNE, Marquess of	Lord Lt. for Wiltshire
LEGGE, Arthur	Steward for Mr Benett at Pythouse
LOVELESS, George	Tolpuddle 'martyr'
LOVELESS, James	Tolpuddle 'martyr'
LUSH, James	Agricultural Labourer, Bishopstone
MACEY, Charlotte	Wife of Samuel Banstone (Macey) Fonthill Gifford
MACQUARIE, Lachlan	Governor, New South Wales, Australia
MAIR, Lt. Col. John Hastings	Army Officer, responsible for security, Salisbury
MARTIN, Charles	Agricultural Labourer, Tisbury
MARTIN, Elizabeth	Wife of Charles, sister of Thomas Vinen
MASON, Joseph	Agricultural Labourer, Barton Stacey, Hants
MASON, Robert	Agricultural Labourer, brother of Joseph Martin
MELBOURNE, William Lamb, 2nd Viscount	Home Secretary
MORRISON, James	Landowner, Fonthill Estate
MOULD, George	Agricultural Labourer, Wardour Estate
MOULD, James	Agricultural Labourer, Hatch,
MOULD, James	Ploughman/agricultural labourer, Tisbury
MOXHAM, Andrew	Agricultural Labourer, West Tisbury
OBOURNE, (Osbourne) Henry	Agricultural Labourer, Tisbury
OBOURNE, Robert	Agricultural Labourer, Tisbury
PALMER, Samuel	Artist
PARKE, Mr Justice J	Special Commissioner
PENISTON, John	Salisbury architect and Lt. in Wiltshire Yeomanry
PENNY, John	Agricultural Labourer, Ridge, Tisbury
PHILLIPS, Thomas	Agricultural Labourer

PITMAN, Richard	Kitchen gardener, Tisbury
PREVOST, The Rev. Thomas	Vicar St John the Baptist Church, Tisbury
RADNOR, Lord	Estate owner, Downton, Salisbury
REBBECK, Richard	Owner, Totterdale Farm, Tisbury
RIXON (Rixen), Thomas	Carter, Tisbury
SANGER, William	Agricultural Labourer, Tisbury
SCOTT, William	Agricultural Labourer, Quarry, East Tisbury
SELF (Selfe) Henry	Tenant Farmer, Fonthill Bishop
SNOOK William	Ploughman, Tisbury
SNOW, James	Mr Benett's employee, Pythouse estate
SORELL, William	Third Lt. Gov. VDL
SPODE, Josiah	Settler, VDL, Superintendent Prisoners' Barracks
STANFIELD, James	Tolpuddle 'martyr'
STANFIELD, Thomas	Tolpuddle 'martyr'
STEPHENSON, John	Surgeon Superintendent 'Eleanor'
STINGEMAN (Stingiman, Stingimore) Thomas	Agricultural Labourer, Tisbury
SWING, Captain	Name given to rioting agricultural labourers
TABART, Francis Gerard	Settler, Fonthill House, Andover VDL
TABOR, John	Licensee Beckford Arms Fonthill Gifford and settler, Longley Arms Inn, Hobart VDL
TALBOT family	Malahide Castle, Fingal and Malahide, Launceston VDL
TALLENTS, William Edward	Lawyer for the Crown
TARGETT, James	Labourer, Hindon
TARGETT, John	Agricultural Labourer, Fonthill Bishop
TARGETT, Thomas	Agricultural Labourer, Hindon
TASMAN, Abel	Founder, Dutch, VDL/Tasmania
TOPP, Jeremiah	Agricultural Labourer, Fonthill Bishop
TOPP, Thomas	Ploughman, Fonthill Bishop
TRIM, Joseph	Carpenter for Mr Benett at Pythouse Estate
TURNER, John	Tenant farmer, Hatch, Parish Overseer
TURNER, George	Gamekeeper for Mr Benett at Pythouse
TURNER, William	Agricultural labourer, Pythouse employee
TURNER, William	Young boy, member of Turner family
UPHILL, John	Shepherd, Pythouse estate
VAUGHAN, Baron	Special Commissioner
VINCENT, Jonathan	Blacksmith, Fonthill Gifford
VINEN (Viney, Vining) family	Harriet Obourne, Elizabeth Martin, Mary Vinen, Thomas Vinen, Henry Vinen, Jean Moxham
VINEN, (Viney, Vining) Henry	Agricultural Labourer, Tisbury
VINEN (Viney, Vining), Thomas	Agricultural Labourer, Tisbury
WELLINGTON, Duke of	Tory Prime Minister
WENTWORTH, Captain D'arcy	Settler, Commandant Bothwell Barracks, VDL

WHITE, Edmund	Blacksmith, Tisbury
WILDE, Mr Serjeant	Crown Prosecutor
WILKINS, Charles	Blacksmith , Mr Benett's employee at Pythouse
WILKINS, John	Blacksmith, Journeyman, Hindon
WITHERS, Peter	Agricultural Labourer, Rockley Hampshire
WOODS, William	Mr Benett's employee at Pythouse
WYNDHAM, Charlotte	Daughter of William Wyndham at Dinton House
WYNDHAM, William	Magistrate, landowner, Dinton
WYNDHAM, Captain William	Leader, Hindon Trooper Wiltshire Yeomanry
YOUNG, George	Agricultural Labourer

1
November 1830 (1)

Wednesday 24th November 1830

THE HOUSE HAD been in turmoil all day, alive with rumours of insurrection, tales of disturbances in Suffolk, Kent, East and West Sussex and Hampshire. Now John Benett, Member of Parliament for Wiltshire since 1819, hears that the rioting in the countryside of southern England is spreading across the county borders into Berkshire and his own constituency of Wiltshire.

The disturbances consist of threatening letters signed 'Captain Swing', public demonstrations with demands for higher wages by agricultural labourers, riots about enclosures of common land, about conditions in workhouses and the administration of the Poor Laws, all resulting in demands for immediate cash payments and the reduction of rents. Labourers are setting fire to hay and straw ricks and even to farmhouses. Worse, they are damaging and destroying the new agricultural machinery including, and particularly, the hated threshing machines.

On the 20th November a 'Swing' letter reaches the Salisbury district. Two days later the area to the north of Amesbury is affected, including demands of money by menace at Figheldean and to the south of the city in Downton, West Dean and Whiteparish destruction of threshing machines occurs. On the 23rd the riots approach Mr Benett's home area, with action in Netheravon, Odstock and then Wilton where, he hears from another MP, angry labourers had entered the big cloth making mill complex in the town and broken non-agricultural machinery owned by one John Brasher – an important Benett constituent. Five hundred men had arrived at the mill announcing that they were going to break his machinery 'in order to make more work for the poor people'.[1] Mr Brasher later estimated his loss at £500, a not inconsiderable sum of money.

Mr Benett had heard Henry Hunt, the radical Member of Parliament for Preston, talking about his travels, saying that he had heard the labourers complaining, but saying 'We don't want to do any mischief, but we want that poor children when they go to bed should have a belly full of tatoes instead of crying with a belly half-full'.[2] Mr Benett is unimpressed by Henry Hunt, who has been travelling around southern England and, in Mr Benett's view, has much to answer for in the matter of agricultural labourers' discontent with their situation. He himself employs a number of labourers, providing them with, in his opinion, 'perfectly satisfactory wages and cottages'. In any case, their wages, now around 7s a week in his area, are made up by the contributions of the local vestry under the auspices of Poor Laws. Those wages are, he has to admit, some of the lowest in the whole country, so he is surprised to find that the labourers of Kent, who are already earning 10s a week, are amongst the most vociferous in their demands for more money.

Like the rest of England's Members of Parliament, Mr Benett has been much taken up with the business of a change of government earlier this year, following the death of King George IV in June. The new King, William IV, doesn't like the incumbent prime minister of the time, the Duke

The Palace of Westminster in 1830

of Wellington, a die-hard Tory, but approves of Earl Grey and his Whig party. Following a general election which is held over July and August, the Duke is returned as prime minister, but there is a gradually growing swell of opinion that reform is going to be necessary. There is concern in the country following the Second French Revolution which had happened in late July 1830, then the Belgian Revolution in August, the creation of the young but militant Trade Union Movement in the north, together with a downturn in trade and now these 'Swing' Riots in the south. Additionally there is a financial crisis in the city of London, which has caused a run on gold. Mr Benett can do nothing about most of this, but he can influence any unseemly rioting in his own constituency.

In the Salisbury area the disturbances continue – on the 24th November there is action at Wilton again, at Burcombe, Coombe Bissett, Broad Chalke, Barford St Martin, and Ebbesbourne Wake. The pattern is spreading west, ever closer to Tisbury and only a very few miles from Mr Benett's own beautiful mansion in the Fonthill area, set in its parkland amongst its own tenanted farms. He has in fact recently been negotiating to buy a substantial part of the nearby old Beckford Fonthill estate, currently available following the recent death of Mr Farquhar who had bought Fonthill Abbey from William Beckford. The agreement is in existence, it is just that he hasn't yet been able to find a mortgage or the cash to finalise his purchase. Still, he considers that he now owns this significant block of land, becoming, in his own view, an even more important landowner. Not a popular one, though, and the prospect of his recent expansion has not gone down very well with his newly acquired tenant farmers or their labourers.

Clearly, he feels, he should be on hand to organise resistance to any unauthorised assemblies. He leaves the Houses of Parliament and on reaching his home in London, no. 19 Albemarle Street, he is dismayed to receive a message that rioting is planned to start in nearby Hindon, and that the now defunct cloth factory at the head of Fonthill Lake is to be targeted. The message is 'that great excitement prevailed' in the village.[3] Mr Benett makes up his mind to travel down to Wiltshire that very night, even though it is by now late in the evening of Wednesday 24th November.

He is taking advantage of a grant of absence made by the House of Commons for MPs to return to their constituencies if disturbances are taking place there. Thirty-eight MPs take leave of absence for periods of ten days to a month from 22nd November to the 6th December 1830.[4]

He could travel by stagecoach – there are some 20 coaches a day leaving London for Exeter; they leave from The Swan With Two Necks in Graham Street, travelling at about ten miles an hour on average from London via Kingston upon Thames, Guildford, Farnham, Basingstoke, Andover and on towards Exeter, conveniently passing through the village of Hindon. However, Mr Benett, although almost always in debt, is considered to be a rich man, and as such, needs to be seen to have his own transport, which might well have been a four seater barouche, the passengers sitting two abreast opposite each with a rainproof hood covering the seating area, or a two seater cabriolet, also with cover. This is of course faster, although there would still need to be stops every so often to change horses on the 103 mile journey from Albemarle Street to Pythouse. It is a jolting, tiring journey taking around ten hours or so, and he does not reach his Wiltshire home until about four o-clock in the morning of Thursday 25th November. Exhausted, cross and worried, although he has been unable to see any damage anywhere en route due to it being pitch dark, he falls into bed.

Thursday 25th November 1830

AT SEVEN O'CLOCK in the morning it is cold and dark – it will not start to get light until after 7.30a.m., but James Cheverill has already started work at Mr Dally's tenanted farm at Ridge, close to Tisbury and to Fonthill Bishop. James is nearly 20 years old and has been working for Mr Dally, at the pottery at Ridge for five years. He sleeps in the stable there and eats his meals with the family. Sometime after seven o'clock but before eight he hears the sound of hunting horns being blown, and on going outside to see what is going on he finds Charles Martin, Robert Obourne and William Scott, all from Ridge, and all of whom he knows well, together with a large mob of other men from Chilmark and the immediate area. There is a great clamour of noise and the mob insists that he should join in with them as they are going, they shout, to break up the machines. Scott and Obourne have small walking sticks in their hands, but Martin does not. This little group, according to James, lags behind the mob and by the time it reaches its first destination some three or four miles from Ridge, James thinks they are about a quarter of a mile behind, but he can see that the mob is intent upon breaking the threshing machine at Down Farm.[5] Down Farm, in Fonthill Bishop is owned by Mr King of Chilmark, but tenanted by Mr Henry Self, who very prudently has himself taken apart his threshing machine because of threatened arson attacks in the area. He has left the base or stage in the barn and this is the only piece of it which is still intact. An agricultural labourer, John Penny, aged 26, gets inside the barn and opens the great doors from the inside, allowing the mob to enter. James Cheverill stays well

Pythouse from the south-east, built 1805, extended 1891

back with his friends, watching for about 15 to 20 minutes. He can see that parts of the machine are being thrown out of the barn and others in the mob are setting to with bars and sticks to smash up the bits and pieces. James is relieved that Martin, Scott and Obourne are with him and not with the mob, because he is aware that they have previous convictions – in the case of Robert Obourne, six months for felony at the Spring Assizes in 1826, and Martin, who received a two month sentence for a similar offence, both with hard labour[5.]

At Down Farm John Targett, a 29 year old from Hindon, together with Jeremiah Topp, 23, and his brother Thomas, aged only 20, both from Fonthill Bishop, are apparently seen by a witness named Michael Bradley, from Chilmark, breaking the threshing machine. They have axes and sticks, and, says Mr Bradley, they are joined by Scott and Obourne, who subsequently deny this charge. Mr Bradley's evidence is later found to be unreliable. Nevertheless, men in the mob have broken up Mr Self's threshing machine parts, in about 20 minutes of violent action and the time is ten o'clock in the morning. It has been noisy, exciting but thirsty work and refreshments are now clearly required. Accordingly the group moves on from Down Farm and Self's house, (probably the house known as Baker's Farm) up through the Fonthill estate, past the lake up to the Beckford Arms Inn, where the landlord, Mr Tabor, prudently provides food and drink. James is still with his friends. He counts about 20 others with them.

Sometime earlier that morning, when it is still chilly and dark, a tenant farmer by the name of Joseph (sometimes known as Richard) Alford, walks into his yard at Withyslade Farm just off Tisbury Row and mounts his horse. [6] Mr Alford is a respectable tenant farmer on a farm owned by Lord Arundell, owner of the huge Wardour estate to the south of Tisbury. Mr Alford is a dissenter, and there are many dissenters in the Tisbury area. It is worth mentioning that the system of Poor Law Relief is run by the parish – in Tisbury's case from the vestry meeting in the Anglican church of St John the Baptist. However, as a local landlord with tenanted farms, Lord Arundell, a sincere and enthusiastic member of a great Roman Catholic dynasty, is aware of the inadequacy of the system for the relief of the poor and indeed had previously held a meeting at Withyslade Farm to discuss with some of his tenants (including Alford) and the parish overseers, the terrible situation the agricultural labourers find themselves forced to accept.[7] Lord Arundell is also Commander of the Salisbury troop of Yeomanry Cavalry, and following information he receives, he arrives in Salisbury on the 23rd November. Immediately most of his time is taken up with yeomanry commitments.

Mr Alford, aged about 50, 5 foot nine inches tall and weighing around 16 stone, heaves himself aboard his white horse and collects a band of men from Swallowcliffe, Ansty and Tisbury. A boy named William Turner, aged nine at this time, reports many years later that the farmer is 'symbolic of Joan of Arc'. This doughty band rides down through Tisbury apparently heading up towards Fonthill Gifford and the deserted cloth mill at the head of Fonthill Lake, in order to break the machinery there, which in Alford's view, has created a loss of employment in the area.

On the way through Tisbury, they are joined by John Burton, a 20 year old, and his neighbour William Snook, a 22 year old ploughman, both of whom live in Church Street, Tisbury. John Burton later claims he was forced to join the mob. Another of Lord Arundell's tenants, James Coombes, joins them but it seems as if the mob is itself taking control of the situation and has more nefarious intentions than the two respectable tenant farmers. Alford and Coombes apparently try to stop the mob from attacking the remaining cloth factory machinery, but then after a short parley with the steward for the Fonthill estate, the mob moves on to Fonthill Gifford, where it joins a great many more agricultural labourers assembled near the lime kiln site. By now Mr Alford and Mr Coombe are losing their enthusiasm for demonstrating, because it looks as though the demonstration is becoming an unmanageable riot. At some stage they manage to slip away. They are both responsible tenant farmers, neither of them particularly short of money and probably concerned about the effect upon their tenancies. In spite of their covert disappearance, a warrant will be issued for the arrest of Mr Richard Alford.

At Fonthill Gifford the Tisbury party becomes part of the noisy rancorous collection of labourers, intent upon inflicting as much damage to machinery as they can. They realise that these big machines require heavier weapons of destruction than sticks and staves, so they break into the blacksmith's shop and supply themselves with iron bars, hatchets, axes and hammers. The large group of men, now apparently 400 strong, is led by Charles Jerrard and his son, also Charles, the latter wearing a coloured sash around his body. Their avowed intention is to break up the threshing machines on the farms in the local area, most of which are to be owned by Mr Benett (who has not yet found the required funds or mortgages to complete his purchase). He is unpopular in the area anyway, reputedly having destroyed a number of the cottages on his land some time in 1817 – an act never forgotten or forgiven. The Jerrards, father and son, are probably still smarting from the fact that their family lost their 59 acre farm and house, Jerrards, some 50 years before. They have in fact assembled the mob very close to this old farmhouse. The mob is working itself up to attack Mr Candy's farm at Fonthill Gifford.

Earlier that morning Mr Benett is rudely awakened from a short sleep by his bailiff, James Jay the younger, who arrives at 7.00 a.m. to report that a large number of people had assembled in the parish of Tisbury with the intention of destroying the cloth factory at the head of Fonthill Lake.[8] Mr Benett gets this information checked by a servant, whilst he eats his breakfast and prepares to leave his house with a servant Thomas Ball, and his steward, one Arthur Legge, a rather elderly and ineffective gentleman. He calls upon local farmers, who refuse to come with him, telling Mr Benett that 'he would be murdered and they did not wish to suffer the same fate', which further angers Mr Benett. The small party therefore proceeds on horseback to Fonthill Gifford where, at the lime kiln, as reported, they find a large mob assembled. It is now after ten o'clock in the morning.

Mr Benett spots the younger Charles Jerrard with his sash. This, to Mr Benett indicates rebellion, anarchism, is a reminder of the French Revolution and the possibility of revolution in England. He apparently rides up to young Charles and tells him

'Young man, that sash will hang you!' to which young Charles bravely, but rashly, replies, 'I don't care about hanging. I don't care!'[9]

Mr Benett then enquires what the men are complaining about and is told that they intend to break all the threshing machines in the county which are depriving them of winter work, and that they want an immediate increase in wages to 2s. per day. A very reasonable request.

In response Mr Benett offers to read a proclamation which he tells them he has brought from London, from the king. The mob is clearly not interested in the king's proclamation but Mr Benett attempts to read it anyway. He tells them that a reward of £50 is being offered to anyone who can give information which results in the detection of a machine breaker and £500 for the disclosure of anyone who has set fire to a property. A voice in the crowd shouts out, 'We don't burn. We have nothing to do with fires. We are Hunt's men' and the men shout their agreement. Clearly this comment refers to the radical speaker Henry Hunt MP, whose rhetoric is having some effect upon the Swing rioters.

Mr Benett then craftily suggests that although he is sure they don't, none of them will now be able to trust anyone else 'for any one of you by informing against ten others would obtain £500'. They should go home, he tells them, preserve their own lives and keep the peace.

Far from doing what the landowner suggests, there are derisory shouts and the men form themselves into groups. One group goes straight to Mr Candy's farm at Fonthill Gifford and proceeds to smash up the drum of the threshing machine (again the machine had already been dismantled by the tenant farmer himself). Another group marches up the road towards the Beckford Arms where in a field behind the inn, Mr James Lampard, the tenant farmer at Lawn Farm, had placed his threshing machine. This is duly smashed up, and the two groups join up to proceed up the road towards Newtown and Pythouse Farm. They are joined by the inebriated group which has been eating and drinking at the Beckford Arms and with much shouting and banging around, they progress up the road.

In order to reach their next destination they pass the lane leading to Lawn Quarry where they see Mr Benett's carter, young John Brickell/Brickle, with his team of six carthorses drawing a cart full of stones from the quarry which are destined to make a new road to West Lodge, Fonthill. The mob, thought by Mr Brickell to be about 900,(but this would seem to be an exaggeration), demand that the carter join them and come and break up some more machines. He desists but they demand to take his horses. Mr Brickell manfully says that, 'where them horses go, I goes'.

He also sees that 'some of 'em are awful drunk', so sensibly he joins in with two of his horses. John Brickell knows a number of the men quite well, young Charles Jerrard, James Blandford, John Barrett, William Snook, Samuel Eyres, James Mould, Thomas Topp, Thomas Vining and

Andrew Moxham. (He later admits that he doesn't see all of these friends or acquaintances being forced to join the mob as they say they are, but he does say that 'several people' were forced to do so).[10]

Mr Benett has reached Lawn Farm before them, where he attempts to address the mob again, but they refuse to listen, being intent upon access to the horse house, dismantling its roof and the piers upon which it stands and attacking the machines inside. Lawn Farm is yet another part of the estate which is being purchased by Mr Benett from Mr Farquhar. Thomas Ball, Mr Benett's servant, later testifies that he sees James Blandford destroying the 'Horse House', and another of Mr Benett's men, James Snow, sees Thomas Vining and Thomas Phillips joining in with this destruction.

Still on his horse, Mr Benett insists upon addressing the mob again – telling them to go home. Shouts demanding higher wages greet him, and more threats of damage to his machines. Many of the men say that as he won't listen to their demands or complaints they will attack his machines at Pythouse Farm and indeed they may attack him. With that they stolidly proceed towards Pythouse Farm to where Mr Benett has prudently withdrawn together with about 20 of his employees.

At this point a separate part of the group splits off and goes across country to Linley Farm, another Benett property on the other side of Pythouse, where there is a substantial threshing machine run by water power. This is some distance away, but James Snow follows and sees the older Charles Jerrard, Thomas Phillips and John Targett there, intent upon smashing up the big threshing machine. The mob, according to John Brickell, then took the Beer Barrel out of the Bailiff's house at Linley, knocked the bung out and 'got more drunk'. The mob then manages to smash the bar of the big threshing machine and they leave through the park for Pythouse, where they make for the plantation.[11]

It is now midday and at Pythouse Farm the remainder of the mob, led by William Snook, pours into the farm yard and smashes up machinery with enthusiasm. Many of them are seen by Mr Benett's employees, including James Cockburn his gardener, William Turner a labourer, John Ford, Charles Wilkins, James Lampard, James and Noah Doggrel, John Jukes, John Uphill shepherd, and William Woods. All these employees of Mr Benett later testified, naming their friends and neighbours as being present at Pythouse Farm, behaving riotously and breaking up the machines.[12]

With his employees around him, and still mounted on his horse, Mr Benett sits and watches for about ten minutes whilst the mob attack his farm machinery and possessions. They stop their work and stare at him. A moment of silence occurs when suddenly a stone sails past Mr Benett's head, followed by another and another, until one eventually hits him in the face. His head drops and his hat falls off. It can be seen that blood is gushing from a wound between his eyes. Mr Benett is temporarily knocked out. Elderly Mr Legge, the steward, is also hit by a stone and so is Mr Benett's horse, which sensibly turns and trots smartly away, only to get caught up in a team of Mr Benett's own cart horses in the lane outside the farmyard. Benett recovers and shouts, 'Another stone and I fire'.

He reaches home, however, barricades the door and gets his wound attended to. The mob prowls around outside Pythouse itself, demanding money and food from the servants. They toss a coin to decide whether to attack Mr Benett's house, or to damage another of his machines – the coin decides the latter course. The little band of Benett employees follows him to Pythouse itself, where Mr Benett tells them he believes the mob will attack and destroy his home. He hears that Linley Farm is under attack too. By now Mr Benett, with his face hurting, is very angry indeed and ready for some form of revenge.

This will arrive in the form of the Hindon troop of the Wiltshire Yeomanry.

2
The birth of Captain Swing

ONE DEFINITION OF a protest movement is of events in one locale at one particular time influencing later events elsewhere.[1] This definition could certainly be applied to the events which culminated in late 1830 in the small rural war in south-west Wiltshire, the effects of which were to be felt by the local population for very many years afterwards. So what were these initiating events that occurred at one particular moment in the history of eastern and southern England in 1830, and how did they arise?

There were a number of causes.

Traditionally many of the low paid workers on English farms had managed to retain some independence and self sufficiency – wages were low but were supplemented by cottagers having a vegetable patch and access to the great open fields of communal land around the village – the best arable land in medieval times was divided into strips which were allocated annually so that everyone had a chance of good growing land on a regular basis. In addition some rougher communal areas were reserved for grazing, (herbage), wood gathering (estovers), turf cutting (turbary) and fishing (pescary). These traditional, long enjoyed rights enabled the villager to keep a cow, a couple of pigs perhaps and certainly some geese to supplement the diet. The cow was all important, providing as she did, milk for butter and cheese, and calves for beef or replacement dairy animals. These rights enabled them to supplement their income with wood for the fire, fish to add extra protein for the diet and gave them some independence. In addition, the

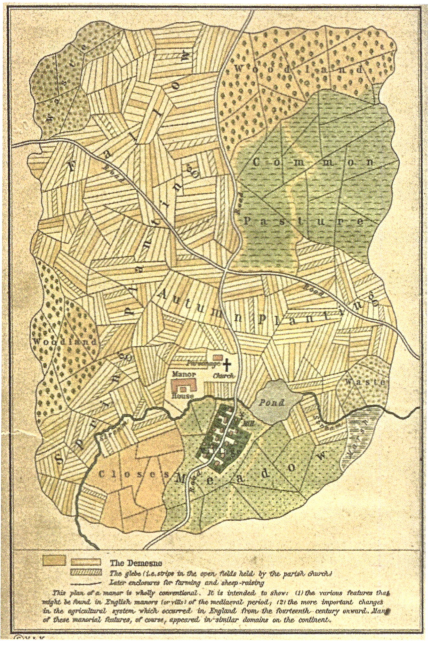

Plan of a Medieval Manor – from Historical Atlas by William Shepherd 1923-26. University of Texas at Austin

peasant was provided with seasonal work by farmers – the sort of work that was not done by living-in servants, for example hedging, ditching, draining, tree felling, hoeing, sowing seed, reaping and harvesting, threshing and

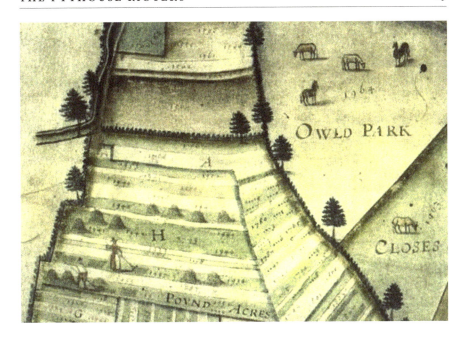
Traditional open field system

shearing sheep. All of these jobs were required each year but the workers, even on a day to day hiring basis, were often fed communally and considered to be part of the farm's workforce. The wives and daughters had work in the dairies, fed the young stock and supplemented the family income with local traditional skills such as weaving, or button making. Farmers had a local pool of labour to rely upon, and the workers had a reliable source of income, fluctuating seasonally but reliable because the jobs had to be done at each specific time of the agricultural year.[2]

In the early 1700s some four and a half million acres of English countryside were still farmed in the old way, the open field medieval system. However, this comparatively happy state of affairs began to change in the late 18th century when the views of agricultural experts, such as Mr John Billingsley of Somerset who was commissioned to write a report on Somerset for the Board of Agriculture in 1795, wrote:[3]

'The possession of a cow or two, with a hog and a few geese, naturally exalts the peasant, in his own conception, above his brethren in the same rank of society. ......In sauntering after his cattle, he acquires a habit of indolence...... . And at length the sale of a half-fed calf, or hog, furnishes the means of adding intemperance to idleness.'

Other agrarian reformists, such as Mr Bishton of Shropshire considered that, 'when the commons are enclosed, the labourers will work every day in the year'.

Reformists considered quite accurately that farming scattered strips and the inefficient use of the commons was not an economic use of the land, and that they should be enclosed into larger unit., This would enable the use of the new machinery that was being developed, with organised use of agricultural labour and with wages being paid, rather than rights of usage in return for labour.

Landowners could see the benefit of this proposed system, returning the use of the common land to them and removing the rights of cottagers, who after all, the landowners thought (if they thought of the peasants at all) would be grateful for such a reorganisation of their labour, resulting in the security of wages. Thus the Enclosures Acts started, slowly at first and then with gathering speed, with a system that of course totally favoured the larger local landowners, and failed to take any resulting deprivation of the cottagers into account. Additionally, the population had grown and a more efficient system of food production was needed.

Enclosure commenced by the local landowner setting out in a petition to Parliament what he considered to be the benefits and reasons why the land should be enclosed. [4] This was done with the help of legal advice, and it could be achieved, before 1774, by one person and his adviser without even the need to let the local cottagers/workers know of his intention. However, a Standing Order was passed in 1774 ensuring that a notice of the petition to Parliament had to be posted on the door of the local church in each affected parish, for three Sundays in August, or three in September. As all arrangements were made in advance though, there was no provision allowed for dissent or disagreement as to the proposals, from villagers or small landowners. In any case, they would not have known how to go about registering such dissent, even if any of them could read the notice.

The petition was now sent to Parliament, where it would be heard and granted leave for the introduction of a bill – to be prepared by the petitioner. The bill would be submitted, read for a first time and a second time, and then referred to a committee, with a Member of Parliament as its chair. The committee was chosen, usually by the Member of Parliament (normally the MP for the country in which the land is situated) plus other local MPs. The interests of the petitioner are therefore in the hands of his immediate friends and neighbours. The interests of the villagers, who have been using the land for centuries, are not represented at committee level. Any petitions against the proposed enclosures were considered but as the average villager could neither read nor write, his views were not taken into account. In theory he could instruct a lawyer, but this was unlikely the costs being so exorbitant and how to do such a thing impossible to imagine. The ownership of the acreage involved was supposed to be the deciding factor but negotiations ensured that this percentage could be ingeniously manipulated in favour of the petitioner and against the interests of the opposing collection of small landowners and users of these common lands.

The committee then presented its report. If the report was in favour of the proposed enclosure (it always was) then the bill would be passed. First by the Commons, after which it went to the Lords, who passed it and it received the Royal Assent.

Now the commissioners, suggested by the committee in the bill, would arrive in the district and allocate the new land ownership. Maps were made with plans of proposed changes. The land was reordered, hedges and trees planted, new farmhouses planned to sit within the new blocks of land. Sometimes the arrival of the commissioners would be the first time the common labourer had heard about the proposed enclosure.[5]

For centuries, even before the arrival of William the Conqueror, the local villager had enjoyed the right of keeping his cow, his pig and his poultry on the common land. And he would have had the right to farm the various strips of fertile land, on which he grew his small quantity of crops. Thus he would he be able to feed his family. It also gave each man a sense of community ownership and a sense of fairness of distribution as the strips were rotated. But now a massive change would take place and sadly, national opinion started to move against the old community system. First, agricultural improvements could not be made easily when so much of the country's agricultural land was worked in the old fashioned way. It was impossible to introduce new ways of working the land, such as those suggested by innovators – Turnip Townshend, for example, Coke of Holkham, Jethro Tull or Robert Bakewell, if the land was still in the hands of those who many considered to be ignorant peasants. And as we have seen, the view of agricultural reformists was that not only were the peasants ignorant, but that they were lazy as well.

A verse written at that time goes –

The law locks up the man or woman
Who steals the goose from off the Common,
But leaves the greater felon loose
Who steals the Common from the goose'[6]
 Anonymous but heartfelt.

In 1688 there had been some 10 million acres of unenclosed 'waste' land from the 37 million acres which comprised England and Wales. By 1850 over 6.6 million acres of common land had been enclosed by act of Parliament.

In 1750-60 there were 56 Acts enclosing 74,518 acres

1760-81   521   752,150
1802-44   808   439,043
1845 and later 508   334,906

In addition 4.5 million acres of open field systems were enclosed under 2,911 separate Acts of Parliament during those years.[7] Hedges became boundaries between men and the land, creating a whole new class of poor labourers whose 'greatest offence against property was to have none'. [8]

During this period there was also considerable concern about possible revolutions; France was undergoing the terrible convulsion of the 1789 revolution, and the belligerent colony of America was gearing up for independence. Clearly, one way of keeping the rural population under control would be by removing their communal rights and making them dependent upon proper employment.

But the change in agricultural practices to allow the newly popular ideas of crop rotation, the use of mechanical seed drills and hoes, and selective sheep and cattle breeding, would also benefit from the movement to enclose these great communal lands. Crop rotation would not only enrich the land by putting back nitrogen into the soil (clover), it would provide cattle feed (clover and turnips) and food for the increasing number of town and city dwellers (barley and wheat) – and this latter number of people would be even greater when the villagers were displaced by the very act of enclosing their food and subsistence provisions.

With regard to animal husbandry, this could benefit from improvement too. Robert Bakewell of Dishley bred a better meat producing sheep (the Leicester) and experimented with Longhorn cattle. The Collings brothers developed Shorthorn cattle. These breeders aimed for increased meat production per animal, with the added benefit of fodder crops grown on the rotation system. More food per acre of land could be produced and indeed this was increasingly necessary as the population of England and Wales grew from about 5.7 million in 1750 to just over 17 million by 1851. With the enclosure of heath and low-lying land, it became possible to create really productive arable farms.

About 3,000 parishes were affected – a few were just tidied up into enclosed fields, but for most parishes it was a complete transformation from

The Harvest cradle – oil on canvas John Linnell 1792-1882 – York Art Gallery.

the traditional open areas with furrows and strips, headlands and cart tracks to neat, squared off, hawthorn hedged, manageable sized enclosures with straight roads running out from the villages rather than the old winding footpaths. New farmhouses were built outside the villages, surrounded by their allocated land and the old farmhouses set in the village streets were deserted, or split into tiny cottages. Of course all this took a few years, but the change was swift, happening in less than one generation.[9] In Wiltshire one in four acres was enclosed but on the higher chalk the rate was one in two. It was in the great midland counties where the most sweeping changes occurred.

The poet, John Clare, an accurate recorder of the countryside wrote

'Inclosures, thou'rt a curse upon the land,
And tasteless was the wretch who thy existence plann'd'.

The land was now irrevocably under the control of the great local landowners, the aristocracy, the Members of Parliament, the Church of England, and the really rich, such as sugar plantation or mill owners, who at this time were buying up country estates in order to build themselves a beautiful mansion, create parkland and gardens and live the sort of privileged, educated, cultured life that was epitomised by the Georgian period.

In Britain the power of the monarchy had been gradually removed – unlike in France where the aristocracy had had privilege but no power, which was in the hands of administrators influenced by philosophers, emancipators (Voltaire, Montesquieu, Diderot, Rousseau) with a decadent monarch. English aristocrats had gradually removed the power of the potentially Catholic monarchs (Charles II and James II), choosing instead the securely Protestant William and Mary, who understood that their position was based upon a limited amount of power, an accession known as the Glorious Revolution – achieved with virtually no bloodshed,(unlike the French Revolution in 1789 which was distinguished by continual and terrifying bloodshed and the eventual beheading of the monarch).

The pragmatic Prime Minister Walpole, realising that Britain, (having appointed as king a foreigner – George I – who spoke no English and actually cared very little for his newly adopted country), needed Parliamentary power to be a collective responsibility vested in its ministers, in the form of a Cabinet government with no direct interference by the monarch.[10] Members of Parliament, chosen as they were by the local gentry of the English constituencies, needed to adopt this idea of power with responsibility and a parliamentary seat became a prize much fought for, granting the incumbent huge local authority to appoint representatives to local and national bureaucratic institutions. Franchise was of course severely limited, the lower classes and women having no right to vote at all. This would eventually have to be addressed, but during the period of Georgian monarchs, franchise was minimal. However, after the French Revolution there was always a degree of fear present in the minds of the English landowners – a terror that revolution could happen in England. Thus it was essential to control the local village labourers, any intellectuals who might come up with revolutionary ideas of extending franchise or privileges to the lower classes, and certainly any foreigners who might be introducing such ideas into the heads of naive peasants.

There were other ways in which the labourer might improve his lot – poaching was one. Unfortunately for him, however, landowners could employ bailiffs and stewards, or a gamekeeper with the right to set man traps. To make matters worse, the very same landowner who might be the labourer's employer, was quite likely to be a Justice of the Peace, sitting on the local bench, so in control of punishment meted out to an unfortunate family man who had taken a pheasant from his employer's woods. For serious offences of this sort, a new system had been set up of a jury, in particular, a Grand Jury, with jurors appointed once again by the Justice of the Peace.

Sometimes the JP did not bother to set up a jury at all, he simply heard, tried and convicted an arrested man and particularly anyone taken with reference to the Game Laws. Thus the law of control came to be the virtual prerogative of the local squires and landowners, i.e. feudalism under a different and less lenient guise than had been the case earlier. JP's were not actually paid either, so of course they had to be financially independent. Buying one's way into local power was necessary, and very much part of owning property and land. At the same time the great schools and universities of England mainly originally set up as communities of learning for the poor, had gradually been taken over by the rich, granting degrees to any who could afford one. So education too had become unavailable to the poor. Except of course, Sunday schools under the control of the church.

So now the countryside, neatly divided into squared off fields the right size for working with the new machinery that was being developed, with its small but elegant farmhouses built in the classical, regular Georgian shape and style, its hawthorn hedges and straight roads, (the minimum width for roads between villages now had to be 40 feet between ditches, the middle 12 feet stoned to a depth of a foot).[11]

Ever wider turnpikes spread out across the countryside, linking newly elegant cities and increasingly middle class country towns to the great industrial metropolises, becoming a less comfortable place to live as an agricultural worker. The country has become a place of culture and pleasure, power and influence, controlled by a small section of the population,

Peasant with a horse drawn plough – Charles Emile Jacques 1864

who are well educated, well fed, well clothed, able to enjoy the luxuries of imported goods such as sugar, tea and coffee, silks, beautiful china, carpets and cared for by an army of servants. The bulk of the rest of the population, however, amongst whom are the unfortunates still living in poverty in the countryside, (who are nevertheless expected to produce food for the nation) are increasingly unable to control the means of their own survival.

The scene is set, therefore, for demands for political and social reform. Deference towards employers such as farmers, towards local magistrates and towards the clergy in particular, declined.

In the north the working class is exploited by the newly rich mill owners and industrialists. Before the advent of mills and machinery, the master cotton spinners for example, although poor and dependent upon the sale of their finished products to the clothiers, were able to work at home, in control of their output and working hours. Now they are labourers in a factory, working unreasonably long hours in dangers and unhealthy conditions, no longer in control. If he did not submit to their strict rules and wanted to complain, the labourer would have to take his grievances before the local magistrates, who were hand in glove with the employers. Dispute was impossible – he could not afford to instruct a lawyer to act on his behalf.

It is hardly surprising therefore to find machinery breaking in the north – which became known as Luddism and the people who broke the machines as Luddites.[12] No doubt the workers in the southern half of England gradually became aware of these groups of men, who had begun to get together secretly and overnight attack a factory, smashing the spinning jennies and the shearing frames. The cover of darkness would hide their identities. These men had been proud of their crafts and independent status and loathe to surrender it, even if wages in the north of the country were better than those in the south.

But this machine breaking was a limited way of dealing with the problems and by 1830 there were quite well organised trade unions in the north, friendly societies, religious and educational organisations, a replacement for the 'moral' spirit of community which had existed before the industrial revolution.[13]

In the south this was only just beginning. No doubt southerners had gradually become aware of the Luddite movement and the subsequent organisations, but in the south men were working in much smaller groups of farm workers, distant from each other. Communication was difficult. Enclosure had produced more food but not for those who were producing it. They needed an increase in wages and some land for themselves to grow their own food. This natural right had been lost. They did not know how to regain their self respect.

In Wiltshire the farm labourers were particularly poor. Close to Tisbury lies the town of Warminster, where a block of common land known as Warminster Common had provided poverty stricken families with a space for one room hovels. Their plight was recorded faithfully by a Methodist minister, William Daniell, known locally as the Bishop of Warminster Common. For some 40 years he held services, built a small chapel, visited the poor and dying and held childrens' meetings, for all of which he was unpaid. He helped to provide drainage and a water supply, eventually being appointed surveyor of highways, overseer of the parish and registrar. His radical views on the terrible conditions of the poor led him to comment on the new enclosures

'Have the poor no rights to be held sacred? And this mode of disinheriting them without the power of appealing at all likely make them peaceable and virtuous?'.

The village of Tisbury was the subject of an article in a non-political newspaper by the name of the *Morning Advertiser*, which was published in London on behalf of the charitable Society of Licensed Victuallers. On the 7th October 1826 a correspondent writes under the title 'Agricultural Parishes' that the village of Tisbury is a purely agricultural one with the exception, he says, of 'the new manufactory at Fonthill'. This statement does ignore the quarries employing stonemasons, the article concentrating on the plight of the agricultural labourers.

The parish, states the writer, is some seven miles long and includes Wardour Castle, Pyt House and part of the Fonthill estate – a total of around 8,000 acres with a population of over 2,000. Poor relief is provided for about 670 of this population – of whom 92 are old and 36 constant workhouse residents. Thu 574 people (over a quarter of the population) needed to have their working incomes supplemented by the poor rate relief. They each receive less than 1s 6d per week, based upon a levy of about 5s per acre of land owned by poor relief contributors and after the cost of maintaining the elderly and workhouse residents is taken into account.

If, as the writer suggests, wages were to be raised by say 2s per week for working men, 1s for working women and 6d for working children, all the population except the sick and infirm could be taken off the relief system. It is not a case of unemployment being a burden to the village, indeed more labourers are needed and jobs are available – it is simply that wages are too low for people to be able to maintain themselves and their families.

'There is scarcely an able bodied person in this parish out of employ, and complaints are often heard of a want of labourers. .... This is one of the most favoured parishes in the west of England, and it may be taken as a sample of the agricultural villages in general. The people look healthy; their houses do not exhibit broken windows, or other marks of extreme wretchedness, and there is nothing in the general aspect of the labourers to excite regret, but the recollection that even the most industrious and excellent workmen, who have families, are compelled to receive assistance from the pay board, and that there are not means with their power by which it is possible for them to escape this degradation'.[14]

3
More hardships

THERE WERE OTHER matters which were causing distress in the countryside.

Farmers themselves had been heavily taxed by a government under Pitt, which sent money abroad, to Prussia and Austria in particular; to assist in the fight against Napoleon. Tax revenue was spent on pensions and sinecures – those secure jobs for cronies and men who had voted for the current Parliament; money was going on the cost of pressing young men into the armed services, on imprisoning poor people for minor crimes and the subsequent cost of transporting them to far flung colonies which themselves were being supported by Britain in the form of governmental structure, policing and providing a military presence. None of the tax money taken went to relieving the poverty of the underclass, or towards educating them, or to improving their standard of living, which had dropped considerably over the period 1795 to 1830.[1]

At the same time, members of other classes – landlords, the judiciary, parsons and the growing middle classes of the towns – lawyers, shopkeepers, industrialists, tradesmen etc. were all better off – particularly those in receipt of government pensions and who held bureaucratic positions.[2] The rich were buying up land and property, building beautiful homes, travelling to Europe on the Grand Tour, bringing back paintings, sculptures, forming art collections and creating libraries, designing wonderful gardens and indulging in intellectual pursuits. Life in towns and cities had become very much more pleasant, fashionable watering places provided the stimulus of company, entertainment and conversation. But the agricultural working class citizen could no long afford to eat bacon, cheese or provide milk for his children. He and his family lived on bread and potatoes.

War with France was expensive and brought into sharp contrast the new difference in status between the now liberated French peasant, with his own cottage and piece of land, no longer a serf under an idle aristocratic landowner, and the poverty stricken English agricultural labourer, so independent at the beginning of the 18th century, who had lost his rights of use of the common lands, and was suffering from only being able to get partial employment, he and his family becoming a burden to the parish.[3] Of course conscription and pressing had provided some security during the actual Napoleonic Wars period, but after 1815 these young men, now conditioned to a fighting way of life, were suddenly discharged onto the streets, swelling the numbers of non and under employed, and putting a further strain on the parish system. Adding to local problems was the fact that these young men had been trained in handling weapons, and in working in teams/gangs. This was to prove useful to them.

Poaching had always been a part of living in the country, but now it became a necessity, to supplement food supplies, and help with income. It had been severely punished after the passing of the act of 1770, and in 1800 a further act had been passed, enabling even more draconian measures to be used, including ironically, one of committal to the Army or Navy for a young man of over 12 years of age. Now these lads were out of the Army or Navy and resistance took the form of gangs forming to poach more systematically, leading to a near war between landlords and their gamekeepers on the one hand, and the poachers on the other. Horrible deterrents were legal to use, including mantraps and spring guns which caused terrible injuries or lonely deaths. Occasionally a spring gun or mantrap would be set off accidentally by a farm servant or a hated gamekeeper, a form of rough justice generally considered to be perfectly satisfactory by the poachers. If caught the poacher could be transported for seven years, particularly if armed with a gun or something with which to bludgeon game. If armed with a net only, the punishment was three months hard labour. If they were caught in a group of three or more, the transportation term went up to 14 years.

Between 1827 and 1830 one in seven of all criminal convictions in England were for offences under the Game Laws, totalling 8502 unfortunate persons, many of whom were boys of under 18. They were tried at the

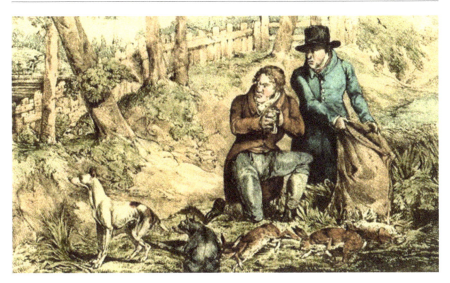

Thos. McLean print of 1826 – Poachers

quarter sessions by a bench consisting of magistrates whose main sports interest was in shooting and hunting. Fair game.

The supplementary food or income provided by poaching, such as snaring an unwary hare, or bashing a pheasant to death, made all the difference between starvation on a wage of 3s a week for a young, unmarried, agricultural labourer, or just about surviving. The sort of work offered by the parish to supplement these low wages was work on the roads.

But the labourer went on risking his freedom and even his life. William Cobbett tells of meeting a young man breaking up stones by the roadside and asking him how long he could live on 2s and 6d a week which the sum the young man was receiving. 'I don't live on it' he replies, 'I poach, it's better to be hanged than starve to death'.

Poaching could even be turned into a business. Enterprising men made contacts through, perhaps, a coachman on the Exeter to London mailcoach run. He in turn might know someone in London with contacts with a poulterer or game dealer at Leadenhall or Newgate Markets, in need of a supply of game at a reasonable price. This was risky, but the poachers obliged, providing the sort of game required in the quantities needed and with a small profit all round. The game would then be bought in London by the kitchen staff of some large mansion and might be served at dinner to the very people from whose land the game had been poached.[3]

But to add to the humiliation of the low wage economy, a system of poor relief had been introduced in 1795 as a result of a meeting held in the parish of Speenhamland (now part of Newbury, Berkshire). The initial purpose of the meeting at The Pelican Inn was to discuss the possibility of raising wages in the area so that they fell into line with the rising prices of corn and provisions. Seventeen magistrates, seven clergy and various other interested parties attended the meeting chaired by Mr Charles Dundas, MP. Somehow, although the intention of the meeting had been good, the second resolution that was passed required only a request to employers to raise wages and to supplement these wages with payments from the parish funds. These payments were to be related to food prices viz. when

'a gallon loaf of second flour weighing 3lbs.11oz shall cost one shilling, then every poor and industrious man shall have for his own support 3s weekly'.

A wife and other members of the family, i.e. children, would receive 1s. 6d each. When the loaf price went up to 1s. 4d the labourer would receive 4s for himself and 1s.10d for each family member. This was based on a man needing three gallon loaves a week and family members one and a half.[4]

This recommendation was seen as fair and appropriate and was soon taken up throughout the whole country (except for Durham and Northumberland). In addition, unemployed labourers (before receiving the parish allowance) had to go 'on the rounds' of the parish seeking day or weekly work, an utterly humiliating experience.

It was impossible for the working man to achieve any change through Parliament. Very few labourers had the vote – electoral franchise was restricted and affected by corruption. 'Rotten' boroughs such as Old Sarum returned two Members of Parliament but had no population at all and the borough was owned by a single landowner. Forty English counties returned two members each, but there was only one polling station for each county. In 'pocket boroughs' votes were bought, the price being negotiated by middle men, and those who did have the right to vote were wined and dined in exchange for their commitment to vote. Slave owners purchased Members of Parliament as did city financiers and even the East India Company, so that their interests were well represented in government. After the Napoleonic Wars ended in 1815 discontent became more visible, with high unemployment and hunger making the population more aware of their inability to change matters, but in spite of this, the Tories held onto power.[5]

Adding to the misery of the Enclosures Acts, the Game Laws, the Poor Relief system, the Corn Laws and the lack of parliamentary representation, the weather in those post war hard years leading up to 1830, was unreliable, causing poor harvests. 1816 saw a decline in agricultural returns and declining prices and 1817 too was considered a bad year. By

1821 the agricultural economy had slid further into depression. There was a very slight improvement for a few years after 1822, but this ceased with the appalling weather that struck England in the late 1820s. 1827 saw the last good harvest for some time, being the best since 1814. However in 1828 it was reported that the harvest was an unmitigated disaster, with scarcely a dry day during the summer/autumn. A mild winter followed, but the summer of 1829 was 'wretchedly wet', and then to everyone's horror, in mid October came frosts and snow, with hardly any of the harvest yet in. The cold and snow persisted until the springof 1830. Cottagers, with no access to the furze and sticks and small wood of the old common land, froze. Heating was impossibly expensive, food scarce and in the local small towns soup kitchens were set up to alleviate hunger, but there is no record of this happening in the countryside.

Understandably the poor labourers felt at a distinct disadvantage. Their 'rights' had been completely wiped out with the Enclosure Acts, they could not grow enough food or vegetables in their meagre gardens, the lack of work was exacerbated by them having to plead for daily jobs before they were able to claim parish relief and now the weather had turned against them. It is surprising that there were no revolts earlier.

Of course it was difficult for uneducated, disconnected people in the countryside to organise resistance, even if they had energy to spare to do so. In the cheap ale houses and in the public houses and inns reform was beginning to be discussed, 'foreign influences' were mentioned – strangers encouraging demonstrations, or rebellious meetings. Reform movements were in fact starting up, mostly led by educated tradesmen or craftsmen in the small towns, encouraged by visiting speakers such as William Cobbett, the reforming journalist, or Henry Hunt MP for Preston, whose work took him travelling around the countryside, or John Thelwall, another Reformist speaker, who toured the countryside giving lectures.

Certainly these gentlemen encouraged the agricultural labourer to think for themselves and they published their own views. Copies of Cobbett's Political Register appeared in the pubs and were even made available on loan. But how many labourers could actually read? The lecture tours were more useful – Cobbett undertook one of the south of England in the autumn of 1830 and it is known that Henry Hunt was talking in Overton and Andover in nearby Hampshire during November.

In Sutton Scotney not far from Andover, a publican by the name of Enos Diddams had set up the Musical and Radical Society, a reformist group which met regularly at local pubs in the area, including in the villages of

Micheldever, Overton and Barton Stacey. They held discussions and heard talks on reformism. The members were mostly tradesmen, who could read and were able to borrow copies of Cobbett's *Political Register*. They included shoemakers, sawyers, harness makers, shopkeepers and smallholders, with a few labourers amongst them. At Barton Stacey the Mason brothers, Robert and Joseph, were to lead a threatening demonstration at the house of the local curate the Rev. Joliffe. The brothers had a very clear idea of the problem facing the proletariat – when the Rev. Joliffe refused to provide food and drink on demand, they responded that

'You have more than we have – you must give us something'[6]

Simplistic but heartfelt.

In Sutton Scotney the meetings resulted in the preparation of a reform petition, signed by members at the Swann Inn – this was just before the start of the riots that were spreading through southern England from Kent, Sussex and into Hampshire.

Cobbett in particular was blamed for the Swing Riots. So much so that later on he was prosecuted for seditious libel – the Attorney General claiming that the Political Register had a 'prodigious effect' upon the rural poor. Cobbett replied that he hoped that it had. Previously, during the actual period of the Swing Riots, he had proclaimed'[7]

'There is not one single village, however recluse, in England, where my name is not known as the friend of the working people, and particularly of the farming labourers, and if ever man deserved any thing, I deserve this character'.

But Cobbett himself was not Captain Swing. The movement developed its own momentum across southern England, with information and discussion passing through village after village, sometimes via the public houses, sometimes through travelling salesmen and sometimes through these reformist speakers. But the villagers knew each other very well, it was a very small world. They also knew through family and friendship ties, people in their neighbouring village. Poaching gangs, which were tolerated by agricultural labourers, since so many of them availed themselves, even in a small way, of poached game, taught organisation, having learned this as soldiers in England's army against the French. They could show how to create a group, how to manage a demonstration and eventually, how to riot and burn a rick or dismantle machines. Some of them, such as John Gilmor, the leader of a mob which attacked the agricultural machinery manufacturer Taskers, at Andover, were competent managers.

Most of the groups which developed across the southern counties in 1830 came together for a short time, held together by intent, family and neighbourhood ties and a communal interest in achieving a better quality of life. Few of them were anything other than labourers, although there was one quite large gang – the Salisbury Fisherton gang, 23 strong, who were committed for trial after the Swing Riots – they were not agricultural labourers, but local tradesmen.

In Wiltshire suspicion fell upon dissenters, Methodists and radicals and Catholics. This was particularly true of the Wardour area of Tisbury, and the local landowner, Lord Arundell, spoke up saying that he denied that

'Catholics and dissenters have occasioned this (the Tisbury) disturbance'.

So the name Captain Swing represented disparate bunches of understandably aggrieved and discontented men. Their way of life had been undermined and their dignity eroded. The stage was set for confrontation, and the final straw came in the form of machinery – the introduction of the threshing machine.

4
'pull down your messhines'.

How did the labour-saving threshing machine become the object of such hatred for agricultural workers in the early 1800s?

On its invention by Andrew Meikle, a Scot, in 1786, farmers quickly realised that such a machine would save the incredible back breaking labour of threshing by hand. This operation was done, as it had been for thousands of years all over the world, by flailing the stalks of corn with a swinging wooden stick attached to a longer pole, known in Wiltshire as a 'vrail'. The swinging stick hit the corn stalks on the floor of the barn, separating the grain from the chaff, or straw. This was extremely hard physical work, done by a circle of labourers squatting in clouds of dust, working for eight hours at a time, and it needed to be done carefully because the swinging stick, if swung too high, could flip back over the labourer's head, hitting his back painfully. Equally it had to be done with skill and care, so that the grain itself was not damaged in its separation, and the straw left usefully as intact as possible. The name – the 'Swing Riots' is in fact derived from the 'swing' of the flail.

It was claimed that the threshing machine could do as much work in one day as could be done with the traditional flail in ten days. However, although dirty and unpleasant for the worker, the long hours of threshing were paid work days and better paid than ordinary field-work, providing some 25% of work available outside hay month and harvest month. Additionally it was carried out over the long hungry winter period, when other work was very scarce.

The agricultural year had followed the same pattern for hundreds of years, although changed slightly from the manorial system. The year began immediately after the harvest was taken in – normally in late September early October, depending upon the weather – after which ploughing could commence. The field worker would spend the long autumn days walking behind the horse-drawn plough, the design of which was only marginally different from that used in the 14th century, although now slightly improved. The newly enclosed fields did make the work a little easier, being of a more manageable size and shape.

Following the ploughing, the seed had to be sown. Traditionally the sower transferred seed from a large sack on the edge of the field into a box or basket slung around his neck or waist. He then proceeded to walk up and down the field all day, scattering the seed rhythmically, left foot up, right hand scattering, right foot up, left hand scattering. Pea and bean seeds however, had to be planted individually, or dibbled, into the ground. So the new seed drill, invented by Jethro Tull in 1701, was considered a wonderful idea. This machine had a hopper to contain the seed, a cylinder which turned the hopper, and a funnel which directed the seed on to the ground regularly. At the front a ploughshare created the seed row, and at the back a harrow covered the drilled seed in soil. At first this was a one-man walking operated machine, but it was refined to provide three rows at a time and became a wheeled, horse-drawn vehicle. Tull went on to create a hoeing device and to improve ploughs.

So now the seed was in the ground, and where this had been done by hand and not machine, harrowing followed. This was done with a sort of giant horse-drawn rake which covered the seeds with a layer of soil. Behind the horse harrow walked a boy, scaring away the birds with a sling and stones.

Draining, ditching and hedging now took up some time in the early winter and then threshing could take place in the barn. The ricks were unpicked and the corn stalks spread over the barn floor. After threshing the ripe cornheads (wheat, barley and oats) were gathered up, stored in bushel weight sacks ready for sale by the farmer. Left over little bits of grain on the floor could be swept up, carefully picked over and bagged up by the workers, ready to take to the miller to be made into a few pounds of flour for the family. Rough chaff was also saved – useful for the chickens.[1]

The crops in the ground, as soon as spring weather softened the earth, had to be weeded (docks and thistles) and in May in the grass

The threshing floor 1898 by Ralph Hedley 1848-1913 Laing Art Gallery Newcastle-upon-Tyne

meadows would be cut for hay. Hay fed the horses and the cattle during the coming winter months, so it was scythed by teams of workers, raked into long rows, turned on a good day to help it to dry out and then stooked up into haycocks. The next operation was to fork the stooks up onto the heavy horse drawn waggon, which was then driven to the rickyard, where the hay was forked off again to form hayricks, which were finally expertly thatched to defend the hay against any wet weather.

Now the corn crops were ripening in the summer sun and in late September the scythes were sharpened again and the teams were out in the hot heavy air, swinging in unison. The cut stalks were raked and formed into stooks, heads of corn upwards of course. Out came the carters with the big waggons, the heavy stooks were forked on, taken back to the rick yard, forked off again and expertly stacked into ricks, to await threshing. Now the teams could enjoy a harvest supper, with much eating and cider drinking. It was the best time of the year, well paid and satisfying, if exhausting.

This romantic view of the countryside is depicted by artists at that time. It is clear that many of them (although not Constable) thought that life was one long bucolic picnic. Samuel Palmer, whose paintings of the countryside are so powerful, saw his beloved countryside through golden tinted spectacles – his painting The Harvest Moon, done in 1833, just after the Swing Riots, depicts villagers stooking the newly cut corn under a moonlit, starry sky probably in the Kent countryside where much of the initial rioting occurred. As Susan Owens says of him in *Spirit of Place: Artists, Writers and the British Landscape*:

> ...he had moved to the small village of Shoreham deep in the heart of Kent, where he sketched ploughmen and shepherds, cornstooks and sheep-shearing, mossy-roofed byres and flowering apple trees. The natural forms he drew and painted are exaggerated, almost hallucinatory, each ear of wheat bulges happily, every farmer's field looks ready to burst with joy. Coming afresh to the body of work he created during these years, anyone would think that south-east England of the 1820s was an early paradise of fecund harvests and contented farm labourers. In reality, it was a place of simmering resentment about terrible working conditions and agricultural mechanisation that was shortly to boil over into the Swing Riots.

Some of the men were experts in their particular trade, such as the rick makers, providing their own tools. They were paid slightly more than

The Harvest Moon 1833 by Samuel Palmer 1805-1881 oil on paper Yale Centre for British Art

ordinary field workers, as were carters, cowmen and shepherds (who did not provide their own tools).²

Before ploughing could begin, there was the jolly task of muck spreading, and then the farming year could start again. But it was autumn, so there was plenty of fruit to be gathered from the countryside, and the children went out to collect blackberries, elderberries and even wild raspberries. All this helped the family's food supply.

Now the carters worked on maintenance of their waggons, cleaned out the horse barns, and prepared for winter, with all the normal feeding, cleaning, mucking out, and strawing down that was needed, both for horses and for cattle when they came in from the fields. Milking cows had to be brought in for winter, with their calves, and also the beef animals. At this period improvements in breeding were happening, providing more milk per lactating cow, and better meat from the selective breeding of both cattle and sheep.

The demand for labour therefore varied during the course of the year according to the way in which it was needed and how people were actually employed.

Farm servants were hired for a year and lived with the farmer's family – low wages but with board and lodging and security.

A regularly employed workforce, more or less kept busy all year round, living in a tied cottage (tied to the farm which employed him), gave less security, reasonable wages but an unsatisfactory, insecure employment state, as losing one's work meant losing one's home.

Casual labour, such families living in a rented cottage, employment found by the day or piece rate gave no security at all and forced the labourer to seek other work in the parish if his usual employer did not need him – otherwise he would be in receipt of poor relief (provided by the parish vestry).

The final group were the independent skilled specialists, such as hurdle makers, thatchers, hedgers etc who were paid as contractors but might have employees (casual or otherwise) of their own.

All these workers contributed to the rural economy but had varied standards of living and would be differently affected by enclosures and now by the introduction of machinery.³

The wonderful threshing machine was enthusiastically taken up by agrarian reformists and following Malthus' prediction in 1798 that population growth was about to outpace the food resources of the country, a brewer and landowner by the name of William Spicer Dix predicted that

Horse powered threshing machine

the threshing machine could double the amount of grain available for sale each year, eliminating the need for importing foreign grain.

During the subsequent labour shortages caused by the Napoleonic Wars, many farmers invested in a threshing machine. They were expensive though, £100 for a fixed horse-drawn or water powered machine, plus the cost of maintenance and probably the cost of borrowing the money in the first place. This machine worked by the corn stalks being fed headfirst into rollers, shaken out by iron rod beaters into a revolving drum; the seed heads then fell down and were funnelled into a hopper or box whilst the straw was fed out of the machine ready to be stacked into a straw rick. Two men, one woman and two boys were needed to run the machine, plus two to four horses to provide the power. The horses walked round and round all day, attached to long beams – as much as 6 yards (approx. 5.5metres) long. Later steam power would replace the horse or the water mill.

Portable threshing machines cost less and could be used in the field, cutting out the labour of one waggon loading procedure. These smaller machines might cost around £30 – £40 – still a considerable sum for a small farmer, so often the machine was hired from a contractor, or the contractor himself came with his machine to do the threshing.

In fact, many farms were of less than 100 acres – even in 1851 the average farm was only 110 acres (44.5 hectares) and 65% of farms were of less than 100 acres, not including smallholdings of five acres or less. With the cost of the machines the maintenance and the damage it often caused to the straw (used universally for thatching or sale) it was not very economic for farmers with less than 110 acres to machine thresh, when wages costs for hand flailing were so low and the balance of the costs of the labourers' incomes was made up by the parish, which, while including contributions from the farmers themselves, was spread around by the contributions of non-farming members of the parish.

Another point which the farmer needed to take into account was the price he could obtain for his corn. The machines did save time making the harvest available for sale much more quickly. As grain prices always began to fall immediately the harvest was in, it was essential for the farmer to sell quickly and the speed at which he could sell made a considerable difference to farm incomes, i.e. between making a profit and making a loss. Prices would gradually rise in the Spring, but farmers had costs and expenses to find in between harvest time and Spring, including rents falling due at Michaelmas. In addition, the corn had to be kept at a reasonable temperature and not allowed to get damp. Nevertheless by 1830 it has been suggested that there were about 1,000 threshing machines in use in central southern England. Manufacturers included Taskers of Andover, the subject, unsurprisingly, of a violent attack during the Swing Riots.

However, the more farmers who had a threshing machine, the greater the competition in getting a quick, good price at sale. Small farmers then began to realise that perhaps things would be better if there were no threshing machines at all and the field would become level again. Thus the tendency during the Swing Riots for farmers to stand aside willingly and watch their machines being broken up – and even on occasions uttering encouraging words to the rioters.

The labourers themselves obviously wanted the machines to go – no threshing in winter meant no money. No wonder the threshing machines became an icon of discontent.

But the Swing Riots did not start with agricultural labourers actually breaking up threshing machines. In Suffolk and Norfolk there had already been brutal suppression of riots on the border area around Diss and Hoxne in 1816 and again in 1822 – wages demands and objections to threshing machines. These demonstrations were put down by the local Suffolk Provisional Cavalry with the rough help of the 9th/16th Lancers. They became known as the 'Bread and Blood Riots'.[4] Each time, after punishment of the demonstrators, the countryside became quiet again. Discontent kept simmering below the surface however and in February 1830 a threatening letter purporting to come from 'Captain Swing' arrived at a farmhouse in Mildenhall, and then another at Brandon at the end of February. This was the first appearance of Captain Swing.[5]

However, it was in east Kent where the start of the sustained rioting of 1830 took place. At Wingmore near Canterbury on the 24th August a

'Swing' cartoon by Henry Heath 1830 – The British Museum – 'A knock-kneed ruffian with a sinister scowl .....'

gang of 24 men descended upon a farm owned by Mr Dodds and destroyed a threshing machine. The long autumn and hungry winter months stretched ahead so something needed to be done.

On 28th August a machine belonging to a Mr Collick, on hire to Mr Inge at Palmsted, Upper Hardres, again near Canterbury, was destroyed by a mob of 57 men, 24 of whom then went on to break up two more machines at Stephen Kelsey's farm at Eastleigh in the parish of Lyminge. Kelsey's threshing barn had been the subject of an arson attack some months previously.[6] Apparently the local Reverend Price, a JP for Lyminge, had been talking with local farmers as to the justice of using these machines – this giving rise to the belief amongst the labourers that it was perfectly acceptable, after attempts to warn farmers that they should stop using the machines, that breaking them up was justified.

By mid September the original gang had been joined by men from other parishes and on 20th September they split into two gangs, destroying at least five machines in one night. They had become more organised now, sending out 'Swing' letters and following these up with attacks in the area between Canterbury to the north and Dover to the south-east. There was one arson attack amongst some 19 attacks on threshing machines in that area.[7]

These early machine breakers set a pattern for the subsequent Swing rioting events. Some were well planned attacks; on arrival at the chosen farm, four men were posted 'a rod and a half' away from the farm gate to keep watch. This would be about 30 feet away from the gate. As many as 30 men now formed a defensive line in front of the farmhouse to deter anyone inside from coming out to see who was actually involved in the operation. Then around 20 other men entered the barn where the dreaded threshing machine was stored, dragged it out and broke it up. This procedure would take about 20 minutes to half an hour, after which the company reassembled by the farm gate and gave three cheers, and then noisily whistling, shouting and singing, dispersed back home, or on to the next target. Frequently they went to the nearest public house for a few beers – there seems to have no attempt to disguise what was going on and perhaps they felt that with this number of labourers involved, no retribution would be taken. Of course, eventually the names of ringleaders became known and they were arrested, but by now there was no question of stopping.

As the movement gained momentum, the organised form of attacking did not always happen. Sometimes the riots were spontaneous, springing up after a few drinks in the pub, or men working themselves up into a state of anger and choosing a farm where they knew there was a machine, set out at night to destroy it. Sometimes, however, a gang started out at one farm in one parish, gathered more men in the next parish, destroyed a machine there, dropped the original team and went on to do further damage elsewhere, covering a considerable distance overnight, but not always with the same people, new men replacing men from a distance away. Labourers, it should be remembered, were used to working in gangs, hay making, thatching, loading, harvest making and flailing. Some of them having been soldiers, were used to being organised and told what to do.

By October 100 machines had been destroyed in the east Kent area and the riots spread westwards across west Kent into Sussex, where the area around Goodwood, Worthing and Yapton was attacked. On the movement went towards Berkshire and Hampshire. By the 17th November rioting had arrived at the area near Sutton Scotney, in Hampshire, where radicals were already raring to go – they had heard Mr Cobbett speak, and also Mr Henry Hunt. Micheldever, Overton, St Mary Bourne and then Andover on the 19th and 20th November; Vernham Dean to the north of Andover, Weyhill to the west and on to Netheravon and Figheldean in Wiltshire. It wasn't always machine breaking of course, demands for more wages, demands for money on the spot or food or drink occurred, but the demands came with threats of arson and machine breaking. Andover was particularly targeted, because at Upper Clatford, a village close by, the company called Taskers was based, known then as blacksmiths, but actually agricultural machine manufacturers. There the rioters attacked twice, damaging the manufacturing of the machines. By the 22nd November the rioting reached the Salisbury area.[8]

1830 had already been a year of change at the highest level of government. In August the Duke of Wellington had managed to retain his parliamentary majority at the general election. At the time the Whig party was in some disarray with no official leader, Earl Grey having relinquished the position in 1824, due to the animosity felt towards him by the then reigning monarch, George IV.

On the death of George IV, in June 1830, Grey, who had the approval of the new monarch, William IV, was able to resume leadership of the Whig party. In November, following the defeat of Wellington's Tory party on the Civil List division, Wellington himself resigned and Earl Grey became prime minister of a coalition government which would go on to promote the reform proposals that Wellington and the Tories had resisted.

Wellington, the hero of Waterloo, had expressed his views on how to deal with the Swing rioters –

'I induced the magistrates to put themselves on horseback, each at the head of his own servants and retainers, grooms, huntsmen, gamekeepers, armed with horsewhips, pistols, fowling pieces and what they could get, and to attack in concert .... these mobs, disperse them, destroy them, and take and put in confinement those who could not escape'.[9]

These views undoubtedly influenced the attitude of many landowners, resulting in behaviour which would affect the lives of the agricultural labourers for ever. However, the new government, despite its apparent enthusiasm for reform, would pursue and punish these troublesome rioters and get them out of the country and out of public consciousness as soon as possible.

5
November 1830 (2)

THE 23RD NOVEMBER falls on a Tuesday, and as is usual in Salisbury, it is market day, as it has been since 1361. The streets in the centre of the city are full of noises and smells – the cattle for sale are tied up in pens on Ox Row, the fish sellers are shouting their wares for sale in Fish Row and the housewives are clustered around the Butter Market at the end of Fish Row. Farmers huddle in the public houses, speaking in low tones about the terrible things that are happening in the countryside – the rumours fly around the city – there have been riots all across the villages edging the Plain, with threats and demands for money by labourers in Collingbourne Ducis, Buttermere, Ramsbury and down the Avon valley as far as Figheldean. Even here in Salisbury there have been threats, and destruction of threshing machines in Great Bedwyn, Ramsbury, Downton, Enford, Idmiston and Netheravon, Newton Toney, West Dean and now Whiteparish – have you heard that arson attacks have happened in Amesbury and Everleigh and yesterday in Winterslow? Where next? They soon find out.

At Downton that day a mob of 20 or so men attack Mr Reed's threshing machine by burning it and the farmer, who tries to put out the flames, is pelted with stones. Another Downton farmer, James Shelley has his machines broken too and 100 people attack a machine at Idmiston.

Talk is that the city of Salisbury is advertising for special constables to help keep the peace and that the magistrates held a meeting yesterday to put this measure in place. None too soon in the opinion of the farmers and the traders. Only this morning a great mob of 150 people had demanded money from a surgeon at Whiteparish and now the talk in the pubs is that a large number of men are approaching along the London Road towards the city, intending to destroy the iron foundry owned by Mr Figes. Stopping at Bishop Down they casually break up a threshing machine.

However, on approaching Salisbury, they meet with members of the Salisbury troop of the Wiltshire Yeomanry, who have been deployed with special constables and accompanied by Mr William Wyndham, the magistrate. In the absence of Lord Arundell, the Commander of the Salisbury troop, it is led by Lt. Peniston (a local architect). After an appeal to the men to disperse fails to move them, Mr Wyndham reads out the Riot Act. This too falls upon deaf ears and it is left to Lt. Peniston to give the order to charge. Stones are thrown at the volunteer soldiers but the yeomanry, with its sabres and the potential of using pistols, prevails – 22 rioters are arrested and brought into Salisbury where 17 of them are committed for investigation.

Now the Salisbury troop starts patrolling the city streets, posting a ten-man guard outside the Council House. The onlookers gawp at the volunteer soldiers, turn away to discuss the whole matter and as the market starts to close, the carts clatter up to collect the remaining animals and hurdles. The farmers disperse home, the housewives gather up the last of the bargains from the traders, and the city is left with the yeomanry to guard it through the night. They are to be relieved in the morning by the Hindon troop led by Captain William Wyndham (eldest son of Mr William Wyndham the magistrate, from Dinton), the troop having arrived in Salisbury that afternoon. Hindon troop are instructed to take over guarding the city and to patrol the streets the next day. The troop has about 60 members at this time, so allowing for absentees, is probably about 55 in strength.

Wednesday 24th November dawns and witnesses an increase in riotous activity in the Salisbury area. About 250 men are involved in damaging machines at Broad Chalke, including unfortunately the water wheel on the farm of Mr Jesse Rumbold. The mob goes on to break machines belonging to Mr John Selfe, Mr Young and Mr Rebbeck at Ebbesbourne Wake and then Mr Thomas Blandford at Fifield Bavant. The members of this mob vary – usually attacking farms in a parish not their own. This is so that they are not recognised easily by the farmer whose machines they are damaging. They also demand money, drink the farmers' cider and as a result become generally rude and unmanageable, refusing to listen to reasoned requests by the farmers.

In the afternoon another large mob collects at Wilton, attacking the cloth manufacturing mill owned by Mr John Brasher. The 18- year-old leader of this mob, John Jennings, announces to the son of the owner that they are going to, 'break the machines to pieces in order to make more work for the poor people'.

Samuel Brasher points out that all this will do will be to throw more poor people out of work. Jennings is not persuaded by this argument and tells Samuel to 'get out of the way or I will break you to pieces'.

Samuel sensibly stands aside and the mob pours in to the factory, spreading through the mill buildings and breaking up the engines and the weaving machinery. Damage totalling about £500 is achieved quite quickly.

At Alderbury a large mob is confronted by local landowners Lord Radnor of Longford Castle and Mr George Fort. Mr Fort is the owner of Alderbury House and a magistrate. He is the son of a previous high sheriff of Wiltshire, Mr George Yalden Fort. This mob has destroyed machines in the area, stopping in Alderbury for refreshment and to collect up prior to moving on to Salisbury. Lord Radnor sends for help and Colonel Baker who is today leading the Hindon troop arrives with his men whilst the mob is still in the pub – drinking the profits from the demands for money made by them that morning from Mr Henry Rumbold. The Hindon troop surrounds the pub and takes 12 men prisoner, allowing the rest to go home. The men are bound, loaded into a farm waggon and taken to Fisherton Gaol under escort, where they arrive at 5.00 p.m.

Whilst all this is taking place around Salisbury more mobs are very active throughout Devizes, Marlborough, Highworth and the Heytesbury areas. Wiltshire seems to be on the verge of revolution.

The streets of Salisbury are again filled with horses, gigs, farmers and landowners, who have arrived to take out insurance policies against damage to their properties from arson, looting and machine breaking. However, shopkeepers have closed their shops, barring the windows and the yeomanry is patrolling the streets – fires can be seen on the hills surrounding the city.[1]

The yeomen are all volunteers – the first unit had been formed in August 1794, all being gentlemen, yeomen or 'any other person approved by the Lord Lieutenant of

Cornet of the Wiltshire Yeomanry: Hugh Evelyn Prints

the county'. A volunteer territorial force, it appeals to those who enjoyed their hunting, coursing and 'any other bold riders'. The first Hindon troop was commanded by Thomas F Grove, Captain, with J H Penruddocke Esq as lieutenant, and a young William Wyndham is appointed cornet. All pay earned whilst on active service is to be divided equally between officers and men without the least distinction. Other rules are

> That they are to find their own horses, saddles, and leather breeches (each Horse to be fourteen Hands and a half high, or upwards), and that whatever Sum shall be allowed by the Committee of the Wiltshire Subscription shall be applied for the purpose of providing such Regimentals, Arms and Accoutrements and other necessaries for the troop, as may be directed by the said Committee.
>
> That they will forfeit the sum of Twenty Pounds in case of non-attendance, without sufficient cause, upon being called out to suppress Riots and Tumults in this County.[2]

So there is every reason for the men of the Hindon troop to ride into Salisbury in support of peace keeping – apart from the excitement of course! It was not often that they are called upon to exercise their authority.

Early in the morning of Thursday 25th November news reaches Salisbury that demonstrations are planned to take place in Hindon itself. It will be market day there, so a decision is made that the Hindon troop, some 45 men strong, should now return to its own village to keep order on its home territory. Accordingly the troop, temporarily based at the headquarters in Salisbury, rises, breakfasts, feeds and waters the horses and by the time they saddle up and leave Salisbury it is already 10.30 in the morning. Even if they ride at the trot the whole way (which is not really feasible), it is about 17 miles from Salisbury to Hindon. At the trot the troop moves at about 7 miles per hour and at the walk, 3.5 – so it takes them some time to reach Hindon.

Many years afterwards, the great countryside writer W H Hudson met an old man in Hindon who remembered watching the beginning of the day's rioting:

'He was but a small boy, attending the Hindon school, when the rioters appeared on the scene, and he watched their entrance from the schoolhouse window. It was market-day, and the market was stopped by the invaders, and the agricultural machines brought for sale and exhibition were broken up. The picture that remains in his mind is of a great excited crowd in which men and cattle and sheep were mixed together in the wide street, which was the market place, and of shouting and noise of smashing machinery and finally of the mob pouring forth over the down on its way to the next village, he and other little boys following their march.'.

On arrival in Hindon the troop finds that after breaking threshing machines which had been brought to the market for sale, the insurrection has moved on and it is already after 12.00 midday. An attack has taken place at Pythouse Farm, and they must now have heard that part of the mob had moved on again and were attacking at Linley Farm, so the troop follow this lead. There is no mention in the records that any battle took place at Linley Farm, or of the presence of the Hindon troop, but there must have been some sort of skirmish there, as musket balls have been found at the site.[3] Firing must therefore have occurred and this would indicate that Captain Wyndham at the head of his troop was quite prepared to give the order to fire when he thought it necessary.

It is well into the afternoon, at about three o'clock, when Captain Wyndham calls on Mr Benett at Pyt House itself, where Mr Benett is resting following the attack upon him at his own farmyard. Mr Benett gets back on his horse, and together with the Hindon troop rides up the lane where it meets the now very cheerful mob, said to total 500 but this is difficult to assess. They meet in the narrow defile between Pyt House and Hatch House, with steep banks on either side and woods to the edge where the banks are fenced. The mob ironically gives a great cheer when the men see the soldiers approaching, all on their horses. Men immediately scramble up the banks, over the post and rail fencing and into the woods either side, where they collect stones. Once again Mr Benett tries to read them the Riot Act, but now the mood of the mob changes to one of sneering anger and stones are hurled at the men on horseback.

The troopers are ordered to fire blank cartridges but this only induces scornful laughter. It is doubtful that they used blank cartridges . Musket balls have now been found in Crosse Close field and smaller lead bullets in East Crosse field. The first volley may in fact have been fired by the troop across the heads of the mob to deter them. Musket balls are lethal to about 175 yards but only 'accurate' to about 100 yards. Volleys aimed at killing are normally fired at about 25/50 yards to ensure accuracy. The musket balls which landed in Crosse Close were, if the Hindon troop were around the wooded plantation area, fired high above the heads of the mob as they land at least 250 yards away. This is a warning procedure only. For half an hour or so the stones fly and the soldiers, riding up and into the woods,

The fight at Pythouse – watercolour – whereabouts unknown

slash with sabres. The mob retaliates by throwing their clubs, sticks and axes, and trying to do as much damage as they can, whilst being cut around the head and shoulders with the sabres of men who are their neighbours and whose families all know one another. Fingers are cut off, and skulls opened.[4]

Captain Wyndham now splits his men into two parties and they go round the back of the rioters, in an attempt to round them up, but movement amongst the trees is difficult for men on horseback, easier for men on foot to dodge around. According to Mr Benett, Captain Wyndham asks him if he should order the cavalry to fire – Benett apparently replies:

'For God's sake not if you can help it, but we must beat them'

Wyndham orders a sabre charge. The mob is running out of missiles and starts to try dragging the troopers from their horses. They attempt to hold the reins of the horses and hit the soldiers, and this is how John Harding is killed. He is from East Knoyle, but is there with his brother from Hatch.

Mr Benett told Parliament later that he had been unwilling to allow the troopers to use their pistols, but inevitably, they eventually do, and John Harding is shot, by a trooper with a pistol the bullet entering his head and exiting on the other side. He dies quickly. His brother is called over to him. The mob is horrified, shocked, many rioters are now wounded, with both sabre cuts and pistol shot wounds.[5] None of the Hindon troop are killed, but many received bruises and scrapes, and Captain Wyndham himself has cuts

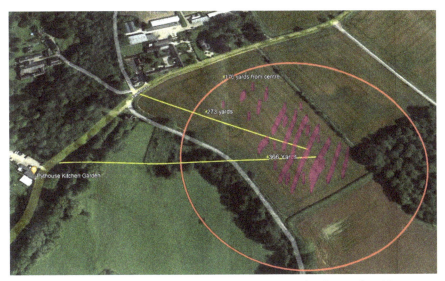

Musket balls found at Cross Close field and trajectory plan by Stephen Toomer, metal detectorist

and bruises to his head.

Finally the mob runs out of steam, and flees in all directions, some towards Hatch, some through Fonthill Woods to Fonthill Gifford, Hindon or Fonthill Bishop and some up the Newtown road towards Tisbury, pursued by the horse borne troopers, who catch and arrest 29 men. Pistol shot has been found in East Crosse Close, next to Crosse Close, on the road towards Tisbury. Mr Benett orders two of his great farm waggons to be brought round with their horses, and the first one is driven by John Brickle. The prisoners are loaded, bleeding and bruised, into the waggons and slowly the sombre procession starts the journey to Salisbury. It is late on the November afternoon and becoming dark. It will take some time to reach Salisbury, driving the waggons through the pitch black countryside. The whole troop of 45 men escort the waggons as far as Fonthill Park, where it is decided that Corporal King and 15 men should return to Pyt House to mount a guard there to protect Mr Benett and his property. Sergeant Goddard is instructed to ride on to Chilmark with nine troopers to guard the property and house of Mr Henry King, a local landowner, friend of John Benett and owner of the property known as Down Farm at Fonthill Bishop. The rest of the troop escorts the two waggons full of miserable prisoners to Salisbury.

John Brickle records the event much later on (he is actually 96 when this is done but he remembers it very well). He mentions that blood 'did trickle out of 'em waggons all the way to Salisbury'. When they reach the pub at Chilmark (he calls it the Black Horse but he is 96 – it was probably the Black Dog) or if it was the Black Horse, it would have been at Teffont Magna; both public houses being on the Salisbury road. He says:

'the prisoners cried out for summat to drink poor Fellows but the Cavalry wouldn't let 'em have nothing – They wouldn't. It were awful cold night and they were most shramm'd with the frost'.[6]

One load of men, the worst wounded, are taken to Salisbury Infirmary, where three or four of them are admitted. Everyone else is carted off to Fisherton Gaol, to join the other Wiltshire men who are already inmates. It is midnight before the demoralised rioters from Tisbury are finally committed and the troopers of the exhausted Hindon troop are able to return to their headquarters in Salisbury.

The following morning Mr Benett is determined to round up the men he considers to be troubleshooters, men who are known to him. A troop of the 9th Lancers is posted to assist Captain Wyndham in this task.

Meanwhile the government appoints a senior soldier by the name of Lt. Col. Mair to supervise troop movements and ensure that peace is returned in the area around Salisbury. He visits the Gaol where he meets the newly incarcerated Wiltshire labourers, where, he reports, they impress him as reasonable men. Their argument is 'that their enemy is capital, and that if some should be allowed on bail to return to their families….. they hoped they would evince by their loyal, industrious and peaceable conduct that they might be depended on'. Mair sees the point of this and allows some to go home. He also subsequently writes to the Home Office on their behalf, saying that they did not receive a 'fair remuneration' and that something should be done to help them.[7] None of the Tisbury men appear to have been allowed to go home.

Lt. Col Mair is a competent military man. He now sets up a plan to police the city. The special constables are to be divided into districts of between 50 and 100 men, classing them according to the vicinity of their habitations. A Head Constable is to be appointed for each district, and each district will be allocated a letter, e.g. A, B.C, and each Constable within that district is to be numbered. One district each night will be responsible for guarding the city. There are to be seven districts, with three superintendents to each one. This solves the security problem to the temporary satisfaction of the householders of Salisbury. He gives precise instructions to the superintendents as to how to keep the peace and draws up a sketch plan of Salisbury divided into chequers.[8]

Mr Benett has not been idle. He explains to Captain Wyndham about the troubleshooters and on Monday the gallant Captain arrests Richard Pitman, said to be one of the leaders of the riot at Pythouse Farm. Richard puts up a valiant struggle but is duly taken. In the evening five more Tisbury men are taken, one of whom attempts to evade his pursuers by hiding in his cottage chimney. Amongst the men taken this evening are the two young men from Church Street, William Snook and John Burton.

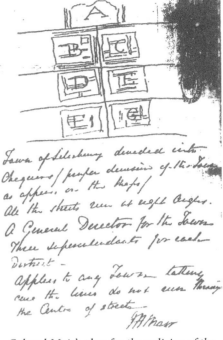

Colonel Mair's plan for the policing of the city of Salisbury PRO HO 40/27 E367

At Tisbury today, an inquest is held into the death of John Harding. Evidence is given that the rioters had jeered at the Hindon troop, throwing stones and missiles. The order to charge and take prisoners had resulted in more resistance it is said, and shots were thus fired. A witness reports that he saw one of the mob holding on to the reins of a trooper's horse with his left hand whilst with his right he attacked the rider with a club stick. The yeoman had resisted for five minutes but then drew his pistol and shot the man. The jury brings in a verdict of 'Justifiable Homicide'. It is worth mentioning that the foreman of the jury is the father of one of the Hindon troop of volunteer yeomanry.

Because of this verdict, the coroner considers the consequence to be an act of 'felo de se' which means that legally he cannot grant a warrant for release of the body for a Christian burial and although he was very sorry, it was his painful duty to tell this to the relatives of John Harding. However painful the duty devolves upon him and he admits he is thus adding to the sorrow of the grieving relatives, the facts are too clear to admit any alternative. However, it later transpires that John Harding's body is actually buried in the churchyard at Hindon although according to the carter Mr Brickle it was Knoyle, as apparently his people came from Knoyle. They were able to take it away for burial in the part of the churchyard reserved for unbaptised infants and those who commit suicide. His brother remains in Hatch. John Harding had presumably been with his brother at Hatch when they decided to join the mob that fatal day.

News of the rioting reaches the Rev. William Daniell at Warminster Common and in his diary on the 27th November he writes:

'This week has been a week of such terrible desolation and fear as the oldest man living never knew. The laboring classes of society have assembled large riotous mobs in several adjoining counties, and they have burned the corn and destroyed the farmers' machinery in every direction. They also levied contributions when they chose and nothing it seemed could resist them.'

Daniell is concerned that the rioting came so near to Warminster – mentioning Heytesbury as being only three miles away. However he is very concerned at what he has heard happened in the Hindon area where, he says the mob daringly attacked the cavalry and regular miliary engagement took place......

'One of the mob was shot on the spot; another was found dead in the adjoining wood; one or two others, they say, have since died of their wounds; several have had their hands and fingers chopped off; about 100, it is supposed, are wounded more or less.'

Clearly the number of dead had increased with the telling of the events. However, Daniell is initially not particularly sympathetic to the mob. He mentions that 'many influential persons took the advantage of a dissatisfied spirit in the poor, and thus led them on to such terrible results.'

However, he subsequently meets with a person who questions his views on the situation in the country, telling Daniell that the poor have no representatives, their cry is not heard. This is a debt, says Daniell's informant, which has been accumulating for years – it is the righteous vengeance and the finger of Almighty God. Daniell goes on to record in his diary that as a result of this discussion he has now begun to agree that the poor should be represented in parliament – are they not, he asks himself, a substantial and very important part of the nation? This is an extremely radical view, but not yet one shared by many of his peers.

By Thursday 2nd December 1830 Fisherton Gaol in Salisbury is full – Devizes House of Correction has received 100 men as a result of the riots and 30 more are at Old Bridewell also in Devizes. The authorities are informed that a special commission would be issued. Trials would be held at Salisbury before a judge, and minor offences tried at Devizes at a magistrates' court hearing.

However, on the 17th December Lord Melbourne writes to the Earl of Radnor of his concern at the state of the local gaols and confirms his agreement with local magistrates that as many prisoners as possible should be tried at the special commission trials rather than his previous preference for reserving minor cases to the quarter sessions. 'The clearance of the gaols will be of the greatest public convenience'.

The first special commission opens at Winchester on the 18th December with Mr Baron Vaughan, Mr Justice Alderson and Mr Justice Parke appointed as commissioners. The Attorney General, Mr Sergeant Wild are amongst the crown Prosecutors. Three hundred Hampshire men are charged, either with extorting money by threats or with breaking machines. Mr Justice Alderson announces that, 'We do not come here to enquire into grievances. We come here to decide law'[9]

But the law as it stood is against the labourers and they are not allowed to give evidence about unfairly low wages or distress through poverty. The judges allow themselves, however, to pontificate about conditions, about the outrage of men trying to compel employers to raise wages by assembly together and making threats, and about the presence of not only agricultural labourers at these riots, but also of tradesmen such as wheelwrights, shoemakers, village mechanics, joiners, carpenters and smiths. The Justices feel that these tradesmen should be even more heavily punished for their temerity in joining in the disturbances. It is the fact that these working men have opinions and spoke about them that disturbs their Honours. The Mason brothers at Bullington come in for special attention – they actually take in a copy of Cobbett's Register regularly and read it aloud to 20 or 30 villagers.[10] A cobbler William Winkworth is another of Cobbett's faithful readers. Joseph Mason and William Winkworth are sentenced to be 'cut off from all communion with society for the rest of their lives' and Joseph's brother Robert gets transportation for life, which is presumably the same as Joseph and William are condemned to suffer.

Six men at the Winchester trials are 'reserved for execution', 95 men transported for life, 36 transported for various other lengths of time, 65 imprisoned in England with hard labour and 67 acquitted. Of the six reserved for execution, four are saved as a result of a public outcry in the local and national press, and only two are actually hanged. However, the hangings are particularly cruel, as the commissioners insisted that all the prisoners be present at the executions. *The Times* of 17 January 1831 reported that 'many of the convicts were weeping bitterly, some unable to stand, leaning against the wall of the prison yard.' This is to be their last view of British justice fairly dispensed.

Fortunately for the men of Wiltshire, incarcerated in Fisherton Gaol and at Devizes, awaiting their own form of justice, the hangings took place after their own trials. But the sentencing at Winchester did not bode well for them.

On Thursday 2nd December it is announced by the local newspaper that the following men from Tisbury (amongst others from Wiltshire) have been committed to Fisherton Gaol during the previous week:

>   Thomas Topp, ploughman
>   William Sanger, agricultural labourer
>   James Mould, ploughman
>   Thomas Rixon, carter
>   Andrew Moxham, agricultural labourer
>   William Gray, agricultural labourer
>   Samuel Banstone, (Macy) agricultural labourer
>   James Mould, agricultural labourer
>   Richard Pitman, kitchen gardener, groom
>   Samuel Barratt, agricultural labourer
>   Thomas Abree, mason
>   James Blandford, agricultural labourer
>   Thomas Vining. Agricultural labourer
>   Samuel Eyres, agricultural labourer

By Monday 13th December another Tisbury lad has been committed:
>   Edmund White, blacksmith

By 20th December:
>   Charles Jerrard, agricultural labourer/carter
>   William Snook, ploughman
>   John Barratt, agricultural labourer, /mason
>   And by 23rd December:

Thomas Birt (Burt), top sawyer
George Mould, agricultural labourer
Henry Osbourne
Charles Martin
William Scott
Thomas Targett, agricultural labourer

In the Minute Book for Salisbury Infirmary for Saturday 4th December 1830, the following note is written:
'George Young Tisbury
Thomas Stingeman Tisbury
Henry Viney Tisbury
Jonathan Vincent Fonthill
Discharged from the Gaol and sent here with wounds upon the heads, hands.'[11]

Henry Viney is another agricultural labourer, listed in the 1841 census Return as living in Tisbury Row. He is likely to be a relative of Thomas Viney. He must have been discharged after treatment, with the three other men, who are not listed amongst those sent for trial. According to William Turner's recollection of the events in his youth, however, Thomas Stingeman was involved in the battle at Pythouse – he is described as 'a veritable Trojan, fighting desperately against five of his enemy And severely wounded'. William also states that 'at trial he was acquitted, his wounds and desperate suffering saving him from a life sentence beyond the seas', but his name is not listed amongst those tried, nor are the names of George Young or Jonathan Vincent mentioned again as rioters. By 1861 Thomas Stingiman (or Stingimore) and George Young are neighbours, living at the Chicksgrove end of Course Street in Tisbury. Both are agricultural labourers, with family nearby. Jonathan Vincent is living with his mother Lucy at Fonthill Gifford, where he is still a blacksmith.[12]

Christmas 1830 in Fisherton Gaol would not be a joyful occasion for the men awaiting their fate.

6
The Full Panoply

THE MISERABLE MONTH of December winds slowly on towards Christmas.

By now the National press is aware of the drama unfolding in Wiltshire. On the 10th December *The Times* reports the attack on Mr Mortimer's woollen cloth making mill on the Fonthill estate, with its broken machinery, now rusting beside the lake, and its emptied cottages. The newspaper comments:

'At Fonthill some thrashers are still working at 7s per week .... The mill at Fonthill has been unoccupied for nearly two years, and very few persons indeed are employed about the grounds. Indeed the whole place seems fast sinking into ruin. The cottages are fast decaying, and the broken windows indicate the extreme poverty of the once prosperous and happy peasantry of Mr Beckford'.

On the 18th of the month Mr William Edward Tallents, a crown lawyer, is sent by the government to Salisbury to start arranging the prosecutions and to liaise with the prosecuting solicitors. Mr Tallents is principal steward and political agent for the 4th Duke of Newcastle. The treasury would be paying him the sum of £1,500 for supervising the special commissions set up for Berkshire, Hampshire and Wiltshire, although in the end he only took responsibility for Wiltshire. He had written to the Home Secretary, Lord Melbourne, that hardly any preparations had been taken towards the trials of the prisoners and there was an expectancy in the county that the bulk of the costs would fall upon the government rather than the county.[1]

The trials are to be held outside the normal bi-annual local court schedule. However, care should be taken that the government should not be seen to be interfering with the normal administration of the law. In addition, the apparent leniency of the punishments meted out to the rioters in Kent for example should not be shown to the Hampshire and Wiltshire offenders, who must be seen to be properly punished for their riotous behaviour. The local magistrates would need to be involved at all levels. Poverty would not be an excuse.

Lt. Col. Mair is to make the arrangements for escorting the prisoners to and from Fisherton Gaol. The 'Nisi Prius' court will have three judges and Mr Tallents will be at the White Hart on Saturday 18th December with a Mr Bingham, Counsel, who will advise on drawing up the indictments for each prisoner together with the Clerks from each magistrate's division where the prisoners live. Great care is to be taken that the special commission shall be an example of British justice.

On the 22nd December the Salisbury Town Clerk issues a Notice that a special commission is to be held starting on the 27th December. All special constables are to be available for the period of the trials, to keep the peace and to assemble at the following Divisional points:

Division A	The White Horse Inn, Castle Street
B	The Black Horse Inn
C	in the Cheese Market
D	at the Goat Inn
E	at the White Hart Inn
F	at the Radnor Arms
G	at the Red Lion Inn

The judges, appointed from the courts in Westminster, are due to arrive at 3.00 p.m. on the 27th December. They are to be met by the High Sherriff and the Under Sherriff of the county and a company of men armed with javelins, who will escort them into the city of Salisbury. special constables and many 'gentlemen of influence in the county' will join to form a cavalcade. The special commission will open formally and the court then adjourn until Tuesday morning 28th December. It is to be an example of British justice, its power and authority, its purpose being to impress the local population and to deter any further unrest. The full panoply of the law will

The Guildhall in Salisbury – 1798 – aquatint 'New Council House' by Francis Jukes (before the north porch was added around the time of the trial)

be displayed. Lord Melbourne, as Home Secretary, is determined to make no major strategic or political changes in the way that popular insurrections are handled.[2]

And in fact, this is how it happens.

Mr Sergeant Wilde arrives from Winchester, the special commission is opened and then adjourned. In the courts, practical arrangements are made to shield their Lordships the judges from draughts, as so many doors open into each courtroom at the Guildhall. However, there is no heating in the form of fires or stoves and the weather is cold.

The judges themselves do not arrive in Salisbury until after midday on Friday 31st December, New Year's Eve. Mr Baron Vaughan, Mr Justice J. Parke and Mr Justice Edward Hall Alderson are met by the mayor of Salisbury and the high sheriff of the county, attended by about 100 of the local nobility, gentry, the magistrates and yeomen all on horseback, or in their carriages. This procession precedes their Honours as the procession winds its way to the cathedral. The streets on either side are lined with about 400 special constables.

At the cathedral the procession is welcomed by the Dean with the Canons and other members of the Clergy. The Rev. Mr Kitson, Chaplain to the Sherriff, gives a sermon based upon 1 Peter, chap ii, verse 16: 'As free, and not using your liberty for a cloak of maliciousness, but as the servants of God' No doubt it has taken him some time to locate what he feels is appropriate chapter and verse and it is much appreciated by the fortunate, free and of course, totally non-malicious congregation that day.

Their Honours now retire to their comfortable lodgings in the Guildhall.

The local newspaper reports that the calendar of prisoners is very heavy with upwards of 300 people committed for trial. New Year's Day would see the first of these trials. A date for the start of trials in the next county, Dorset, has been set as 10th January, but it seems very unlikely that the Wiltshire trials will be completed by that date.[3]

On Saturday, the commissioners, Mr Baron Vaughan, Mr Justice Parke, and Mr Justice Alderson, together with the Marquis of Lansdowne (Lord Lt. of Wiltshire), the Earl of Radnor, and Mr T G B Estcourt all take their places in the Nisi Prius court room at the Guildhall. Nisi Prius – a trial of the issue of facts before a single judge or jury.

The court is to be held in the Oak Room, in the new Council House, at the Guildhall, built in 1795. This room is an impressive reproduction of a court in the Old Bailey and has its substantial, raised oak panelled Justices' bench set diagonally in one corner, looking down upon the assembly, which maximises space. It is intimidating and with the full majesty of the bewigged and robed judges, is designed strike awe and terror into the hearts and minds of anyone unfortunate enough to be called before the bench.

Below the courts are the cells where the prisoners will wait to be called. These are tiny, chilly and damp. There is insufficient room for all the prisoners for each day to wait, so they will have to be retained in prison vans outside, awaiting their turn. Hygiene facilities are basic.

The next step is the swearing in of the Grand Jury, and the following names are called:

A court room – the Oak Room

John Benett Esq. MP
Sir Edward Booth, Bart.
Wadham Wyndham Esq. JP
P. Methuen Esq
William Wyndham Esq
E Warrener Esq
George Eyre Esq
W H Ludlow Esq
George P Scrope Esq
Charles Wyndham Esq
Thomas Grove Jun. Esq
George Matcham Esq[4]

Sir J. D Astley, Bart, MP
Sir E Antrobus, Bart.
Robert Gordon Esq MP
G W Wroughton Esq
Alex Powell Esq
Harry Biggs Esq
William Fowle Esq
T B M Baskerville Esq
Fulwer Craven Esq
George Monkland Esq
Charles Hussey Esq

It will be noted that this is a Grand Jury composed of local (i.e. Wiltshire) Members of Parliament, Justices of the Peace and local nobility and landowners. Hardly a trial by their own peers for the local agricultural labourers. Mr John Benett MP is appointed Foreman of the Grand Jury.

Having sworn in these gentlemen as the Grand Jury, Mr Justice Parke addresses them at length, welcoming the collection of such a 'respectable body of the gentry of this county'. He regrets

'the spirit of subordination and tumult which has prevailed in many parts of the kingdom'.

During the course of his long introductory speech he points out that the spirit of disorder has not been confined to those who are distressed, and although distress may have had some share in producing these calamitous events he notes the importance of the role played by town and village craftsmen among the rioters and that such men have been the foremost in the destruction of the threshing machinery and the violent and often felonious acts which the mob, in the pursuit of that purpose, have so often committed. He exhorts the Grand Jury to look at the evidence and consider each case with calmness and deliberation. He reminds them that the crime of

A cell in the basement of the Guildhall

arson is justly punished by the death penalty, as are riotous assemblies that result in the destruction of houses or property or for a riotous assembly to remain together for an hour after the Riot Act has been read. At some length he reminds them that the repression of crime will ensure the peace of the country and obedience to its law.[5]

The Grand Jury now retires to the impressive Grand Jury Room above the court room to consider the first bill.

When the Grand Jury returns to the court room after three quarters of an hour's deliberation, it presents a bill against 23 men for destroying a threshing machine belonging to John Benett Esq. at Pythouse Farm, Tisbury on the 25th November 1830. Seventeen of these men are in custody and are now brought up from the cells and placed at the bar. They are:

James Blandford, Samuel and John Barrett, Samuel Banstone (Macy), Richard Pitman, the two James Moulds, one from Tisbury and the other from Hatch, Thomas Vining, Thomas Topp, Samuel Eyres, Thomas Rixen, Edmund White, the younger Charles Jerrard, William Snook, Thomas Burt, John Targett and Andrew Moxham.

All the prisoners plead 'not guilty'.[6]

The Attorney General opens the case against them, summarising it by saying that all of these men were part of a larger mob which had assembled near Hindon and walked to various farms in the area where they broke up machinery and committed other outrages.

The first witness to be called by the prosecution is Mr John Benett himself. He is examined by Mr Sergeant Wilde and describes meeting with the mob at Fonthill Gifford, trying to persuade them to disperse and then following them around the various farms until they reached his own farm at Pythouse, where they pulled down part of the roof of the building housing his threshing machine and destroyed the machine.

The next witness is John Brickle, the carter employed by Mr Benett, who goes through his evidence of working at Lawn Quarry for Mr Benett, seeing Jerrard, Blandford, John Barrett, Snook, Eyres, James Mould of Hatch, Topp, Vining and Moxham. Brickle tells the court that the mob took his six horses out of the team and forced him to go with them to Mr Benett's farm. He admits, on cross examination, that he had seen several people being forced to join the mob, but none of those were amongst the prisoners at the bar.

At this point James Mould from Hatch says he saw Brickle with Thring who was reasoning with the people and that the nearest Brickle got to the farm gate was a quarter of a mile away.

John Jay, the third witness, son of a Tisbury farmer, says that he arrived at Pythouse Farm at about midday and estimates that about 500 people were there. He says he saw Mould of Hatch with a hatchet forcing out a piece of wood which connected the horse house with the barn. Vining, he says, was throwing down the wall nearest to the horse wheel, using a pickaxe. Mould of Tisbury, says Mr Jay's brother, had a stick and he saw Charles Jerrard breaking the threshing machine.

John Jay's brother James Jay, Bailiff to Mr Benett, is called next. He testifies that Banstone and Snook were breaking the machine wheel. He admits he did not see Mr Benett struck but did see his employer's face streaming with blood, caused, he supposes, by the stones thrown at him. He also saw Mr Legge (Mr Benett's steward) being hit on the head by a stone. He also claims he was himself hit on the head that day, but not at Pythouse Farm.

Next in the witness box is Thomas Ball, Mr Benett's coachman, who witnessed Snook, who he says he knows very well, and had seen four or five times already that day, enter the farmyard and when asked by Mr Benett if they had come to beat down the machine, Snook agreed that this was so and immediately commenced breaking it up. Ball also testifies against Topp, saying that Topp threw the first stone at Mr Benett. He then brings out a large flintstone, weighing about 2lbs. This, says Ball, hit his employer in the face, between his eye and nose, whereupon Mr Benett's head fell forward, his hat fell off and his face was covered with blood. Ball says that he attempted to retrieve the hat, pointing his finger at Topp in accusation. He says that Topp then came forward and struck him with the handle of his sledgehammer.

John Uphill, a shepherd from Hindon is the next witness, identifying Burt, Blandford, Banstone, John Barrett and Vining as taking part in destroying the machinery. He had not seen Topp touching anything. Blandford attempts to cross examine the shepherd, saying that he had heard Uphill encouraging the others to destroy the machinery. Uphill denies this, replying that he

'said no such thing ……my master Benett was near me and had set me to watch those who came in to the yard'.

Blandford responds that John Uphill was a 'false swearer' and was backed by Topp and another prisoner.

Another Benett employee, George Turner, speaks next. He had been beaten up by the mob. He produced a club taken from one of the men. It was about 5' in length and 2' in diameter, with a large, double fist sized knob at one end. He identifies John Barrett.

Charles Wilkins, a blacksmith is called next. He says he was at the farm at the time and saw Pitman breaking the machine. He had also seen Topp and John Barrett but did not see Topp breaking anything, only the mob breaking the machine.

William Woods, a labourer who works for John Turner at Hatch Farm, identifies Blandford, Eyres and Rixen, whom he saw machine breaking, and also Banstone but did not see Banstone breaking anything. He does tell the court that he heard men in the mob telling others to 'keep their matches in their pockets' although none of the prisoners at the bar was amongst these.

John Duke is next. He had been at Pythouse Farm that day and saw Jerrard and Topp machine breaking. He knows Banstone but had not seen him there that day.

John Wilkins from Hindon testifies similarly having seen Edmund White striking the cast iron roller of the machine.

James Snow from Tisbury reports that he saw Targett tearing the thatch off the horse house and Noah Dogrell says he saw Banstone, Moxham and Topp, Banstone having three big stones in his left hand and a stick in his right. He also saw Charles Jerrard and Burt the sawyer.

James Dogrell, Noah's brother, had also seen Burt, chopping with an axe at the timber connecting the horse house and the barn. He had also seen Moxham and Vining destroying the horse house wall and Jerrard, with a piece of broken machinery in his hand.

James Green (there is also a member of the jury that day called James Green) says he had seen Banstone throw a stone at Mr Benett's head and the last witness Joseph Trim from Tisbury saw the mob destroy the machine and Vining beating down the wall and the beam of the horse house with a very heavy sledge (hammer) whilst the mob was breaking down the machinery.[7]

Most of the witnesses, it can be seen, are employees of Mr John Benett and indeed in some cases there is evidence that he has himself taken their sworn and signed statements at Pyt House.

The defendants are now allowed to speak in their own defence. There has been no arrangement made for them to be properly represented in court, they are expected to organise their own defence whilst waiting to come to trial and are not kept informed as to the nature or any details of the case against them.[8] These are under-educated, illiterate workers for the most part, probably completely daunted by the formal and frightening situation in which they now find themselves, unable to respond coherently to the charges being brought against them. They are not allowed to refer to their poverty or distress or refer to the damage that the threshing machine is doing to their livelihood. Only a very few had appeared before a court before and then only for minor poaching offences. Most are clearly intimidated by the proceedings and can only apologise or deny being present, or insist they were pressed to join the mob. Every prisoner expresses his regret – for example, William Snook says

'I am very sorry I was in the case. The mob knocked at my door early in the morning and said they would break it if I did not get up and go with them. I did go, against my will, but I did nothing'.

Thomas Burt – the top sawyer, says:[9]

'My Lord, I found work very hard to find in Fonthill, my own parish, for the last three years, and having a wife and three children to support, I was glad to go to work wherever I could get it. I had got some work at a place four miles from my house. I was going there that morning, before daybreak, when I met the mob. I got inside the hedge, intending to keep out of the way, but some of them saw me, and called out to me to join them. I wanted to get away, but they said that if I did not go with them they would kill me, so I was obliged to go. I tried to escape, but they would not let me. It is a hard case with me, my Lord, I was glad to get work, though I could only earn seven shillings a week, and it cost me one shilling a week for iron, so that I only had six shillings a week to support five persons'.

And Andrew Moxham –

'I am sorry that I was there, but I was going on an errand for my master when I met the mob, and they made me go, but as soon as I could I got away. I met one of my children and took it home. I have a wife and three children. I hope my Lord will consider me. I was never before my Lord before this, nor yet in a prison'.

Thomas Vining has the courage to say –

'I am very sorry that I was there. There was a great number of farmers there in the morning encouraging the people to go on, and if they did not give them that encouragement, or if they had told them not to go on, I do not believe they would have done any harm, or gone about. I am very sorry that I was there, but it is my first offence of any kind'.

After each prisoner has spoken one or two character witnesses are called to speak on behalf of individual prisoners –

James Target speaks for Richard Pitman, saying that he lives at Hindon and knows Pitman well and that Pitman's wife had just called her husband in for his dinner when men from the mob swore he should go along with them and started pushing him down the street where Pitman had been at work. He did not go willingly.

Mr Lambert, a gentleman from Hatch, speaks for James Mould of Hatch – he knows him well as a carrier, honest, sober and quiet – a jobber in pigs and cheese' with a house of his own. Mould at this point denies that he had a house, it had been sold, he says and he is not worth £5.

Lord Arundell also speaks for Mould, who had worked for him as a labourer. Mould is now very poor, he says, with a wife and six children, but two of these children had died of typhus whilst Mould was in Fisherton Gaol. His family would now have to be supported by the parish.

Mr Augustine King speaks for William Snook, who he says, has worked for him for many years. Snook lives in Church Street, Tisbury with his father. He is unmarried. Mr King hands in a written character reference.

James Cuff speaks for Thomas Rixon – a quiet man, says Mr Cuff, worked for me for five years – I sent him out to his work at 8.00 that morning.

John Wilkins, John Benett and William Jeffery spoke for others and a blind gentleman spoke for Thomas Burt.

The trial is now drawing to its close and Mr Baron Vaughan points out the laws relating to the offences and sums up the evidence, detailing it for each prisoner.

The jury has no difficulty in coming to its conclusions, finding all the prisoners 'guilty' except for Edmund White and Andrew Moxham, who were both found to be 'not guilty'.

This trial has taken all day and as it is now 9.15 p.m. the court adjourns until 9.00 a.m. on Monday 3rd January 1831.[10]

The prisoners are taken back to Fisherton Gaol to await sentencing, including Edmund White and Andrew Moxham, who whilst having been found not guilty of the offence at Pythouse, were also charged with machine breaking at Linley Farm and other places.

7
The Visitations of Providence

DURING THIS COMING week the special commission works hard, sitting again from 9.00 a.m. on Monday 3rd January 1831, hearing the cases concerning machine breaking at William Nash's woollen cloth mill at Quidhampton, John Brasher's woollen cloth mill at Wilton, extortion at Stapleford and threshing machine breakage at Corton. These trials take up the whole morning and at one o-clock Mr Justice Alderson and Mr T G B Estcourt move from the Nisi Prius court to the crown court to hear the first case there.

At the bar are Thomas Abree, John Barrett, James Blandford (again), James Mould of Tisbury, Richard Pitman and Edmund White. These men are charged with destroying a threshing machine, the property of John Benett Esq. at Linley Farm in the parish of Tisbury on 25th November 1830. This is the second appearance in court for all of them except for Thomas Abree.

Mr Serjeant Wilde opens the case before the jury, stating that if people who engaged in breaking machinery laboured under a delusion that the machines reduced the availability of labour, they were mistaken; in his opinion the introduction of machinery had tended to cause an increase in labour, since the introduction of machinery had enabled the more efficient production of various articles which could then be exported to other countries, rather than Britain having to import such articles.

John Jay is called as the first witness. He says that he was at Linley

Farm at about 3.00 in the afternoon and saw 700 – 800 men who had destroyed the machines there. He saw James Blandford. Abree told him they were going to Pythouse again, 'to have a bit of a row'. Blandford now speaks up, telling the court that Jay has sworn falsely and that he was never near the barn and Jay had never seen him there.

William Wood, second witness, says he saw John Barrett with a stick, which he produces. It is 5' long, 6' in circumstances (sic) and weighs about 6 or 7 lbs. He identifies Abree, Pitman who was in the barn near the machine and Blandford who was beating the machine. Blandford interrupts again, absolutely denying being there and Pitman agrees, saying 'Lord, your soul is gone, man'.

Charles Wilkins testifies that he saw Blandford with a large sledge hammer in his hand at Linley Farm, beating down the wheels and also James Mould with a small stick beating the machinery. Mould denies this.

Thomas Jay now testifies, producing an iron bar which he says Edmund White had been carrying. It was normally kept in the barn.

John Wilkins says he saw White beating the machinery with a sledge hammer.

John Ford, the sixth witness and George Turner, the seventh, both identify Abree as being with the mob in the barn and breaking machinery.

None of the prisoners defend themselves further but Mould says

'I was pressed by the mob and obliged to go with them'.

Building at Fonthill Gifford / the blacksmith's shop? Robin Webster

Character witnesses are now called, among them Lord Arundell, who speaks for Abree. Lord Arundell says he has known the prisoner for about 12 years and employed him for most of that time. Abree is a mason, very honest, quiet, steady, sober and industrious and a very regular chapel attender.

Lord Arundell also gives Edmund White a good character, as do other character witnesses, including John Snow, William Jeffery Bailiff to Lord Arundell, William Lambert, Matthew Coombes and John Gray.

John Williams now speaks for James Mould, who has worked for Williams' father for 12 years and Henry Bristow, the overseer in John Barrett's parish also gives Mould a good character – he is very poor, says Bristow, earning only 5/- a week and has a wife and a child.

At the end of these speeches Mr Justice Alderson sums up the evidence and the jury find all the prisoners guilty but recommend White, Abree, Mould and Barrett to mercy.

Mr Justice Alderson now addresses the gaoler, saying that the prisoners were still handcuffed when they were at the bar, which is very improper. When placed upon his trial says the judge, a prisoner should be perfectly free. The gaoler apologises and said the prisoners had been brought up in such a hurry he had not had time to take the handcuffs off. He is warned about allowing this, and vows that it will not happen again.[1]

The prisoners are taken down.

The court next tries a case of arson and machine breaking in West Grimstead.

After this it is the turn of the men charged with machine breaking at Down Farm, Fonthill Bishop, the machine being the property of Henry Self. These men are:

Charles Martin, John Penny, Robert Obourne, William Scott, John Targett, Jeremiah Topp and Thomas Topp. These men are fortunately represented in court by a Mr Williams, a magistrate, who has been retained as a defence lawyer and appears for defendants in a number of other cases where it is apparently thought to be appropriate. Clearly his expertise as a defence lawyer has been judiciously selected for certain trials only.

The first witness to speak against these men is Michael Bradley from Chilmark, who tells the court that on the morning of 25th November he is at work in a plantation, near Down Farm which is occupied by Henry Self. He sees, he says, 50 people with tools in their hands approaching the barn. John Penny goes inside and opens the door from the inside, the mob gets in and breaks up the machines. They throw out the parts and all beat

Mr Candy's barn at Stop Farm – Historic England

them to pieces and chop them up. Amongst the men are Jeremiah and Thomas Topp, Scott, Targett, Martin and Obourne, who, says Bradley, has an axe.

Mr Williams cross examines Bradley, who admits he told different people about the action, not Mr Self who lives two and a half miles away from him, but Mr King, his master at Chilmark. No, he had not seen a paper offering any reward for information. He admits that he was once a witness against men for sheep stealing – a crime for which they were acquitted.

Jeremiah Topp, Martin and Scott all deny being there. Obourne says he did not have an axe, Penny admits to having a hedge stake. Targett had been working two and half miles away and Thomas Topp says he was three miles away.

Mr Williams, on behalf of Martin, Scott and Obourne, now calls James Cheverell, a potter, who says he, Martin, Scott and Obourne were forced to go with the mob and had nothing in their hands. The mob first went to Mr Self's, but these four were, Cheverell claims, a quarter of a mile away from the mob and never went near the barn.

Cross examined by Mr Serjeant Wilde for the prosecution, Cheverell says he has known the others for five years and they are steady, industrious men. He himself works for Mr Dally at Rudge (sic) in the potteries. He repeats his version of events, saying that they stood about a quarter of a mile from the barn for about 15 to 20 minutes, then went down to Mr Self's house and from there to the Beckford Arms at Fonthill Gifford where he ate and drank with the three others. There were around 20 other men present. The mob, he says, then went to Lawn Farm, then Pythouse and then Tisbury. He says he went part of the way to Linley Farm, then

Farm buildings at Lower Lawn Farm – photograph by author

'ten or twelve of us went back to Tisbury. We were pressed between 7 or 8 in the morning and did not leave the mob until 3 in the afternoon. I am near 20 years old. I lodge at Mr Dally's, at Rudge. I sleep in his stable and eat my victuals in his home. My friends live at Tisbury. I do not know that the prisoners were ever in prison before'.

The court now hears from a Mr Thomas Bishop from Frome in Somerset, a baker and a sheriff's Officer. He swears he knows the witness Michael Bradley and

'would not believe him upon his oath'.

On cross examination by Mr Williams Mr Bishop reveals that Bradley denounces men for sheep stealing and then asks them for £10 in exchange for not witnessing against them. He heard Bradley do this in a public house in Shaftesbury. When he, Bishop, gave evidence on behalf of men falsely accused, the prosecutor, a Mr Steed, said that it had been on Bradley's evidence alone that the men had been prosecuted for sheep stealing and he, Steed, desired that a bill be preferred against Bradley for perjury.

Bradley now denies all this and blames Bishop. Mr William Dowding, the Deputy Governor of the gaol, is called and remembers Martin and Obourne being convicted for a felony in spring 1826, Charles Martin being sentenced to two months and Robert Obourne six months imprisonment with hard labour.

Mr Justice Alderson now sums up the case. The jury retires and returns with a verdict of 'Acquitted'.[2]

The morning of Tuesday 4th January sees the full complement of judges on the bench of the Nisi Prius court – Mr Baron Vaughan, Mr Justice Parke and Mr Justice Alderson, together with the Marquis of Lansdowne, the Earl of Radnor and T G B Estcourt Esq. The men from Tisbury, convicted the day before, are brought up to be sentenced and addressed at length by Mr Baron Vaughan:

He tells these young men that they are convicted for the crime of breaking a threshing machine, the punishment for which is transportation for seven years, and that they are fortunate, since they are also guilty of the offence of personal violence which might well have led to them losing their lives. He points out that it has been suggested that they are suffering great distress as agricultural labourers, but to suppose that this distress is caused by the use of machinery is a most gross delusion. Everyone knows that the times are not favourable, but people must submit to the visitations of providence and he hopes that the fate which awaits them will serve as a warning to other persons in their condition of life.

He now sentences James Blandford to 14 years' transportation and all the others except Eyres and Targett to seven years' transportation. These two receive sentences of 12 months' imprisonment in the House of Correction with hard labour.[3]

The prisoners are taken away, back to Fisherton Gaol to await transportation. It is market day again in Salisbury. This would be their last glimpse of life in the busy, noisy, smelly little city. It seems unlikely that any of their families would see them again. The driver whips up the horses, and the prison van rattles away down Fisherton Street.

The trials of the Wiltshire men accused of machine breaking, arson, rioting and robbery grind on through the week.

On Friday morning 7th January Thomas Topp and Henry Obourne (presumably Robert Obourne's brother) are brought up from the cells to stand at the bar. They are indicted for destroying a threshing machine belonging to Henry Self of Down Farm in Fonthill Bishop parish. James Blandford is not in court for this trial, as he has already been capitally convicted. However, on taking the stand, Mr Self tells the court that there was only part of a machine in his barn at the time, as he had removed it. He says

'My reason for removing the machine was on account of the fires there had been. I believe that the breaking of the machine in taking it down was accidental'.

Because the machine had already been rendered useless by the owner before it was broken further by the mob, the jury, on the direction of the judge, Mr Justice Parke, finds Topp and Obourne 'not guilty'. [4]

Uriah West, also before the bar that morning, and Obourne, are both discharged as there is no other indictment against them. Uriah West has already been acquitted for breaking machinery at Broad Chalke.

Pressure on the special commission to complete its work at Salisbury is now great, as the judges are expected at Dorchester on Monday afternoon. The following morning, Saturday 8th January therefore sees an extra judge sitting and this means using the Grand Jury Room upstairs as a court, in addition to the other two courts, the Nisi Prius and the crown court.

Mr Justice Parke presides over the crown court and after a number of cases are heard, three Tisbury men are brought up to stand trial on the charge of destroying a threshing machine, the property of James Lampard (of Lawn Farm) at Tisbury, on 25th November. They are John Burton, Andrew Moxam (sic) and George Mould, an offence for which they are acquitted. John Burton however, is put to the bar again to face a charge of rioting at Fonthill Gifford, to which he confesses, and is allowed to enter into recognizance of £100 and charged to keep the peace.[5] He is very fortunate.

That morning *The Times* publishes an article by its special commission correspondent which comments on the difference in demeanour between the Hampshire and Wiltshire labourers during their trials. The Wiltshire men, he says, are

'more athletic in appearance and hardy in manner, turning to the witnesses speaking against them with a bold and confident air, cross examine them and contradict the answers with a confidence and a want of common courtesy in terms of which comparatively few instances occurred in the neighbouring county'.

However, he puts this down to 'a very low state of moral intelligence' in Wiltshire.[6] Those prisoners would need all their boldness and confidence to face what was going to happen to them.

By 8 o'clock in the evening the three judges, having worked hard all day hearing cases and pronouncing sentences, are able to retire to their lodgings, the court adjourning until 8.30 a.m. on Monday 10th January.

And so it is that on Monday 10th January 1831 the special commission meets again to sentence the remaining convicted prisoners of whom there are very many, including two men who are probably going to be condemned to death – Peter Withers, from Rockley in the north of the county and James Lush from Bishopstone near Salisbury. The first batch of

THE PYTHOUSE RIOTERS   71

prisoners is dealt with, convictions given and another group brought up, 26 men in all, including Withers and Lush.

After a very long speech, specifically addressed to the two

Farm buildings at Pythouse Farm before (above) and after conversion (below)

unfortunate men convicted of felony, the three judges put on their black caps, and the other two commissioners their hats. Mr Baron Vaughan reruns through the reasons why the punishment of these two men must be carried out.

Peter Withers has been convicted of assault with intent to do grievous bodily harm and although some consideration could be given to points in the case raised on his behalf, he should not expect leniency.

Lush has been convicted of one of the most atrocious cases of robbery to come before the Special Assizes.

Mr Baron Vaughan tells them that laws must be enforced and obeyed, riotous assemblies put down. The object of the law, he says, is not the punishment of the individual, its wish is to operate by example. Eventually he announces that they are to be taken to a place of execution and that there they are to be hanged by the neck until dead and the Lord God Almighty have mercy upon their guilty souls.

The effect of these dreadful words upon these naïve men is terrible to see. Lush is scarcely able to support himself at the bar, uttering loud groans and rocking his body backwards and forwards, weeping. Withers has gone pale, sweating profusely and sinking to his knees, apparently fainting. He is handed a glass of water by a court attendant. He cries out 'Lord have mercy upon us'. Lush says 'It was other people that did it and not me, my Lords'. The noise in the court is silenced.[7]

They are taken down.

The rest of the convicted men are sentenced to transportation for life. Upon hearing this, women in the court burst into tears, crying and wailing, and trying to reach the men before they are removed from the court.

Mr Baron Vaughan now concludes the business of the special commission in Salisbury by thanking the constabulary force for its excellent arrangements and discipline in organising the hearings. It is ten o'clock and the judges leave the Guildhall immediately to start the whole procedure over again at Dorchester, where they are expected at 3.00 in the afternoon. The court empties.

Outside the Guildhall wait a crowd of women. When the cell doors open the prisoners appear, chained together. The women weep and try to embrace their men – husband, father, brother, son. Children are howling. The men are swiftly loaded into the waiting prison vans. One woman goes up to a van, bangs on its side and attracts the attention of one of the prisoners.

'Your wife is confined' she says and the prisoner bursts into tears

'Yes, and she is dead and the baby too'. And with that, the driver flicks the reins and the horses clatter off.[8]

Withers and Lush are condemned to die on 25th January but in the meantime a petition to save them from the gallows is organised by ministers of the churches in Salisbury, the Rev. Greely (Church of England), two dissenting ministers, Mr Good and Mr Jeffrey and also James Marsh Esq. The petition is signed by 2,000 people from Salisbury including the mayor, and the cathedral canons and clergy. This petition is delivered on the 18th January to the Home Office in London. The Under Secretary of State promises it will be laid before the king without delay.[9]

On Monday 19th January 12 judges meet to consider the case of Peter Withers, but come to the conclusion that' the law must take its course'.

The same day sees two prison vans, each drawn by six horses, loaded up with 36 men from Fisherton Gaol, set off for Portsmouth to be locked up in the prison hulk *York*, which is anchored off Portsmouth.

These two vans include most of the Tisbury men:

Thomas Abree (Abrey), age 32 bricklayer/mason from Wylye, but working at Wardour	7 years
James Blandford, 28 ploughman, from Tisbury	14 years
Samuel Banstone (*alias* Macey), 41 farmer's labourer from Fonthill Gifford	7
Samuel Barrett, 30 agricultural labourer from Ansty	7
John Barrett, 24 agricultural labourer from East Hatch	7
Thomas Burt (Birt, Burke), 26 top sawyer from Fonthill Gifford	7
Charles Jerrard (Gerrard), 22 carter from Tisbury	7
James Mould from Hatch, 39 ploughman /grocer from Hatch	7
James Mould from Tisbury, 23 labourer from Tisbury	7
Richard Pitman, 29 kitchen gardener/groom from Hindon	7
Thomas Rixen (Rixon), 44 labourer from Tisbur	7
William Snook (Snooks), 22 ploughman from Tisbury	7
Thomas Topp, 20 ploughman from Fonthill Bishop	7
Thomas Vining (Viney, Vinen), 19 labourer from Tisbury	7
Edmund White, 20 blacksmith from Tisbury	7

The Tisbury men not transported are:

John Burton, 29 labourer from Tisbury	– £100 recognizance to keep the peace
Samuel Eyres, 30 labourer from Tisbury	– 12 months' imprisonment/hard labour
Charles Martin, agricultural labourer from Tisbury	– discharged
George Mould, 35 agricultural labourer from Wardou	– acquitted

Andrew Moxham (Moxam), 25 agricultural labourer from West Tisbury- acquitted
Henry Obourne, agricultural labourer from Tisbury – acquitted
Robert Obourne, agricultural labourer from Tisbury – not guilty
John Penny, from Ridge - acquitted
William Scott, agricultural labourer from Quarry E. Tisbury – acquitted
John Targett, 29 labourer Fonthill Bishop – 12 months' imprisonment/hard labour
Jeremiah Topp, 23 agricultural labourer from Fonthill Bishop – not guilty

And on Friday 21st January a further 32 men leave Fisherton Gaol for Portsmouth.

On Monday 24th January the convictions of Lush and Withers are 'respited during His Majesty's Pleasure". Both men, on receiving this news, thank God and promise to dedicate their future lives to His service. They are to be transported for life.

On Wednesday 26th January 33 more men are moved to Portsmouth and another 34 on the following Monday.

8
Setting an Example

IN TOTAL 153 men from Wiltshire were condemned to be transported to the other side of the world immediately following the Swing Riots – their crimes were mainly machine breaking and other offences such as assembly and demanding money and of course higher wage rates. Most of them were agricultural labourers who can have had no idea of the severity of the punishments which were to be given them, these being excessively severe in both Wiltshire and Hampshire.

The earlier Swing rioters were met with a much more conciliatory attitude by land and tithe owners; demands for higher wages quite often being met – for example on 15th November on a market day in Chichester a meeting of labourers from Arundel, Bognor, Bearsted, Felpham and Yapton in Sussex demanded a rise in wages from 10s. per week to 14s per week and the justices in that area and the principal farmers employing them accepted these terms.[1]

By the end of the rioting there were about 100 men arrested and awaiting trial in Kent, 165 in Berkshire, but in Hampshire and Wiltshire 300 in each of those counties. The end was now approaching, Captain Swing's pendulum had reached its apogee and was slowing down. Throughout 1831 there were sporadic attacks each month, some of arson, some of wage demands and some of illegal assemblies, but by the beginning of 1832 it was all over.[2] Most counties had been affected by these attacks but in totals of single or low double figures varying from two in London and, eight attacks in

Warwickshire to 88 in Norfolk. Nothing compared with the southern counties of Berkshire 165, Hampshire 208, Kent 154, and Wiltshire 208. In Norfolk, Kent and Sussex the punishments were less severe, the magistrates more sympathetic to the distress of the labourers.

However, a change was to occur. On 22nd November there had been a general election, returning the Whig party in place of the Tory party. The attitude of the newly elected Whigs under Lord Grey, who replaced the Duke of Wellington (himself a man of iron attitudes and no understanding of the suffering of the poor), was to be very much the same as the Tory one i.e. examples must be seen to be made to deter any further rioting.[3] The gentry was worried by demands in the country for political reform. The general elections in 1830 in July and August, and then again in November, had raised expectations and resentments. But because the new government could not afford to be seen to be weaker, it became even more determined to ensure that peace should return to the countryside, at whatever cost to the rural population. The newly appointed Home Secretary, Lord Melbourne, regretted that funding of the local militia had been withdrawn from the counties, which left them without peace-keeping abilities and prone to rioting and disturbances. This had caused considerable anxiety amongst the upper classes, who felt vulnerable without the protection of at least a local yeomanry force. There were no police forces at that time either, the local constabulary being raised voluntarily when necessary. Decisions had been made 'on the hoof' by local magistrates in different counties, whose views varied considerably. With regard to militias, Wiltshire had managed to keep its yeomanry, and as we shall see, the Wiltshire Yeomanry unit from Hindon played a large role in 'keeping the peace' at Fonthill.

Lord Melbourne's views on the keeping of law and order were strict and narrow, in spite of his membership of the Whig party. His views, however, were not unusual amongst the nobility or gentry of England. Although they knew that the labouring workforce could hardly be expected

Lord Grey – Prime Minister by Samuel Cousins 1764-1845

to exist on wages of 7s a week, somehow they were unable to see why these same labourers, or paupers, had any right to complain or to ask for a higher wage rate. In Wiltshire in particular, low wages had led to poor health and lack of energy. In 1813 the steward for the Marquis of Bath at Longleat had commented that although they were strong and robust, they were slow – in Norfolk for example a ploughman and his horses moved at three and half miles per hour – in Wiltshire at little more than two. Farmers were complaining:

'that the labourers do less work than formerly, when in fact the labourers are not able to work as they did at a time when they lived better'[4]

Damp conditions made suffering from rheumatic aches worse, their cottages were cold from 'lack of firing' i.e. wood, and their diets completely unbalanced and inadequate.

A comparison of the wages of agricultural workers in Wiltshire with the rest of England is interesting:

Wiltshire		*Highest*	*Lowest*
1768-70	7/-	9/- (Notts)	6/- (Yorkshire)
1824	7/7	12/6 (Yorkshire)	7/1 (Herefordshire)
1837	8/-	13/- (Cheshire)	7/6 (Dorset)
1850-1	7/-	14/- (Yorkshire)	7/- (Wilts and Glos)
1892	10/-	18/- (Cumb and Lancs)	10/- (Wilts and Dorset)

Lord Melbourne was determined that the magistrates should stiffen their resolve and on the 24th November, immediately after the election, sent a circular to lord-lieutenants and magistrates recommending 'in the Strongest Manner' that they should in future use firmness and vigour in quelling disturbances, and virtually promised them immunity for illegal acts done in discharge of their duty. *The Times* Special Correspondent in Wiltshire wrote amusingly of suspicion of everyone since Lord Melbourne's recommendations – gentlemen in chaises or gigs holding a cigar were as much under suspicion in case the cigar was used as an incendiary device to ignite haystacks as they passed, as were grumbling labourers speaking to one another in country churchyards.[5] Everyone was a possible suspect.

The rick burning and demands for higher wages over a large spread of the countryside continued into December, with Swing letters delivered in the midlands. *The Times* leader once again risked opprobrium from the government by commenting, on 6th December, that never had such a dangerous state of things existed to such an extent in England:

'Let the rich be taught that providence will not suffer them to oppress their fellow creatures with impunity. Here are tens of thousands of Englishmen, industrious, kind-hearted, but broken-hearted beings, exasperated into madness by insufficient food and clothing, by utter want of necessaries for themselves and their unfortunate families'[6]

But the Home Office needed to be seen to react firmly, and so Lord Melbourne, who felt that the magistrates in Kent and Sussex had proved less than firm, determined to change matters. He encouraged the arrest of known troublemakers, or men who had been previously convicted for offences like sheep stealing, poaching, or robbery.

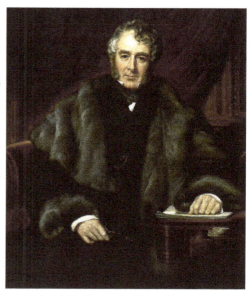

Lord Melbourne – Home Secretary by John Partridge

On 8th December therefore Melbourne issued a further circular directing that magistrates should not advise on wage rises, which could he said only lead to the most disastrous results.

'It is my Duty therefore to recommend in the strongest Manner, that for the future all Justices of Peace, and other magistrates, will oppose a firm Resistance to all Demands of the Nature above described, more especially when accompanied with Violence and Menace; and that they will deem, it their Duty to maintain and uphold the Rights of Property, of every Description, against Violence and Aggression'[7]

This quickly put paid to any hope for the awaiting prisoners of a defence of distress and hardship.

By this time over 1900 labourers were in prison awaiting trial. Melbourne was concerned that the local magistrates, in spite of his circulars, were still not powerful enough or determined enough to impose the severe penalties required by the existing laws. In some counties magistrates had divided loyalties and were, Melbourne decided, dragging their feet. Indeed, one magistrate in Norfolk had the temerity to write to the Home Secretary that if when the riots commenced on Monday the 22nd ult. at Beeston in

Norfolk, ' the magistrates had remonstrated with the people but' been able to tell them that their wages were to be increased as they had demanded, rents and Tythes reduced and thrashing machines laid aside, they would have quietly dispersed and committed no further violence'. [7]

An agricultural labourer at home in 1830 – the herring dangling on a pipe was an icon for extreme poverty. Bodleian, Oxford

Lord Melbourne did not agree to these radical notions and decided to create a special commission for the counties where he felt the worst of the damage to property had been committed. These would be Hampshire, Wiltshire, Berkshire, Buckinghamshire and Dorset. Norfolk, Kent and Sussex were not included, as judicial proceedings were already underway in those counties.

Two senior Army officers, Lt. Col. John Hastings Mair (a veteran of the Portuguese campaign) and Col. Brotherton, had been sent to Salisbury and Warminster respectively to command and supervise the return of peace in Wiltshire. Lt. Col. Mair reported that by the end of November in Salisbury

'the labourers are returning to work and everything is becoming tranquil.'[8]

And Brotherton from Warminster wrote that the energetic action taken by a 'few' magistrates and a widespread compliance with the labourers' demands had helped to check the insurrection. He also felt that these insurrections were not directed by any 'plan or system, but merely actuated by the spontaneous feeling of the peasantry and quite at random.'[9]

But the insurrection still spread to Dorset, south towards Blandford and Wareham on the south coast. Via Shaftesbury it pushed out to Winterbourne Kingston and Bere Regis, Puddletown and westwards through East Stour into Somerset.

It was now necessary, thought Melbourne, to make examples in order to stop the momentum of Captain Swing. Melbourne was enthusiastically backed by a number of members of the upper classes, particularly in Wiltshire and specifically by Mr John Benett. The system of seeking 'existing' troublemakers was definitely taken up by this local landowner. In Hindon he was instrumental in having seven men arrested – all of these had previous convictions for poaching.[10] Prisoners were encouraged to witness against their own friends and neighbours, although many refused and were convicted as a result; rather than receive an acquittal or a lesser sentence – brave men.

Prisoners already in Fisherton Gaol were forbidden to see their own lawyer (if they could afford one) except in the presence of the gaoler or a gaol servant.[11] Throughout the trials in fact, landowners were able to influence outcomes and manipulate the witnesses, as most of the witnesses and some prisoners were in fact their own employees or lived in cottages owned by them, the landowners themselves now sitting on the bench, or being members of the Grand Jury. Benett was actually appointed chairman of the Grand Jury. Afterwards there were accusations of self-seeking and manipulative behaviour by local and central government officials keen to

Fisherton Gaol, after it had become an army recruiting centre

bolster their own reputations and thus allowing behaviour that was probably legally wrong.

The new government however, under the Whig party, bears the responsibility for the harsh punishments administered. It over-rode local magistrates and judiciary, appointing the special commissioners and instructing the suppression of the riots by deterrence, i.e. the severe punishments meted out to the rioters. There seems to have been little confidence in the ability of local judiciary to achieve the necessary standard of prosecutions and convictions.[12]

Central government was prepared to pay the costs of providing the special commission, where two thirds of those apprehended were actually convicted and over half transported. Those convictions, by the special commissioners, were the highest in the whole country.

The law of the land as it existed at that moment had been set out in Acts of Parliament passed in 1827 and 1828 and meant that any man of whom it could be proved that he had broken machinery (other than threshing machines) or destroyed barns or buildings, or 'robbed' or extorted money by threats or simple riots, was liable to suffer the death penalty. If he was part of a crowd by whose collective action extortion, violence or physical assault took place, that person was also liable to the death penalty. For breaking a threshing machine the law had been fixed as seven years' transportation. [13]

At Salisbury later that month, Mr Justice Parke set out the views on the law as the judges saw it –

'If that law ceases to be administered with due firmness, and men look to it in vain for the security of their rights, our wealth and power will soon be at end, and our capital and industry would be transferred to some more peaceful country, whose laws are more respected or better enforced'.[14]

From the beginning the special commissioners made it clear that the distressful conditions under which the agricultural labourers had to live, their level of income and lack of ability to improve matters, were not to be part of the proceedings. As Mr Justice Alderson said –

'We do not come here to enquire into grievances. We come to decide law'.[15]

It is quite clear that the penalties were to be a deterrent to mob rule, to inspire shock and awe, to terrorise and to make examples of those who had the nerve to try to change matters, and to make examples enough to stop the rioting in its tracks.

In Hampshire 156 men fell under the horrible death penalty laws, and in fact 101 of them were convicted of capital offences. Six of these men were actually executed, 69 sentenced to transportation, 68 to imprisonment in England, two were fined and 96 acquitted, discharged or bound over.

In Wiltshire 336 men and three women came up before the bench. This was by far the largest number, 239 of whom were charged with machine breaking (219 with threshing machine breaking), 66 charged with 'robbery' and eight for rioting. Of these 90 men were liable to suffer the death sentence – this number was probably because they were involved in breaking mill machinery. Here the special commissioners were slightly more compassionate than they had been in Hampshire, but they were hard on craftsmen and other tradesmen, i.e. those above the level of agricultural labourers. Fifty were capitally liable, but only two actually sentenced to death. 150 men were transported, 46 went to prison in Devizes and 133 acquitted or bound over.

In Dorset 57 were tried, of which most were charged with breaking threshing machinery. Seven were were charged with 'robbery' of which six were sentenced to death but no-one was actually executed. Fourteen went to prison and 30 were acquitted.

In spite of the attacks being as numerous and as violent in Berkshire and Buckinghamshire as they were in Hampshire and Wiltshire, there the commission judges were different from those in Wiltshire and Hampshire and sentences were much more lenient. *The Times* commented that the Berkshire commission was 'a merciful contrast' to that in Winchester. Bargains were struck with prisoners if they agreed to plead guilty. Many cases were dismissed.

By the time the special commission was wound up in Aylesbury, Bucks, the commissioners had been sitting for nearly four weeks. They had tried 992 cases, sending 252 to prison, fining two people, virtually dismissing about 378 and sentencing the rest to transportation or death. Actually 227 people had been sentenced to death but in fact only 11 of these continued towards execution.

Now the government began to receive a huge number of petitions for reprieve or mercy. In Salisbury, as we have seen, the condemned prisoners Lush and Withers were eventually reprieved and their sentences commuted to transportation for life. But from Gosport and Portsmouth, from Romsey, Whitchurch and Winchester a petition signed by bankers, low church clergy (not the cathedral clergy) and tradesmen was sent. 15,000 residents of Reading appealed for mercy and from Newcastle upon Tyne a Radical petition came which reminded the newly elected government that it had pledged to a redress of grievances and should not commence its work 'with evil auspices, by measures of severity'. At Shaftesbury in Dorset, very close to Tisbury, a town meeting promoted a petition to the king that said:

'in no instance, during the late riotous assembling, had it been the object of the distressed peasantry to shed the blood of their supposed oppressors'.[16]

This campaign, by and large, was successful. Eight of the eleven men condemned to hang were reprieved, including Lush from Broad Chalke and Withers from Rockley.

Three men were executed however, one a man from Kintbury in Berkshire, at Reading on 11th January. Henry Cook and Thomas Cooper were hanged on 15th January in Winchester, witnessed, as mentioned before, by their fellow rioters just before their own transportation.

Throughout the whole country a total of 1,976 prisoners were tried in 90 different courts sitting in 34 different counties. The total punishments meted out to the Swing rioters were as follows:[17]

Sentenced to death	252 (but 233 commuted)
Executed	19
Transportation	505 (but only 481 actually sailed)
Imprisoned	644
Fined	7
Whipped	1
Acquitted or bound over	800

Wiltshire and Hampshire suffered the most severe punishments with a degree of maliciousness and bitter vindictiveness by the landowning jurors and the judicial commissioners not apparent in other counties. In some small communities the population of young men between 18 and 30 was decimated, leaving behind misery, incomprehension, anger, worse poverty and affecting the futures of many young children and wives left behind to face no income, no husband or father and parents with no hope of help in their old age. Change, in the form of better education, welfare benefits, trade unions, and eventually universal suffrage, would come, but these improvements would take a very long time to achieve.

9
Overspill and the Criminal-Waste-Management System

Hold me now
Oh hold me now
'Til this hour
Has gone around
And I'm gone
On the rising tide
For to face
Van Diemen's Land

(*From: Van Diemen's Land: Lyrics Clayton, Evans, Mullen and Hewson: U2 Rattle & Hum Album 1988*)

IF THE YOUNG men who were incarcerated in Fisherton Gaol in Salisbury in late 1830 as a result of the Pythouse Riots thought they were now getting used to prison conditions, the next few weeks were to disillusion them. Fisherton was run in a very humane way for the early 1800s, having been newly built in 1822 to replace the terrible old Salisbury gaol, Fisherton Anger, the necessary money being raised rather reluctantly and slowly from the ratepayers of the city. With no sanitary facilities or washing arrangements, no medical examinations and only one hour's exercise each day in a tiny yard – the old prison, sited between Fisherton Bridge and the Salisbury Infirmary, was thankfully destroyed, apart from the clock tower which still looms over one end of the bridge. The new prison would be built further out, at the end of Fisherton Street, where the city then ended and the road lead on to Wilton.

It was a large, square building, three stories in height with rows of barred windows and a central entrance. Surrounded by high brick walls, there was space inside the walls for exercise yards. Prisoners were provided with a better diet than in the old gaol, 1 ¾ lbs. of bread each day plus oatmeal gruel night and morning. 4 oz. of meat per person was provided on Sundays – the meat being ox-head, which was probably more difficult to sell, but it was at least meat. Exercise had to be taken twice a day for two hours each by walking in the yards. Clean clothing, washing at a cistern in each yard with soap and towels provided, the prison was kept clean and the cells whitewashed every year. [1]

Unfortunately for the convicts it would seem that the term of their sentences did not actually start until the prisoners boarded the prison hulk or the ship that would take them to their transportation destination.[2]

So it was probably a mixture of reluctance and relief that the men from Tisbury felt when the morning came for them to be loaded into the prison vans which would take them to Portsmouth and the start of the term of their sentences. They were chained together in groups of six, the chains being locked into the outside of the fabric of the van. It would be a long and bumpy journey from Salisbury to Portsmouth, uncomfortable and crowded, but nothing compared to the life that was to come.

It is unlikely that these young men had seen the sea before their arrival in Portsmouth. Most of them had led a restricted life geographically, being unlikely to have travelled further than about a ten mile radius from their homes. They can have had no idea of the distances involved in their transportation. Now the guards unlocked the chain from the van, but they were still weighted down with the one that locked them together and it was probably difficult to scramble down onto the chilly quayside. They would become accustomed to being chained together. They were cramped, hungry and cold as they waited for the longboats which would take them across the harbour to the prison hulk.

The huge prison hulk *York* eventually loomed above them, wallowing in the choppy grey January waters of Portsmouth Harbour. It was huge, like a floating slum housing rookery, its solid oak frame hung about with platforms, lean-to sheds sticking out from its sides, bedding and washing strung from mast to mast, flapping wildly in the wind. Its old gunports were now obscured by iron bars and what once had been a proud

Prison Ship York at Portsmouth Harbour c. 1828 – plate from Shipping & Craft by Edward William Cooke 1811-1890 National Library of Australia

third rate 74 gun ship of the line had become a filthy, unhygienic overspill prison.

York had been built at Rotherhithe and launched in 1807, seeing service with the Royal Navy in the West Indies and the Atlantic. She had been a prison hulk since 1819, moored in Portsmouth Harbour with other hulks, all strung out in a sad line between Portsmouth Docks and Gosport. Portsmouth was just one of a number of British ports where the hulks lay, holding convicts awaiting transportation – *York* alone could hold 500 of these wretched people.

How did these ships come into service as overflow prisons and why? Before the War of American Independence, the American colony had happily taken prisoners from Britain to work for free settlers as indentured servants. After the War of Independence the Americans, who had previously been happy to accept these convicts, now decided that it was much cheaper all round to stick to importing slaves from Africa, who did not have to be indentured, but would be owned by their employers entirely and unpaid. Britain had been sending its convicts to the colony for some 60 years, totalling about 40,000 people. But now America could choose to import some 47,000 slaves from Africa each year instead. Much more economical, but a disaster for the prison population in Britain, where increasingly large numbers of people convicted of comparatively trivial misdemeanours were sentenced to lengthy jail sentences. The prisons were very soon full and overflowing.[3]

Where to send them and how to maintain them while decisions were made about the future of transportation?

Luckily Britain had many waterways and many old ships due for decommission. In 1779 an act of Parliament (the Hulks Act) was passed to enable these old, decommissioned vessels, both naval and commercial, into 'overspill' prisons, which could be moored in various convenient waterways, close to major towns and cities near the coastline. Thus the prison hulks came to be moored in the busy waters of Plymouth, Portsmouth, Gosport, Cork, Sheerness, Deptford, Chatham and most importantly Woolwich. They were, according to the Hulks Act, to provide 'security, employment and the health of the persons confined therein'. The convicts could usefully be used for such hard labour as dredging channels, dock repairs and road building. [4]

Useful certainly but now even the hulks filled up. What was the government to do with these wretched people? Pressure was put upon the prime minister at the time, William Pitt, to find a solution and eventually, after various places were suggested and rejected, – Gibraltar, the west coast of Africa and eventually Australia were the final three venues selected. All were considered but rejected for various reasons.

One of the problems was that in America the convicts had been 'bought' by the existing free settlers and therefore the costs of maintaining them for their allotted term of imprisonment fell from the hands of the British government onto the hands of the American free settlers. But in Australia for example there were as yet no free settlers to employ the convicts. The cost of maintaining them would therefore devolve upon the British government.

However, the pressure grew and eventually, partly because Captain Cook during his second voyage had discovered a wonderful supply of huge pine trees on Norfolk Island, 1,000 miles east of the Australian land mass, and where flax also grew in abundance, it was felt that these assets would be immensely useful to the ships plying British trade routes, especially for the East India company. Spar timber was in very short supply in the northern hemisphere. A settlement in Australia might provide a safe haven for refitting and repair of trading ships and also a base from which to protect British interests in the Far East. The idea would be to encourage settlers – British farmers/peasants and loyalists rejecting the new state of affairs in America would be welcomed and encouraged to settle. This scheme was proposed by an American-born administrator, James Mario Matra, who had been a midshipman on Cook's ship *Endeavour* – so he had at least actually been to Botany Bay. However, Lord North was not impressed with these ideas, rejecting them immediately.

In 1783 North was replaced by Lord Sydney as Home and Colonial Secretary and he, faced with continuing pressure to solve the prison problem, was instrumental in getting an Act of Parliament passed – the Transportation Act of 1784, which provided that transportation should be 'to what Place or Places, Part or Parts beyond the sea' the crown might decide. A step forward, at least.

Now an employee of the East India Company stepped up – Alexander Dalrymple was employed as a hydrographer and was opposed to the idea of colonising Norfolk Island (an East India Company possession) and suggested that spar timber for masts was easily obtainable in Borneo and Sumatra, flax could be grown more economically in England than by bringing it from Norfolk Island – 1,000 miles from Botany Bay – and anyway, coir from Asia was as good – after all Chinese and Asian shipwrights depended upon it.

There were now two places left in the running for transportation destinations. One in West Africa called Das Voltas Bay was proposed, and this was generally felt to be more suitable than Botany Bay, but after an exploratory expedition by a sloop sent out to survey the area found it to be too dry and infertile, Botany Bay was back as the favourite destination, although the second choice.[5]

The First Fleet was sent to Australia in 1787, hardly too soon for the prison authorities, as in many prisons typhus had taken hold. The government chose a leader for the first transportation to the new Colony. He was a 48 year old semi-retired naval officer, a farmer living at Lyndhurst in the New Forest – Captain Arthur Phillip. So now the government could keep the flow of prisoners in and out of the hulks under some form of control.

Conditions in the prison hulks did not improve a great deal however between the sailing of the First Fleet and the moment the Tisbury men arrived.

From the cold quayside the prisoners were loaded into a longboat, chained to each other, and rowed across the expanse of Portsmouth Harbour to the waiting hulk of *York*. Once aboard they were mustered /assembled on the quarterdeck, where all their money was taken from them and handed to the Captain 'for safekeeping'. Old hands, prisoners already on board, then descended upon the new boys, confusing them with requests and information whilst pocketing any useful object the new boys had brought with them – a comb perhaps, or needles and thread, perhaps a small knife. This was tolerated by the guards. The newbies would have to learn to fend for themselves.

Prisoners then underwent a haircut, a cold bath and a change of clothes from their own garments into the hulk uniform – canvas trousers, a coarse shirt and grey jacket and a pair of shoes, unfitted of course, which caused immense problems particularly when you remember that the prisoners were wearing leg irons as well. The captains of the hulks had commercial deals with old-clothes merchants and sold off any good clothing they were able to take from new prisoners.

A 14lb leg iron was now riveted around the prisoner's right ankle (increased to double fetters should a punishment be needed).

The food provided on board the hulks ought to have been adequate but the prisoner was unlikely to actually receive his full ration of 14 oz. of meat three times a week, as a system of siphoning off took place; the steward, the cook, the inspector, the boat crew and the dock overseer all took a cut, so the prisoners ended up with perhaps 4oz. of meat served with a lump of what was called bread, but was made from sawdust and mildewed wheat.[6]

Sleeping arrangements were exceedingly unpleasant. Below decks were wire cages either side of each deck with a corridor in between. These cages held the mens' hammocks, which were visible to the guards at all

Sleeping quarters on a prison hulk – historycollection.com/australia

times. The close proximity of the hammocks and the numbers of men housed in each deck made the spaces disgustingly smelly and the sanitary facilities below consisted of a bucket or two, the contents of which were chucked over the side in the morning. To add to the discomfort, decks above were sluiced with sea water, which leaked down onto the hammocks. Decks ought to have been stoned clean, but sea water was quicker. No smoking was allowed. There were no lights so it was continuously dark. Until the 1830s young boys of 12/13 were housed with the older men and this gave rise to a great deal of sexual violence by older prisoners. Brutal floggings for minor misdemeanours were common – punishment for dirty leg irons, for wearing a hat incorrectly, for wearing a neckerchief tied the wrong way – all these merited extreme punishments, in front of fellow prisoners.[7]

There was no question of imprisonment acting as a reforming situation, except where one prisoner might be able to influence or help others. They worked every day but at night they were free to talk amongst themselves, to discuss politics, to plot but also to commit acts of violence against each other or bully the younger or newer members of the community – country bumpkins were a particular source of merriment – teasing taking on a much more malicious form, since rural people were considered to be particularly stupid.[8]

Illness and death rates were obviously high. Human waste was everywhere, fresh water in short supply, rats lived very comfortably with the prisoners and a real punishment was to have to wash other people's lice ridden shirts and trousers, often stiff with dead lice. Sores were a particular problem from the chains on legs and ankles. Death may have brought relief to the man concerned, but it could also bring a profit to the doctor – bodies were sold to hospitals for dissection.

At 5.30 am each morning the prisoners were awakened and rose from their uncomfortable hammocks to wash themselves and dress. Breakfast of boiled barley in water was followed by a return below decks to clean the sleeping areas. Work began at 7.30, when they were rowed ashore to break stones, dredge channels, repair roads and quaysides and at noon there was an hour's break for a meal of bread and water. After this a further three or four hours' work was undertaken and then they were able to return to the hulk for another wash and the evening meal, which was equally uninspiring or nourishing. After this about two hours of the day remained when prisoners could take part in a religious service, or self education, or mending. At 8.00 p.m. in the winter and 9 p.m. in the summer they were back in their bunks and locked in for the night.

Some men never left the hulk at all during their imprisonment, serving out the whole sentence aboard. But for others release, of a sort, arrived in the form of transfer to the ship which would transport them to their new far away life. Many, in spite of leaving their families and familiar territory, were delighted to be going.

The rioters from the Tisbury area did not have to wait for very long on board the *York*. They had arrived on Wednesday 19th January 1831 and by the 5th February they were already loaded on to the ship that was to take them to Van Diemen's Land – 101 men from Wiltshire and 123 from other parts of southern England.[9]

The ship Eliza in full sail – William Howard Yorke 1847-1921
National Maritime Museum Greenwich

The *Eliza* left Portsmouth on 6th February. She had previously been called 'Alert', launched in around 1802, a 511 ton sailing vessel built in Calcutta, India as a merchant ship. By 1813, renamed *Eliza*, she was assigned to convict transportation, undertaking her first convict transport voyage in either 1813 or 1819 – there seems to be some confusion about how many voyages she actually made, some convict records saying as many as ten trips, some only five plus one voyage undertaken on behalf of the East India Company (in 1825-6). Ownership of the vessel changed over the years between her launch as Alert and the 1831 voyage of the Wiltshire machine breakers. By 1831 the owner is listed as Mr Heathorn, her Master is John Groves and the surgeon for this voyage is William Anderson. They departed from Portsmouth on 6th February 1831 with 224 convicts onboard and 224 convicts arrived safely and alive in Hobart on 29th May 1831.

The speed at which the Wiltshire rioters were removed from England reflects the anxiety of Lord Melbourne that the insurrection be dealt with and wiped from the public mind as quickly as possible. Much concern had been expressed at the severity of the punishments meted out to these unfortunate workers, requests for clemency had been surprisingly numerous and successful (so far as the commutation of death sentences were concerned) and petitions had been signed and submitted by all sorts of extremely respectable members of society from landowners and peers of the realm, such as Lord Arundell, magistrates, jurors and church officials. All the time the prisoners were in England though, they were in the disapproving minds of the influential. Out of sight, Lord Melbourne reasoned, out of mind. People would soon forget if they were not continually reminded.

Henry Hunt, MP had proposed a motion to be heard in the House of Commons, requesting a general amnesty for all the rioters. This was scheduled for the 8th February. Hence the speed at which the men were loaded on to *Eliza*, which managed to leave two days before the House of Commons hearing. A second ship, the *Eleanor*, was also quickly loaded and took a further batch of the machine breakers away 11 days later. It was implied that the colony of Van Diemen's Land needed the agricultural labourers urgently, but in fact some of these men were not going to be very useful on farms or estates – for example there were three amputees amongst them – one, John Eyres from Enford, had lost a leg and two others only had one arm each, two more had each lost a hand and two men were completely deaf. On the whole though, they were a healthy tough lot, well able to withstand the voyage.

The journey to the other side of the world could be a very long one – conditions varied with the weather, the health of the convict cargo, and the necessity to make stop overs, some of which went on for weeks if there was illness on board. Some ships stopped off in Spain, the Canary Islands or West Africa, South Africa, nearly all in Rio de Janeiro. Over a period of 80 years, 168,000 people were moved in some 800 voyages. These were sporadic to start with, but at their peak in the 1830s, there were dozens of voyages each year.[10]

On arrival on board the convicts, even in the early days of the transportation system, were sluiced down with sea water on deck, their clothes taken away and fresh ones issued. This was to deter lice and parasite borne disease. During the voyage of the First Fleet in the 1790s run by the government, the number of deaths had been acceptable, but the Second

Fleet sailings had seen a complete failure of convict health, the ship *Neptune*, for example, arriving with 165 dead out of a cargo of 500 men. The contract for the provision of transport ships for the 2nd Fleet had been awarded to a private company, which was paid £17 for every convict arriving on board. They were kept below decks, chained in cramped squalid conditions in the dark with very limited fresh air and no exercise.[11] Because the provision of food bit into the profit margin, the diet was very poor and very minimal.

Records for this voyage from the point of view of the prisoners are very few since most of them were completely illiterate. The arrival of the ships caused a scandal, but nothing was done to improve matters and the contract for the Third Fleet sailings was given to the same company, which had previously run slaving ships and no-one was held responsible. Between 1795 and 1801, 385 of the 3833 people transported died en route or as they actually arrived in the colony.

Conditions started to improve when a surgeon was deemed a necessity. He would be paid a bonus of 10s. for every live convict delivered to the colonies. In 1815 the surgeons were given total authority on board with regard to hygiene, discipline and medical matters. In addition payment to the contractors would in future be made only for each convict delivered to the colony safely alive.

Occasionally of course there would be a mutiny, but these were rare and not very successful. Mutineers were, if caught, automatically hanged.

William Anderson's journal of the February to May voyage of the *Eliza* in 1831 has not survived. But on the following voyage of the ship the new surgeon Thomas Bell recorded that

> every possible care was taken to keep the prisoners on deck as much as the weather would permit. The prison and hospital were kept clean and well ventilated and the bedding was frequently aired and shaken before being returned to the berths. The prisoners were shaved three times a week and their hair kept close cut.
>
> The bathing tub was made use of every morning; one half of the prisoners bathed every other morning, two men were appointed to wash with pipe clay and a brush the person in the bath, which they stood much in need of.[12]

It seems very likely that William Anderson would have had the same arrangements in place, as now there were financial incentives to ensure that prisoners arrived alive, and in any case, a surgeon would want to make sure that the men entrusted to his care were fairly treated.

Chained convicts

Meals were properly cooked and served at regular hours with beer or wine and lime juice (the latter preventing scurvy) and the former presumably because they were cleaner than water. Checks were made to ensure that the lime juice and wine were not sold or bartered between prisoners. Leg ulcers caused by the chains, and constipation or dysentery were some of the problems besetting the men and these were treated by the surgeon.[13] There were inevitably cases of consumption, (tuberculosis), which could not be successfully treated, and indeed a few men subsequently died of this after arrival in the colony.

Because headage payments were made on delivery of healthy convicts, it was very much well worth the efforts of the surgeon to keep the men in good physical health. Transportation had become an extremely successful criminal waste-disposal arrangement and was known as the System. During the period 1800 – 1840 the population of England had nearly doubled. Falling wages, rising prices, the Napoleonic Wars, mechanization in the countryside had all given rise to unemployment and thus an increase in what was considered to be criminal activity. The colonies, the government reasoned, needed agricultural labour and the idea of transportation was perfectly acceptable to the average Englishman. It was a perfect System of waste management. After the 1840s however, the anti-slavery movement influenced political thinking and transportation with its overtones of slave ships, became much less acceptable. As far as Van Diemen's Land is concerned, transportation ceased in 1853.

Whilst the Tisbury lads lay in chains below decks on the *Eliza*, or took their baths and exercise on deck, arrangements were made to pay the men who had claimed rewards for assisting in the capture of the Wiltshire rioters. These started with a claim by one George Hunt, a victualler and Thomas Batt, a carpenter, both from Amesbury, that they alone without any assistance apprehended a man called Thomas Pigott, chimney sweep of Netheravon, who had eventually been convicted of breaking machinery at a clothing mill in Figheldean near Amesbury) on 22nd November 1830. They received a payment of £50.

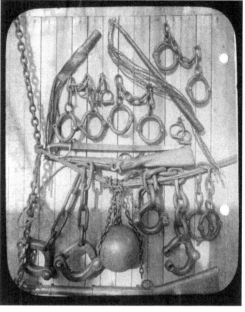

Relics of convict discipline – 1904 photograph by J W Beattie of objects held by Library of Congress, Hobart, Tasmania

At Wilton four men received £50 each and no fewer than 20 people were awarded £10 each for information provided that had resulted in the arrest and conviction of men for machine breaking at Crow Mill, Wilton.

On the 8th April 1831 a number of men, nine at least of them either employees of Mr Benett, or his tenants, were rewarded as follows:[14]

William Woods, Tisbury	£102
Charles Wilkins, Tisbury, blacksmith	68
John Jay, Tisbury, Linley Farm tenant	102
Noah Doggrell, Gamekeeper, Ruddlemoor Farm	42.10s
James Doggrell, Mr Benett's Farm Bailiff, Noah's father	68
George Turner, gamekeeper, employed by Benett	68
John Brickell, Mr Benett's carter, Kinghay	85
James Jay, Bailiff and tenant farmer, Linley Farm	34
Joseph Trim, Carpenter, Pythouse Park	25
John Ford, agricultural labourer, East Hatch	34
James Snow, Tisbury	17

James Foyle, Course Street, Edmund White's neighbour	34
Thomas Ball, Mr Benett's coachman, (later his butler)	51
John Wilkins, Hindon, blacksmith/journeyman	17
John Uphill, Hindon shepherd (later moves to Wales)	17
Thomas Jay, Fonthill Gifford Farm Bailiff	51
James Green crown St. Westminster	34

There can be no doubt that these men were pleased to receive this money – the sums were considerable in relation to the weekly wage in the area. However, it must have made friendships and acquaintanceships extremely difficult in the small area of Tisbury, making the community even more divided. These employees or tenants of Mr Benett's would have found it impossible not to accept the rewards, their job and homes depended upon their employer's favour.

However, for the children, the wives and the parents of the departed rioters, the money given to the witnesses rubbed salt into their already open festering wounds. Their menfolk had been desperate on behalf of their families and their future prospects. They were not taking part in a national revolution to overthrow the monarch or the government, they simply needed higher wages and continuous work, unimpeded by the advance of the dreaded threshing machine. They were crushed, had become outcasts and so their families inevitably suffered too.

10
Heroes? – the Landlords

BY TODAY'S STANDARDS of what might be considered an acceptable public life, the profile of the average 19th century politician does not look good. The pyramid representing the population of the United Kingdom at that time had a very sharp point – the top of the triangle consisted of a very small number of rich aristocrats and landowners, men who came from powerful families which had always been the ruling class. Below them, there was an increasing crowd of lesser gentry vying for parliamentary seats which were still largely in the gift of those same landowners and peers at the top of the pile, who also had the power to provide paid sinecures within the communities they controlled. To become powerful, a man needed land, money and a recognised power base in his community.

Below the ranks of the powerful stood the professions such as lawyers, church dignitaries, but not Roman Catholics of course, men of middling property and some education, the new industrialists. These gentlemen, whilst still very protective of their own interests, had begun to realise that change, or reform in the way the rest of the population in the country was represented and governed, was needed. The bottom layers consisting of workers, had no say in how the country was run. There was more awareness of the terrible conditions of the slave trade than there was of the living conditions for the poverty-stricken workers.

But matters were changing gradually, with radical thinkers, for example the Spinners union, the embryo Trade unions, the Birmingham

Political union and religious dissenters such as the Methodist movement, which were based mostly in the northern newly industrialised cities and the great towns of the midlands. In the south however, the workers' situation was, as the Marquis of Salisbury admitted in the House of Commons on 29th November 1830 – 'in a deplorable state'.[1] In a long speech that day he proposed the appointment of a Select Committee to inquire into the Administration of the Poor-laws, since in their current form they enabled the imposition of low wages and threw the onus of keeping the working peasant alive upon the vestry system. Earl Grey offered no opposition to the proposal, the motion was agreed and a committee appointed. This was good news, but came too late for the Tisbury rioters, where the labourers' conditions were graphically described by Henry Hunt MP in his speech to the House on the 8th February 1831 when he appealed for an Amnesty for the convicted rioters. He told the House:

> He had got from the overseer of the parish of Tisbury, an account of the rate of wages paid to the agricultural labourers of that parish. It showed distinctly the desperate state of poverty to which those labourers were reduced, who committed the greatest acts of violence in the county of Wilts. The paper which he held in his hand contained an account of the allowances agreed to be paid to the poor of that parish on the 1st of November, 1830, on which day was held the last parish meeting, previous to the breaking out of the disturbances. John Barrett, for himself, his wife and child, was to receive 5s. per week. William Sanger acquired for himself and wife 1s.8d. each per week.
>
> Now, the greatest misfortune attending the rate of allowances in this parish was the way in which the wages of the labourer had been paid in it. He had heard the hon. Member for Somersetshire say on a former evening, that it was a hardship on the landed interest that it should be burthened with the payment of all the poor-rates of the county. He denied the existence of this hardship, for proof of it he could find none. Where was it to be found? Was it in the parish of Tisbury?
>
> Let the House look to what was the practice there. He did not mean to say that the hon. Member for Wiltshire, who resided in that Parish, paid the rate of wages which he had mentioned. Perhaps, as that hon. Gentleman was a man of opulence, he paid his labourers a higher rate; but the rate which he had mentioned, was the rate at which the labourers were to be paid, according to a settlement signed by the hon. Member for Wiltshire, as chairman for the county. The labourer received 6s or 7s a week as a

remuneration for his labour, and how did the parish make up the rest of his subsistence? By allowing him tuppence half-penny per week for each head in his family. The overseer of the parish, from whom he had received this statement, was ready, if necessary, to swear to the truth of it. In some parishes, only tuppence half-penny a head was paid; and in other only 2d. and the half of a farthing a head.

He appealed to the House – nay, he appealed to the gentlemen of the landed interest themselves – to remedy this dreadful evil of paying industrious and hard-working men out of the poor-rates. It was a most horrid and degrading thing, that a man who worked hard from an early hour on Monday morning to a late hour on Saturday night, should only receive 7s a week, and should then be compelled to look to the parish for the scanty aid which was necessary to enable him to eke out a wretched and miserable existence.

This was placing him in a worse situation than that of any slaves in the West Indies.[2]

Mr Hunt is clearly referring here to Mr John Benett, MP for Wiltshire, and owner of Pythouse, Tisbury.

However, there were other landowners in the immediate area whose reputations were perhaps enhanced by their responses and behaviour at the time of the riots.

Mr Thomas Grove of Ferne House Donhead, born 1759, and a considerable landowner in the area, had been, with his family, a close friend of John Benett and his family, and the original Captain of the Hindon troop of the Wiltshire Yeomanry. The two families met frequently, enjoying social occasions, balls, dinners and visiting one another's homes, together with the Arundells of Wardour, the Knellers of Donhead Hall, the Selyars of Sedgehill House and the Gordons at Wincombe Park.

Thomas Grove had been one of the proposers for Benett's candidacy as an MP as early as 1818, but did not perform the same service for Benett in the 1819-20 elections, in fact backing a different candidate, since Benett's performance as an MP had failed to meet with Grove's approval and by the 1830s he disagreed with many of Benett's opinions. The friendship had lapsed.[3]

Thomas Grove behaves very differently from Benett during the days of the rioting in the area. On the 25th November, the very day of the battle at Pythouse, according to the *Devizes & Wiltshire Gazette*;

'the men of Donhead St Mary, Donhead St Andrew and Semley

Thomas Grove 1758-1847 by George Romney 1788 Detroit Institute of Arts

gathered today. They were addressed by Mr Thomas Grove. He allowed them to burn his machines and then they returned peaceably to their homes'.

A peaceful solution, but an expensive one. The day after this meeting Lord Arundell of Wardour, writing to John Peniston the Salisbury architect and prominent member of the Wiltshire Yeomanry states that the day before he himself had visited Benett at Pythouse, who was complaining that none of the people, farmers or gentry, would come to his assistance, although a small party, 20 in number, did go afterwards and were sworn in as special constables. Lord Arundell goes on to say that after an announcement by himself at his Chapel at Wardour, Thomas Grove and he administered the oaths to 200 men of Ansty, Hatch and Tisbury, formed them into squads and gave them leaders'

The Grove family were assiduous diarists, the family diaries spanning the period from 1809 to 1925. Between the years 1809 and 1858 the diarists were Harriet (during 1809 and 1810) and then Charlotte her sister, writing between 1811 and 1860. Both were Thomas Grove's daughters, Charlotte marrying the Rev. Richard Downes who became the Rector of Berwick St John, the nearest village to Ferne House. They had no children. Her diaries cover a very long period, one or two years being missing – 1827 for example, the year of her marriage and move to the rectory at Berwick and curiously, 1830. The latter is a great loss as she would have known exactly what happened between Thomas Grove and his tenant farmers and their agricultural workers, and Thomas's alleged acceptance of the burning of his machines

In her diary of 1831, Charlotte starts the year by recording on 1 January that their largest pig was killed and she saw the winnowing in their barn. She reports that the judges are now at Salisbury trying the late rioters. Her brother Thos. she says, is one of the Grand Jury. This Thomas Grove is virtually the same age as Charlotte having been born in the same year –

were they twins? No mention is made of this, perhaps Charlotte was born in January of 1783 and Thomas in December. He is listed with the other Grand Jurors, and is named as Thos. Grove jun. Esq.

On January 4 Charlotte notes: 'Tom has succeeded in getting off the farmers at Tisbury whom the mob accused wrongfully'[4]

There is no mention in the records of the trials of any charges specifically against tenant farmers of farms on the Ferne estate. However, on Tuesday 4 Jan. the records do state:

> Mr Justice Parke observed, that in a case which was tried last night an intimation was thrown out that encouragement had been given to the mob to break these machines by the farmers. The judges had since then made inquiry into that case, and found that there was no grounds whatever for believing that any encouragement had been given. The farmer, in that case, gave the mob cider, but it was under the influence of intimidation. The Attorney General said that the law officers of the crown had made similar inquiries, but had not been able to trace any case of encouragement of this kind by the farmers.[5]

Perhaps this is the success that Charlotte refers to, but there are no names or farm names to confirm this.

In Tisbury a Nightly Watch from 10.00 pm to 4.00 am is established and by the 31st January 1831, a newspaper report states that 'not the slightest depredation has been committed'.

Lord Arundell's comment upon Thomas Grove's action of allowing the men of Semley and the Donheads to burn his machines is a succinct, 'So much for conciliation'.[6]

Lord Arundell himself was considerably involved in the Pythouse riots, but clearly had a very good relationship with his tenants. His huge Wardour estate, mostly situated to the south and east of the village of Tisbury, had been in the hands of the Arundell family for at least 250 years, being the most important Roman Catholic stronghold in the south of England (excluding London) and probably in the kingdom. The family were absolutely loyal Roman Catholics, whose faith never faltered and they provided a haven for members of their faith – by 1839 80% of all the Catholics in Wiltshire lived within the Wardour estate. The Arundell title included Count of the Holy Roman Empire. In 1811 James Everard had married Mary Grenville, the only daughter of the first Marquis of Buckingham and sister to Richard, Duke of Buckingham. By 1817 he had succeeded to the title.[7]

James Everard, 10th Baron Arundell

When James Everard, the 10th Lord Arundell, inherited the titles and the Wardour estate, Wardour totalled some 30,000 acres and his predecessor's income had been £20,000 per annum. But the 8th Lord Arundell, Henry, had built a magnificent, expensive mansion to replace the old ruined Wardour Castle. The new mansion had its own exceptionally beautiful Chapel, a Gothic temple, an Ice House, Camellia House, American Garden, a Banqueting House and Grotto (the last two amongst the ruins of the old Wardour Castle - together with an impressive three-seater privy). All this expense left the new 10th Lord Arundell very short of money. He had to sell the Ashcombe estate and then the one-acre site of the Arundell-Panton estate in the West End of London (on the east side of the Haymarket, from James Street in the south, up across Coventry Street and Piccadilly, as far as Archer Street in Soho) a hugely valuable piece of urban land.

However, his financial affairs still did not improve sufficiently to pay the debts accrued by the estate and although he was always considered to be a thoughtful and caring landlord, he was forced to spend much time abroad to avoid being cast into a debtor's prison - it was probably cheaper to live abroad, and he could, he hoped, let his magnificent Palladian mansion, New Wardour Castle, designed by James Paine. He offered it to Earl Grosvenor, but sadly the peer did not want it. However Mr George Mortimer, who had inherited part of the Fonthill estate from his uncle Mr John Farquhar, was keen to rent it. Mortimer was running the woollen mill (the manufactory) he had built at the south end of Fonthill Lake and improving the remaining Fonthill Pavilion. Lord Arundell was not impressed with the idea of a cloth manufacturer renting his mansion, writing sadly: 'I am humbled but not so low as to put a Scotch Weaver in my House - sooner shall it fall piecemeal to ruin'.[8]

His finances remained ruinous for the rest of his life. However, he had compensations. He was a keen historian and antiquary, writing for the Colt Hoare *History of Modern Wiltshire* 1822 -42, his chapter being on the 'Hundred of Dunworth and Vale of Noddre'.

Another of his interests was in the Wiltshire Yeomanry Cavalry and after joining it in 1824, by 1830 he was Captain of the Sarum troop. At the beginning of the Swing Riots Lord Arundell was not in fact in England, and command of the Sarum troop was undertaken temporarily by Lt. John Peniston, the architect at Salisbury, who, writing on 19th November 1830 having heard the dramatic news of the insurrections, confessed that he did not know 'whether Lord A be at Wardour' so he asked the recipient of his letter, the Rev. R Parker, to ensure that Messrs Stringfellow and Jeffery ' hold themselves in readiness for active service at the shortest notice'. Peniston conveys this information to Captain Wyndham at Dinton House and suggests that he too might consider giving his troop similar orders. He also keeps the mayor of Salisbury and his patron the Marquis of Bath informed of the situation approaching the city.[9]

On the 22nd November Peniston suggests to the Marquis of Bath that it is time to assemble the other troops of the Regiment i.e. not just the troops stationed in the south of the county but also those of Swindon, Marlborough, Devizes, Warminster, Melksham, Chippenham and Malmesbury, with a constant chain of command by orderlies.[10]

In spite of his financial difficulties, Lord Arundell, who had maintained a close connection with his tenant farmers and estate workers, now heard about the problems besetting the area and returned home. He first led his Sarum troop to the defence of Mr Eyre Coote at West Park, Rockbourne near Fordingbridge, where two attacks had taken place. There he left a detachment of 12 men under the command of Lt. Peniston, to guard West Park. Arundell returned to Salisbury to direct the troop's movements. He requested that Mrs Hannington of the Black Horse Inn in Winchester Street, Salisbury, should arrange a Mess Dinner for 6.00 p.m. on the 26th November (the day after the Pythouse battle) for ten officers of the Wiltshire Yeomanry. The diligent Lt. Peniston, who obediently writes the letter to Mrs Hannington, mentions that their Mess Dinners at Devizes have previously had a cost of 'six shillings, exclusive of waiters'. [11]

On the 8th December Lt. Peniston accepted Lord Arundell's invitation to spend a day at Wardour and expressed his regret at Lord Arundell's comment to him that 'all is not yet sound in my neighbourhood'. Lord Arundell had been concerned as to the progress of one of his troop members, Sgt. Mackrell, who was wounded during one of the disturbances. Peniston reported that the Sgt. Is not yet out of danger but his medical attendants have great hopes of him.

Now Lord Arundell's concerns were extended to his own estate workers, particularly those caught up in the riots. He had, prior to 1830, already described Tisbury as 'a parish in which the Poor have been more oppressed and are in greater misery . . . than any other parish in the kingdom'.[12]

Had the noble lord not been occupied in directing his Sarum troop during the rioting, but actually present at home in Wardour on the 25th November, it could be speculated that the result might well have been a much more peaceful one. He now held meetings at New Wardour Castle with witnesses, with suspects and with lawyers, to ascertain what actually happened, the conditions and wages and family commitments of the men awaiting transportation.

Amongst those he examined was a witness, John Uphill, the shepherd, who had been at Pythouse Farm Yard and saw Thomas Burt, the sawyer from Fonthill Gifford break up the threshing machine.

On January 13th 1831 Arundell took the trouble to write to Whitehall, via Colonel Mair, with recommendations for mercy for seven of the now convicted Tisbury men, James Mould of East Hatch, Samuel Banstone (Macy) of Fonthill Gifford, Thomas Abree, mason of Tisbury, Thomas Rixen of Tisbury, James Mould of Tisbury, Edmund White the blacksmith from Course Street, and Thomas Burt, the sawyer from Fonthill Gifford. He carefully sets out their occupations, wages and details of their families and whether they were in work or not at the time of the alleged offences. He particularly urges mercy for Abree and White.

Colonel Mair writes to Whitehall too, backing Lord Arundell's request and stating that His Lordship has a 'deep interest and kind attentive solicitude for his tenantry and a thorough knowledge of their personal character'.[13]

'Had his Lordship been on the spot, instead of attending his duty with the troop, he commands with so much zeal, much of the . . . would have been prevented by his influence'.

Lord Arundell himself was disturbed by the behaviour of the Hindon troop of the Cavalry at Pythouse, and at the lack of goodwill towards Benett by his farmers and neighbours. With regard to the troop's conduct, Lord Arundell mentioned that he found at home two men who had not been taken prisoner by the Hindon troop, one with a slice taken off his head and the other with his hand cut off. He had heard of many others wounded.

As one of the examining magistrates during the special commission, on 1st December Lord Arundell was sitting with the Earl of Radnor. That day Thomas Abree appealed to Lord Arundell, who gave him a very good character reference – mentioning also that when repairs to Salisbury Cathedral had been undertaken, it was Abree, a stonemason, who had been 'hauled to the top in a basket' to repair, presumably, the spire of the cathedral.

Arundell's last act concerning the Pythouse riots came when a report (a rumour, fortunately) was printed in the local paper in December 1831, some time after transportation had occurred, that the ship *Eliza* had been lost. Lord Arundell wrote immediately to Lord Melbourne, the Home Secretary, to ensure that an official contradiction be published. He remained popular in the district until his untimely death in Rome, in June 1834. He is buried at the entrance to the chapel of Sacred Heart in the church of the Gesu.

The remaining relevant landowners in the area were John Benett and James Morrison, but both of them at this time were in the process of buying part each of the Fonthill estate formerly owned by William Beckford. John Benett was not yet the legal owner of the Fonthill Abbey site and adjacent land and James Morrison was buying the northern portion of the Fonthill estate including the lake. His land would border Fonthill Bishop, Fonthill Gifford and Tisbury. Benett, on whose family land the Pythouse riots actually took place, cannot be said to be a hero, and James Morrison was hardly involved at all.

Thomas Grove clearly felt he had acted with compassion and understanding, but it would be extremely interesting to have been able to read Charlotte's diary entries for November and December 1830. They might have thrown a completely different light upon her father's actions.

Whilst Lord Arundell could be included as a local hero, there were others who were not local people but whose influence can be seen in the progress of the revolt. Some behaved well, dealing with matters so that they ran smoothly, some were important parts of the whole reform movement. Of these, the man who may be the best known, acted consistently on behalf of the poor and underprivileged throughout his life – the farmer, innovative journalist and radical thinker William Cobbett.

11
Influencers and Bloggers

William Cobbett – Influencer

It is of course impossible to know whether the men who took part in the Pythouse riots knew of William Cobbett, but Cobbett certainly knew and understood about their lives, the conditions under which these labourers lived, the impossibility of living on the wage they were able to achieve and the humiliation involved in requesting help from the parish. He had tried to help with his book The Cottage Economy, but books have to be read and for the illiterate labourer, a book would have to be read to him. Cobbett's love of the countryside, his compassion for his fellow men and his detestation of greedy statesmen, corrupt clergymen and sleazy middlemen dictated his whole life's work.

As a young man William Cobbett leaves his father's farm and inn in Farnham, Surrey and influenced by reading Jonathan Swift, sets out for London where he joins the Army and is sent to New Brunswick. During his eight year period as a soldier he discovers the corrupt administration which happens as a matter of course in the Army, when food destined for the troops is diverted to make money for the officers, thus starving the men. Or the cost of equipment meant to be provided by the Army is deducted from the men's pay. This first detection of the corruption which dominated 19th century life makes him more aware of other unpleasant facts – the disaster of the Enclosures Acts, the Roman Catholics who were denied representation, the plight of paupers in appalling workhouses, and the exploitation of the factory workers in the newly industrialised northern towns and cities. He starts to publish articles and as a result of this he is forced to go into exile for a short while to France and then twice to the United States of America but eventually he is tried and sent to Newgate Gaol, where he learns even more about the sufferings of the poor and needy.

This sentence for sedition is imposed because of his protests at the 500 lashes awarded to five soldiers at Ely, who had protested

William Cobbett
by John Raphael Smith 1752-1812

at the cost of their army knapsacks being deducted from their pay. Cobbett serves only eight months of his two year sentence and with the help of his friends he pays the £1,000 fine, but he is left bankrupt for the second time. During this period he writes The Life of William Cobbett, under the pseudonym 'Peter Porcupine'.

All the time he is endeavouring to stand for Parliament and would have preferred to stand for a constituency in his beloved southern England. Eventually he manages to become an MP, but for Oldham, an impoverished industrial town in the north.

He is an adventurous and brave man, self motivated and impulsive, but with a very good mind, an acute awareness of his surroundings and a desire to improve life for the poor. At one point he tries to settle down in the countryside and buys a farm at Botley, near Southampton in Hampshire, but within a couple of years he is back in the public eye, an acknowledged Radical thinker and journalist, writing and publishing an independent periodical, the Political Register. In the 1820s he begins the journeys which become, with his writing, his life's work, travelling through the countryside on his horse, with his man George alongside him, or one of his sons with him, recording his thoughts, impressions and the facts about the agricultural situation of the time, as he sees the lives of his fellow farm workers. He records the changes after enclosures, changes in the way tithes were now handled by the Church of England, the way the poor relief system

(Speenhamland) humiliated and belittled the labourers and encouraged the farmers to pay low wages, the lack of work and the progression towards mechanization. Reform is obviously needed, and as soon as possible for those dependent upon agriculture for their very subsistence.

He chooses to travel across country from village to village, avoiding the new turnpike roads, describing the beautiful man-made landscapes of the south and the various fortunes of those who live in it. He discusses the way that agriculture is administered, the greed (as he sees it) of the great landowners, the rotten boroughs that prevent ordinary people from voting or becoming a political representative, he hates the game-laws, the venality of the current church and the way that small local crafts which once earned an agricultural labourer or his wife a small extra income, have been swallowed up by the appearance of the new machines, for example, spinning machines.

He writes all this down and publishes it in his Political Register which is taken and paid for, in spite of the stamp duty imposed upon periodicals, by educated members of the working class and read aloud to groups of others workers in the ale houses or inns, thus influencing and giving shape and a voice to their own thoughts. Among these are the rural workers who will become the Swing rioters. During the 1820s and 1830s Cobbett's words become effective prompts to the embryo rural radicals, backing up their newly found opinions and informing their actions.

In 1826 Cobbett's travels take him down the Avon valley, a land, he observes, rich in agricultural products, foodstuffs produced by the worker, sent to the towns and cities to feed the masses, but not benefitting those who have produced it, the workers being, as Cobbett notes, all skin and bone: 'By some means or other there must be an end to it and my firm belief is, that the end will be dreadful'.[1]

It was certainly dreadful for the Tisbury men and the women and children left behind and although Cobbett does not seem to have actually visited the Tisbury area, he passes down through the Avon valley to Salisbury and he certainly knows of John Benett MP, referring to him as 'gallon-loaf Benet'.[2]

In fact the riots did lead to a slight rise in wages in the south of England and to a feeling of shame and sadness amongst some of the farmers who in a number of instances, had almost supported the riots, allowing the machine breaking to occur. Middle class views were changing, and in the Political Register on 4th December 1830, Cobbett writes

The important feature in the affair is that the middle class who always, heretofore, were arrayed, generally speaking, against the working class, are now with them in heart and mind, though not always in act ... Amongst the tradesmen, even of the metropolis, ninety-nine out of a hundred are on the side of the labourers.[3]

In July 1831 Cobbett undergoes another trial – this time he was prosecuted for the articles he had written in his Political Register. But Cobbett was by now completely unafraid of the authority of the government arrayed against him before Chief Justice Tenterden, who was bitterly against reform of any sort. The prosecuting Counsel is Sir Thomas Denman, who did manage to treat Cobbett with respect, referring to him as 'one of the greatest masters of the English language'.

As prosecuting Counsel Denman paraphrases some of Cobbett's articles and comments upon their effect. But Cobbett is well able to defend himself and points out, during a magnificent speech, that Lord Chancellor

William Cobbett as Peter Porcupine from The Life of William Cobbett written by himself in 1809 under the pseudonym of Peter Porcupine

Brougham himself, as President of the Society for the Diffusion of Useful Knowledge, had asked for and received Cobbett's permission to reprint his Letter to the Luddites, citing it as the best means of stopping the labourers from machine breaking. Denman had not been informed of this and now finds himself facing an impossible task, since Cobbett, having demolished Denman's star witness, goes on to destroy all the other charges against him.[4] Cobbett's triumph against Denman, who had been one of the harshest of the presiding judges at the special commission, is utterly satisfactory, although too late to reprieve the rioters, who by this time had been duly delivered to Van Diemen's Land.

Cobbett's influence extended over many years, from the Napoleonic Wars to the passing of the Reform Bill in 1832. He died in 1835. Cobbett was an impulsive thinker and doer, writing in simple English, ensuring that his audience would be able to understand a concept easily, not condescending to them or patronising them. His prose is lyrical, particularly when writing about the landscape of England, precise when explaining ideas, startling and argumentative when he is angry or excited about unfairness or the wretchedness of human behaviour. Read me, he says, I am making clear to you what you are already forming in your own mind. Together we can change things. He is the great communicator of the period.

The Bloggers of Fetter Lane

IF THE GOVERNMENT thinks that the matter of the Swing Riots is ended by the labourers' transportation to Van Diemen's Land they are sadly misinformed. Now they make the mistake of deciding to prosecute two more people for inciting the rebellion. These two are William Cobbett as we see from above, and Richard Carlile.

Richard Carlile is a publisher based in the Fleet Street area, and a valiant champion of freedom; he has spent some years in gaol as a result of his publishing the writings of Thomas Paine and William Hone, as have, sadly his wife, his sister and the men who work for him in his publishing shop where he writes and publishes the periodical the 'Republican'. After the Peterloo Massacre he had been very vocal and keen to promote the people's right to rebellion. He is something of an individualist though and reluctant to admit to the benefits of political discussion, consultation or any organised party, although a member of the Radical Committee which meets at the White Lion in Wych Street, London, which has been regarded as an 'underground' radical movement particularly during the 1820s.[5]

'Reform' writes Carlile at the time 'will be obtained when the existing authorities have no longer the power to withhold it, and not before'.

He puts forward the idea of holding radical meetings throughout the kingdom – all on the same day. Most of these were to be in the north or the midlands where the reform movement has been at its most active. These meetings were, however, undermined by Henry Hunt, who felt he was losing control of the reformist movement. By the summer of 1820 Carlile is in prison for publishing the 'Works of Paine' and for being part of a seditious and blasphemous press. But his imprisonment does not slow down the reform movement, which although quieter, does not stop growing.

In London, coffeehouses double up as radical reading rooms, with periodicals and newspapers available. In the north there are dedicated Reading Rooms, such as John Doherty's Coffee & Newsroom at his Manchester bookshop – 96 newspapers were taken there every week and available for anyone to read.[6]

William Cobbett too is at the forefront of the radical press. His '2d. Register' printed between 40,000 and 60,000 copies per week in the period October 1816 to February 1817. His 'Cottage Economy' sells 50,000 copies in 1822.

William Hone, who voted with Hunt in the 1831 Amnesty Debate, was an accomplished satirist, although he had not anticipated being imprisoned for his satirical writing and in fact tried to withdraw his work when, in February 1817, the government was clamping down upon such publications. But Carlile republished Hone's parody on the Lord's Prayer for Members of Parliament:

> Our Lord who art in the Treasury, whatsoever by thy name, thy power be prolonged, thy will be done throughout the empire, as it is in each session. Give us our usual sops, and forgive us our occasional absences on division; as we promise not to forgive those that divide against thee; Turn us not out of our places but keep us in the House of Commons, the land of Pensions and Plenty, and deliver us from the People. Amen [7]

As a result, poor Hone, who was in bad health, was remanded in prison from May to December 1817, because he could not raise the £1,000 bail money. Whilst in prison he worked hard on his own defence, collecting examples of other parodists' work. When his trial came, he defended himself brilliantly before the ill natured Lord Chief Justice Ellenborough, reducing the court to laughter by reciting previous idiotic parodies – so much so that the sheriff had to threaten to arrest 'the first man I see laugh'. Hone was found not guilty and now all parodies, satire and squibs were to be published without fear of prosecution. Private Eye must be eternally grateful to Hone.

By 1821 publisher Carlile's wife, sister and his 'shopmen' plus about 150 local printers, newspaper sellers and other volunteer shopmen were keeping his Fleet Street publishing shop open whilst he served his prison sentence, in spite of the government's wish to stop the business. Some of these volunteers actually travelled down to London from Lincolnshire, Leeds and Liverpool and up from Dorset to help. These were the 'freethinkers', the circle of Godwin and Mary Wollstonecraft, an intellectual pro working class radical movement.

12 – An Organiser and a Windbag

Lt. Col. John Hastings Mair – the organiser

BY FRIDAY 26TH November Salisbury is in a state of anxiety and a degree of chaos. So the arrival of an Army officer by the name of Lt. Col .John Hastings Mair may initially have gone unnoticed. The Colonel has been sent to Salisbury by Lord Melbourne, the Home Secretary, with instructions to report direct to the Home Office. He is accompanied by his brother officer Col. Brotherton, who is to be based in the north of the county. They are sent to Wiltshire to supervise the movement of troops in the disturbed area and to see that peace returned. Colonel Brotherton proceeds to Warminster and Lt. Col. Mair makes his headquarters in Salisbury[1].

Mair is a career soldier, about 40 years old, born in Ireland. He joins the 21st Fusiliers at a very young age in 1805. In 1807 he sees the capture of Copenhagen, goes to America in 1808 and Portugal in 1810. During 1815 to 1818 he is with the Army of Occupation in France; is posted to Ireland and takes part in a diplomatic mission to Greece. He becomes judge Advocate for the Army.

By 1830 he is a seasoned campaigner, respected, reliable and a great organiser. He is a sensible, calm man, a man used to dealing with stressful situations and disposing of his troops in a manner making the best use of whatever is available to help him to do so.

On his arrival he immediately assesses the situation with regard to his available troops, i.e. the volunteer Wiltshire Yeomanry, and in particular what has happened the day before at Pythouse. He asks Lord Arundell to return home to Wardour, thinking, as Lord Arundell explains to Peniston in one of his letters, that his Lordship's presence might help to calm the foment existing in Tisbury. Mair's instructions are that the noble Lord should return to Salisbury the following day[2].

Mair himself also rides to Tisbury with the intention of seeing the MP Mr Benett at home in Pythouse where Benett is 'actively engaged in taking up prisoners and sending them under detachment every hour'. Mair expresses anxiety that Benett's actions 'might lead to bad consequences', so his visit is aimed at calming down the volatile MP before further damage is done.

Also on the 26th, Mair writes to the Home Secretary that he 'suspects that small farmers, if they do not aid, are evidently glad to see the labourers at work (breaking machines) fancying it will tend to their benefits, lowering tythes etc.'[3]

The competent Colonel now offers advice to a brother Colonel, who is in Berkshire, proposing a civil police force there, to be funded by the Grand Jury. As a result of this advice being followed, Reading remains calm.

Now Mair starts to undertake the policing of Salisbury during this difficult period. He is very occupied with organising this volunteer constabulary, starting by dividing the city into seven chequers, the streets, luckily, in Salisbury being straight and at right angles to one another, although as he notes in his sketch, this arrangement could work in any Town even if the streets are not as straight. He appoints a General Director for the city and three superintendents for each district/chequer with a central spot in each district for assembly. These are as follows:

    Division A – at the White Horse Inn, Castle Street
    B – at the Black Horse inn
    C – in the Cheese Market
    D – at the Goat inn
    E – at the White Hart Inn
    F – at the Radnor Arms
    G – at the Red Lion Inn
    Each constable is to bear a number.

There are to be 100 to 50 volunteers for each district. Should riots take place in any particular section he says, the leader of such section is to send, or communicate information by means of a well mounted and confidential man sent to the other sections, so that they may assemble as quietly as possible at a General Rendezvous point in the city. However, if the Leader of the district think that with the co-operation of one or two adjacent districts he can control the uprising, he should do so without recourse to assembly at the General Rendezvous. One division each night is responsible for special duty. Movements should be by way of footpaths, woods, fields, by-ways etc. if a meeting at the General Rendezvous becomes necessary. A mounted look-out should precede each group Strictest silence must be observed. Any prisoners taken are to be sent under proper escort to the General Rendezvous. He points out too that 'all should bear strongly in mind that acting with the Law and the Civil Power to aid them, their energy and power will inspire a confidence which the dread of illegally acting and fear of punishment on their opponents must have a weakening and cautionary effect'.[4]

Colonel Mair's volunteer constabulary is so successful that Salisbury is immediately comforted, calmed and the shopkeepers and residents are reported as feeling secure.

On the 27th November a request for assistance at Devizes is sent to Salisbury and the Colonel orders the Hindon troop to deploy to the town. Almost immediately he receives a further message from Colonel Baker at Devizes to say that the situation has been greatly exaggerated, so Colonel Mair, unruffled, orders the Hindon troop to return to base.[5]

On the 28th November, with the special commissioners on their way to Salisbury to start the trials, Mair arranges for the prisoners to be escorted from their various gaols (Devizes, Marlborough and of course Fisherton in Salisbury) to the Guildhall on the appropriate day. He also arranges protection for the witnesses and their Lordships who will sit in judgement upon the unfortunate men.

On the 1st January he is present at the opening of the trials.

At the request of the Home Secretary, he sends Lord Melbourne a Return on the Conditions and Wages of the accused; he visits Fisherton Gaol, commenting favourably upon the demeanour and behaviour of these young men. He is clearly sympathetic to their plight, perhaps able to understand their sufferings, having looked after his ill-educated, poverty stricken and pressed soldiers over a long period. The interviewing of the arrested men in Fisherton Gaol was to have been undertaken by the crown lawyer Tallents, but Tallents delegates this task to Lt Col Mair. On the 6th January Tallents writes to a Mr Phillips at Whitehall for the attention of Lord Melbourne that he had been ill and therefore himself unable to undertake a Return of the Conditions, Wages etc. of the several prisoners so had asked for Col. Mair's assistance. However, he ends this paragraph with the comment that 'I am concerned however that the principal offenders cannot truly plead actual distress in extenuation of their crimes'.[6]

Mair's opinion is different.

After the tumult of the trials and sentencing is over, Colonel Mair returns home to High Wycombe, where he receives a letter from Lord Arundell requesting mercy for a number of the men, most of whom are either Arundell's tenants or estate workers. Colonel Mair is happy to concur with Arundell's request that the letter be forwarded to Lord Melbourne as quickly as possible, and he adds his endorsement to the request for mercy. Sadly the men are, by now, either on the *York*, or on their way to Van Diemen's Land. No-one extends mercy to them.

A sane, sensible, kindly, extremely competent man, Colonel Mair brings a breath of cool fresh air to the febrile atmosphere of the city of Salisbury during that awful winter. Following the agricultural riots the Lt. Col. is promoted to Military Secretary in Gibraltar and in 1835 to be Lt. Governor of the Island of Domenica. Sadly, Mair dies in Domenica on the 21st March 1836, after a very short illness. His obituary is printed in the Gentleman's Magazine:

> The urbanity, the kindness, the high minded feeling and demeanour of Governor Mair had obtained for him the esteem and affectionate regards of all those whom either the duties of his profession or the courtesies of civil life had brough him in contact. As a soldier his name stood deservedly high; in his civil capacity he was universally respected and beloved'.

Salisbury had been lucky to have his presence during the difficult Christmas period of 1830.

Henry Hunt – influencer and windbag?

IF WILLIAM COBBETT is the voice of journalism for the embryo radicals of the early 19th century, Henry Hunt is the voice of their broadcasting medium, an orator of considerable talent, speaking in a comprehensible, understandable but gentlemanly language the opinions and suggestions that the radicals themselves wanted expressed publicly. At the same time Hunt ensures that whilst he encourages others to take part in physical demonstrations and even at times violence, he carefully disassociates himself personally from extremists.

Hunt is born in Upavon, Wiltshire, in 1773 to a landowning family with sufficient money to ensure him a comfortable lifestyle, at least to begin with. Hunt however develops, to his credit, radical, reformist opinions. He is not a peaceable man, he falls out over the years with his friend Cobbett, with other radicals/reformists such as Burdett, or Francis Place, and sometimes he and Cobbett together fall out with other radicals. There is no leadership amongst these reformists and all of them to some extent vie with one another in the popularity stakes. Hunt opposes both Whig and Tory parties.

Whilst still a very young man, he falls foul of his

Henry Hunt – oil on canvas, English School, Harris Museum and Art Gallery Preston

fellow Wiltshire landowner John Benett MP and this animosity lasts for the rest of their lives. They are both landowners in the Enford area but Benett holds the title of Lord of the Manor, thus having historic rights denied to other landowners. In 1815 Hunt opposes Benett over the Corn Laws question (Hunt being opposed to these proposed regulations of the import of foreign corn and to price stabilisation) and Benett finds various ways of undermining Hunt's burgeoning influence in Wiltshire. One is to take him to court over the fishing rights in the river at Enford – Benett claims £1,000 damages against Hunt for fishing in his Manorial waters. The court, while finding in favour of Benett, awards him a derisory and humiliating sum of one farthing in damages.

On another occasion Hunt claims to have been 'attacked' by Benett's gamekeeper. This was not a good idea because in fact Benett had told his gamekeeper to give Hunt notice that he was not allowed to shoot on land belonging to the Manor. Apparently the gamekeeper, following Hunt to serve the notice upon him, tried to put the paper in Hunt's pocket. Hunt, angrily dismounting from his horse, responded by striking the gamekeeper. He was found guilty of assault and sentenced to three months in prison with £200 surety to keep the peace. So Hunt had no love for his fellow Wiltshire landowner.[7] This was Hunt's first taste of prison, and where he met Colonel Edmund Despard, a member of a dissident Irish/English group – the United Englishmen – with links to French Jacobins. It was Despard who persuaded Hunt of the rightness of the radical and reformist ideas which informed the rest of his political life. Despard himself goes to the scaffold in 1803 for high treason, together with six other men, three of whom are Methodist dissidents. They had all been held without trial at the Coldbaths Field prison. By May 1803 France was again at war with England. Hunt was perhaps fortunate not to become too embroiled with Colonel Despard.

Hunt now starts campaigning for political reform and as early as 1806/7 he is appealing to the freeholders of his native Wiltshire to follow the example of the 'Westminster Committee' regarding how to run elections fairly – there should be no bribing of electors, no treating them to dinners or beer, no paying of counsellors by candidates, or paying constables or groups of horsemen to defend the candidate's interests – in short no money should be spent by candidates except sums approved by the whole election committee. Canvassing was to be reformed so that no candidate would benefit from their wealth or influence, or be able to buy votes.[8]

In the winter of 1812 Hunt was to be found in London, at the Spa Fields disturbances, speaking on corruption in public life and taxation. In Bristol in the same year he fights an 'impressive campaign' as a Radical but is not elected. He advocates universal suffrage and annual parliaments and the tactic of mass pressure by the public for change, which he feels could drive the movement onwards without recourse to violence. He is a popular and excellent speaker.

A rather different radical, Samuel Bamford, a weaver from the midlands, reluctantly admits that Hunt is 'a handsome man, gentlemanly in manner and attire and six feet and better in height'.

However, when he speaks, reports Bamford, he becomes overexcited, the kind smile exchanged for the curl of scorn, or the curse of indignation. He bellows, his cheeks flush and his blue eyes start from their sockets, becoming 'blood streaked'. He gives the impression of powerful energy struggling for utterance.[9]

When speaking in public Hunt chose to wear a white top hat – he stood out anyway with his unusual height and fine clothes. He loved

Cartoon – the Peterloo Massacre – print by Richard Carlile

the popular acclaim that his speeches brought him and delighted in the nickname 'Champion of Liberty'.

However, in Manchester in 1819 he meets opposition – at a meeting which becomes known as Peterloo, or sometimes the Peterloo Massacre. Hunt is a guest speaker at this meeting in Manchester which attracts a huge crowd of workers and their families. It is known that Hunt requested that the crowd attend unarmed and in a peaceful manner, but the local authorities, in trying to control the crowds, bring in the local undisciplined yeomanry on horseback, who attack men and women and children indiscriminately, causing death and horrible injuries. During the melee Hunt's beautiful white top hat is stoved in, but luckily it protects his head. For his part in this event Hunt is arrested, tried over a period of over two weeks and sentenced to two and half years in Ilchester Gaol. He had requested that the trial be held in Yorkshire rather than Lancashire, but before the trial he makes a triumphal coach journey through the Lancashire cotton towns – a public progress when he acknowledges the shouts of the crowds of 'Hunt for Ever'. These fired-up young workers unharness the horses from his carriage and themselves drag the carriage into the little town centres, singing

With Henry Hunt we'll go, we'll go
With Henry Hunt we'll go

We'll raise the cap of liberty
In spite of Nadin Joe

He is so popular in Manchester that the monitors at the Manchester Radical Sunday School wear lockets with Hunt's portrait in, rather than crucifixes.[10]

Unsurprisingly Hunt's vanity is growing. He expresses and plays with the emotions of the crowd, which they themselves are unable to put into words. E W P Thompson in *The Making of the English Working Class*, states that:

the charismatic orators were those with a taste for self-dramatization' but 'the demagogue is a bad or ineffectual leader. Hunt voiced, not principle, nor even well formulated Radical strategy, but the emotions of the movement ... he was not the leader but the captive of the least stable portion of the crowd

Hunt's living style is becoming extravagant – it is of course true that travelling around the country speaking at meetings, publishing leaflets and

A Peep inside Ilchester Bastile – from a pamphlet by Henry Hunt 1821
British Library

dealing with correspondence costs money, but Hunt becomes incapable of differentiating between personal and public costs, funds raised by radicals being used for personal expenses. He starts up a business manufacturing, amongst other things, 'radical breakfast powder' made from roasted corn, which was to be a tea and coffee substitute for the poor, avoiding tax on imported goods. He makes herbal tea, he makes a 'blacking' shoe polish. These products give him a very good excuse to be travelling through the countryside in pursuit of his business interests.

After his release from Ilchester Gaol he is welcomed to London and takes a role on The Committee of the Useful Classes, run by one John Gast. This is a forerunner of a trades council, which in 1825, after the repeal of the Combination Acts, publishes its own 'Trades newspaper'. He continues to attend public meetings, moving on to appeal not just for household suffrage, but for manhood suffrage, speaking at the meetings of the Radical Hampden Clubs in London and in the midlands. In 1828 he is concerned with changes to the Game Laws, reform of which proposed to reduce the prison term for a third offence from two years to one year. However the House of Lords finds this too much to take and turns down the reforms, the term remaining the same at two years. No doubt Hunt is reminded of his younger self being served with the notice forbidding him to shoot over Benett's land.

He is thwarted in his desire to become an MP for a Wiltshire constituency but in 1830 he finally obtains a seat in Parliament, standing and winning the election for Preston, a northern industrial town.

1830 is, of course, the year of Captain Swing. If before this the south had been unaware of Henry Hunt, he is now seen everywhere (even when he is not there). But he is certainly at Overton in Hampshire on the 18th November. Following an uprising in the town centre by several hundred agricultural labourers demanding money, food, and a rise in wages, the crowd eventually disperses after offers by shopkeepers of food and money and a wage rise by the farmers. They all go home. Hunt arrives by stagecoach the following day to find the mob reassembled, this time armed with flails, sticks and staves. The local farmers ask Hunt to act as arbitrator. He proposes a rise in wages from 9s. per week to 12s. per week, the farmers to pay the labourers' house-rents and to give them each 2s. for the loss of work occasioned by their own rioting. This strikes everyone as satisfactory, and unsurprisingly is greeted with cheers by the crowd and mutual expressions of good will all round. The mob, within ten minutes according to the local newspaper, departs, leaving the market place in peace and quiet again.[11] This act of mediation gives the labourers locally the hope of success for themselves and the riots spread further into Hampshire and towards Wiltshire.

On the 19th November Andover is targeted and once again Hunt is apparently present. His speech, not an inflammatory one, does not sufficiently satisfy the rioters and they move on to destroy the machinery at Tasker's Waterloo Foundry. By the 25th November Hunt is in Warminster where troops are sent to keep the peace at the request of the magistrates.

There is no record of him being in Tisbury, but commenting upon the death of John Harding at Pythouse, Hunt states that the foreman of the jury at the inquest in Tisbury is the father of one of the Hindon troop of the Wiltshire yeomanry.[12]

Hunt moves on to Exeter where he is said to be 'stirring up the lower classes' and to Taunton where he advocates parliamentary reform and condemns the burning of ricks – incendiarism he says, is not 'manly, peaceable and Englishman-like in manner and not the way to right grievances'

Like Cobbett, he disassociates himself from any involvement in fire raising, as had the young rioters at Fonthill Gifford on the 25th November. – 'we are Hunt's men'.

In spite of his conciliatory words Hunt is, in the opinion of some landowners, clearly responsible for some of the rioting. He insists he is only travelling in these areas because of his business interests.

It is interesting to speculate on the extent of his influence on the Swing rioters, and in particular, how the Pythouse men had known of him, had they heard him speak somewhere, or been told of his meetings? It is possible that a farmer as well educated as Alford, a member of the Methodists, and a moderate reformer, would have heard of him, but the majority of the men from the Tisbury were very poorly educated, probably quite poorly informed, and motivated not by politics or the desire for parliamentary reform, but from a simple need to improve their living standards.

By the spring of 1831 the rioting had largely subsided, but Hunt takes a very full part in the debate in the House of Commons held on 8th February. He alleges that the farmers had actually encouraged or stood by whilst the rioters smashed up the threshing machines. This comment may relate to the small tenant farmers, rather than the landowners who actually owned and could afford the machines. He comments at length about the whole Pythouse riots, and on the fact that those with previous poaching convictions are immediately arrested afterwards – in Hindon seven men had been arrested and every one of them had a small previous conviction.

Hunt claims that he had spoken to the wives of the convicted Hindon men who told him that their husbands had been selected for punishment because of their previous poaching records. In fact this view is confirmed by a letter from the Chilmark landowner Henry King who, writing on 29th December 1830 to the Clerks for the special commission states that he hopes the prisoners 'will receive the Punishments they merit' since, he says 'several of them have before Trespass'd against the Laws of their Country'.

It would seem to have been a very good opportunity for the local landowners to rid themselves of possible troublemakers. Hunt is of course opposed at equal length by Benett. This long debate is a wonderful example of Hunt's oratorical style, but the departures for Van Diemen's Land of the ships *Eliza* and *Proteus* had rather spiked the debate. Hunt was not a popular man in the House of Commons, but his views and comments were always widely reported in the newspapers and periodicals of the time and this had served in this instance to keep the issue in front of the public mind. Hunt had only one supporter in the House, Mr J Hume. Against the motion were the Attorney-General Denman, Lord Melbourne's brother George Lamb the Under-Secretary at the Home Office and local landowner John Benett.

During the debate Benett defended his position as both foreman of the Grand Jury at the trials and as prosecutor in the cases of men who had attacked his own property. He gave his version of the riot in which he himself was involved, and pointed out that he had pleaded on behalf of some of the men, requesting bail for them. He gave a lengthy account of the actual fight which involved the Hindon troop of the Wiltshire Yeomanry, commending its brave commanding officer's good sense and humanity who, said Benett, had directed that his men should strike only side-blows so as to wound the rioters in the arms but not at their heads when a blow might be murderous. He then said he had since taken into his own service some of the men in the disturbances who had asked him for steady employment, and in reply to Hunt's allegation that Benett had in fact excited the mob by the low wages he paid, Benett replied he had raised him employees' wages since the riots had happened.

George Lamb spoke against Hunt's motion for amnesty for the rioters and in doing so joked about the illiteracy of the rioters – in particular the letters written by Looker – who was now en route to Van Diemen's Land.

Attorney General Denman spoke with pride of his actions in relation to the riots and poured scorn upon those who looked with sentimentality upon the rioters.[13]

The motion was of course defeated – by 269 votes to 2.

The Hammonds in *The Village Labourer* note that Hunt's wisdom was not equal to his courage and thus spoilt his natural eloquence. His vanity was indeed considerable but he preached reformism to the tradesmen and embryo middle classes in a style they could relate to.

Whilst an MP, and between February 1831 and August 1832, he made over 1,000 speeches in the House. But when the Reform Bill comes before Parliament for consideration he criticises it as insufficiently radical and says it will fail to benefit the working classes. Amongst bills he proposes is one for womens' suffrage; he calls for justice following the Peterloo Massacre.

In 1834 Hunt becomes poorly, is unwell for about a year and in early 1835 he suffers a stroke and dies, at Alresford in Hampshire. He is buried at Parham Park in Sussex.

His influence was considerable, but he was not always popular, particularly with those who had to listen to his very long speeches – Eric Hobsbawm rather unkindly calls him 'a rhetorical windbag'.[14]

13 – John Benett – Anti-Hero?

A THOROUGH WILTSHIREMAN, JOHN Benett was born in May 1773, the second son of Thomas and Catherine Bennett of Pythouse, an estate in the south-west corner of Wiltshire, near Tisbury. The family had inherited land at Norton Bavant which had been held by them from the late 14th century, having made their money as clothiers and as farmers. In 1725 John Benett's grandfather, another Thomas, bought the Pythouse estate, which had in previous centuries been owned by a different branch of the family – the Bennetts (double n), but who had been forced to sell it in 1669 having backed the wrong side in the Civil War and been heavily fined by the Commonwealth, since they were keen supporters of the monarchy.

Benett inherited Pythouse on the death of his father, as his older brother had died earlier. He also inherited land at Semley, Chicklade, Sutton Veny and Warminster, the Manors of Kingston at West Stour and South Litchfield, and another mansion and park at Kingsclere in Hampshire. On the death of his aunt Catherine, he also acquired the family land at Norton Bavant with its Manor and further land at Enford, north of Amesbury.

Benett now extended his Pythouse mansion, designing the alterations himself in the fashionable Greek revival style, retaining some of the old building inside the new one. He kept the old orangery to the west of the new house, the old gate piers with their bands of rusticated stone, and in 1801 he installed marble chimney pieces from nearby Fonthill Splendens which was being partially demolished by William Beckford. At the request of his father in law he added a Gothic style chapel in the grounds

Now he was established as the owner of a large, splendid country mansion, overlooking its own parkland, backed by woodland and farmland, so he bought more land in the immediate area, 335 acres of Semley and 29 more of Tisbury. In order to achieve this local expansion (he was also entering into negotiations to buy manors, lordships and advowsons in Berwick St Leonard and Pertwood), he put his Hampshire land up for sale – South Litchfield and Freemantle Park at Kingsclere. He also planned to sell Wincombe Park farm (162 acres) in Donhead St Mary, this property selling in 1807.

Eventually completing the purchases of Pertwood and Berwick St Leonard in 1809, he sold a further 293 acres and the advowson at Pertwood the following year, making a good profit on the turn round. In 1808 he had bought 206 acres in Semley and 250 acres of Lower Linley and Upper Linley Farms, immediately adjacent to Pythouse. Further small sales and purchases went ahead, another 22 acres in Tisbury and then, as the enclosures awards occurred he was allotted 770 acres at Enford and Fifield as he held the title of Lord of the Manor there. Similarly at Norton Bavant as Lord of the Manor he received 1275 further acres.

Whilst these negotiations were proceeding, Benett and his wife Lucy Lambert from Boyton (who he had married in 1801), were increasing the size of the Benett family, with four daughters being born, the last of whom died in infancy. In 1809 they had a son, John, and then another boy, Thomas Edmund. The family was involved socially with the Grove family at Ferne, the Arundells at Wardour, the Knellers at Donhead Hall, the Helyars at Sedgehill and the Gordons at Wincombe Park.

Benett now becomes a magistrate and seems to be set to become a successful landowner, farmer and local bigwig. He is particularly interested in agricultural reform, soon becoming a member of the newly formed Bath & West of England Agricultural Society.[1] He creates and chairs The Wiltshire Society for the Encouragement of Agriculture and the Rewarding of Faithful and Industrious Servants, which has as its patron and President the Marquis of Bath, and as Vice Presidents Lord Arundell, the Marquis of Lansdowne, Sir Richard Colt Hoare and the Marquis of Ailesbury. But notably not Lord Radnor or the Earl of Pembroke. This Society meets at Devizes and runs amongst other things, ploughing competitions which Benett's agricultural workers frequently win.

However, Benett is not an easy man to deal with. He falls out quite early in his life with the vicar of Tisbury, Thomas Prevost, over the question of tithes. It had become the practice for the church to accept money instead of the animals or produce which had been the custom in the past. But Prevost refuses to accept money and brings a case against Benett and another local landowner, John Bracher, in the Episcopal court in Salisbury. This becomes a longstanding dispute and grudge between Benett and the church authorities and was to lead to the reform of tithes. Certainly reform was necessary. For every man to have to give the church one-tenth (a tithe) of his earnings to the local parish was deeply unfair to the poor. Following Tyndale's translation of the New Testament into English, it had become clear that the payment of tithes was based upon an interpretation by St Paul, in a letter to the Corinthians, of a sentence attributed to Moses. The massive wealth of the church was based upon this interpretation of a Greek phrase into Latin, and it was becoming increasingly apparent that the whole structure was unreasonable and unstable. The Rev. Prevost clearly felt that accepting goods rather than money was a fairer way of paying tithes, but values had been set and Benett and Bracher thought they should not be changed.

John Benett Esqr.M.P. 1773-1852 – engraving from his portrait at Pythouse – Trustees of the British Museum

Benett now upsets the Archdeacon of Wiltshire, William Coxe, by writing an essay on the unfairness of tithes being payable to the church at all, which in his opinion did nothing towards the costs of agriculture and says that it causes more dissension from the established church. Coxe dismisses these theories and the argument rumbles on for many years in the form of published letters and articles.

Towards the end of the Napoleonic Wars, the price of corn had dropped from £5.9s. a quarter to £2.5s., causing considerable distress in the countryside, both for farmers and for their workers. The introduction of the Corn Laws was an attempt to restrict the import of foreign grown corn and to stabilise prices. Benett, as a large landowner and agricultural reformer, is called to give evidence to a Parliamentary Select Committee and it is during these hearings that he is asked: 'What Quantity of corn per week do you think that a labourer in husbandry ought to earn?'

To which Benett responds: 'A bushel'.

Was this sufficient for the maintenance of a man, his wife and two children, he is asked.

'Yes, certainly. It is what we calculate; we calculate that every person in a labourer's family should have per week the price of a gallon loaf, and three pence over for feeding and clothes, exclusive of house rent, sickness and casual expenses.'[2]

This reply by Benett led to him being called by William Cobbett 'the gallon loaf man' and was highly publicised. It was an epithet that stuck – here was a landowner who thought that the labourer and his family were able to survive on a starvation diet, with no surplus money to pay for house rent or other normal costs of living. Benett becomes an icon of the unpopular landlord and employer and this, together with his support for the Corn Laws, leads to his effigy being burnt in several towns, according to the *South Wilts Journal* in 1819.

He was deemed even more unpopular when he addressed the Poor Law Committee in 1817 – stating that if Parliament amended the Law of Settlement to allow settlement by length of residence, he would pull down all his labourers' cottages on his own estates. On the committee's comment that if there were no cottages there would be no labourers, he replied that it did not matter how far a labourer had to walk to get to work – indeed he had labourers who walked three miles to get to work on his farms every morning even in winter (they worked, he said, from 6am to 6pm) and back at night and 'they are the most punctual persons we have'. These comments as may be imagined, did not go down well with the labourers of Wiltshire. It was said that he had already pulled down some of his labourers' cottages, but this is not actually verified. However, in defence of his wife Lucy, she gave clothing to the poor each year and even Benett, in February 1816, gave the poor an ox.

In 1808 Benett falls out with Henry Hunt, as mentioned before, over the fishing and shooting rights Benett holds as Lord of the Manor of Enford. Another long standing grudge developed.

Benett had joined the local Wiltshire Yeomanry as a private, when he reached 21 years of age. He knew every member of the Hindon troop and in 1800 he was promoted to Cornet, and to Lieutenant in 1804.

This volunteer troop was to provide a useful support during his attempts to become a Member of Parliament and indeed Benett is prone to using the troop as a private militia on other occasions. In spring 1817 Henry Hunt is due to speak at a meeting in Devizes, but Benett is determined Hunt should not be heard and arriving with his supporters (including the members of the Hindon troop in mufti) gives them instructions to 'shout, hoot and bellow' during Hunt's attempts to speak. Hunt refers to Benett as 'Black Jack, alias the Devil's Knitting Needle'. The sheriff, Lord Pembroke, reads the Riot Act and orders the arrest of Hunt, but Hunt is rescued by the crowd, who had come to hear him speak and is carried away to safety.[3]

In 1818 Benett decides to stand for election to Parliament as a county representative. He holds dinners for his supporters at Devizes and at Salisbury and whilst canvassing he makes good use of the Hindon troop of Wiltshire Yeomanry (out of uniform but mounted) to intimidate the supporters of Wellesley, (the other candidate and nephew of the Duke of Wellington). Ribald songs are written and sung about both candidates, slanderous and cruel, but apt:

> A-canvassing around the County, we see
> A long, lanthorn-jaw'd, wretched creature.
> A-straddle across a poor beast – (who but he?)
> Of a gentleman – blest with no feature.
>
> His coat it is blue, and was formerly new;
> His hat is a gift of his scout, Sir;
> His breeches are brown, and well known to each town,
> Which this ill Weed has canvass'd about, Sir
> He's tall and he's thin, and his legs are a-twin;
> His visage, the picture of grief Sir.
> He seems like a thing that's committed a sin,
> And less like a Gent than a ------------- Sir![4]

It is certainly true that Benett is very thin and very tall and does look quite out of proportion. At this election he is defeated, the county returns Paul Methuen and Wellesley. Benett however still has to show his gratitude to his supporters, holding a huge dinner for 700 people in a marquee in the grounds of Pythouse; he gives bread and beer to the inhabitants of Warminster and a further superb dinner to county gentlemen and the cream of the Salisbury area in the Assembly Rooms there. They toast 'The Wiltshire Cossacks', John Peniston the Salisbury architect and Henry King, landowner from Chilmark – both of whom had provided the Hindon troop accompanying Benett on his canvassing.

Benett goes on to stand for two further county elections spending huge amounts of money in his attempts to become an MP. Eventually, in spite of the animosity towards him, on the 4th August 1819 he is finally elected as an MP. He gives his friend Henry King an inscribed tankard for the support given by King and the 'Wiltshire Cossacks'. In Tisbury all 23 freeholders vote for him (including, surprisingly, the Rev. Dr. Thomas Prevost). On the side wall of the Boot Inn in Tisbury is inscribed 'Benett for Ever'. In Semley 16 of the 18 freeholders vote for him. He visits the various Wiltshire towns and gives thank-you dinners. These jolly dinners add to the depletion of his funds.

In Parliament Benett votes with the Whig party. He is in favour of Catholic emancipation (this would be a sensible choice for him, bearing in mind his staunchly Catholic Arundell neighbours) and he votes for electoral reform. Locally he is appointed a member of the Grand Jury in Salisbury – not only a member but the Foreman. He attends meetings all over the county, enjoying the annual Venison Dinner at Devizes, and going to Bible Society meetings. He votes for a reduction in the Standing Army numbers and speaks in the House on many occasions – and at great length. However, all this expensive activity and the maintenance of a London address plus the Pythouse costs are beginning to cause him some financial anxiety so he starts to campaign for a reduction in taxes.

By now Benett is Captain of the Hindon troop of the Wiltshire Yeomanry Cavalry, which by law must be on permanent duty for six days in any given year, so it needs to train for this commitment. The troop is paid at the same rate as regular Army soldiers for these training and duty days, and at the end of a joint training session in 1822 with the Salisbury troop under the command of Lord Arundell, the troops are entertained at Wardour Castle at the expense of the noble Lord, (who is equally short of funds). Shortly afterwards, Arundell, who had run into considerable debt, is forced by his creditors to pay 13s.4d in the pound to settle these debts and subsequently leaves Wiltshire to live in France, where living costs are much reduced. Benett too is permanently in debt, juggling his investments in farms, land, and advowsons by judicious borrowing and selling.

In 1823 he arranges to buy Middle Linley Farm close to Pythouse but in order to do this he has to arrange a sale of 2378 acres of land locally in Berwick St Leonard, Chicklade and Boyton, plus Motcombe, Stour and Keynton in Dorset, all to John Farquhar, the exceedingly rich man who

Ruins of Fonthill Abbey – John Buckler 1825 lithograph print British Museum

was in the process of buying Fonthill Abbey and its immediate land from William Beckford. These sales put him in funds to the sum of £100,000. Benett now becomes Farquhar's tenant at a rent of £3663 per year. He also tries to buy the advowson of Tisbury, but fails in this. One may imagine the relief felt by Dr the Rev. Prevost at St John's.

Now he could afford to become a member of Brooks' Club in St James's Street and the newly founded Athenaeum Club in London where he could rub shoulders with the very top aristocrats and politicians of the day. He is also now first registered as living at 19 Albemarle Street in Mayfair. [5] He keeps up his farming interests, being that rare owner at the time, a truly hands-on farmer.

In November 1825 the great tower at Fonthill Abbey collapses, and although Mr Farquhar appears to be undisturbed by this momentous event, he does decide to sell. Benett agrees to buy 2,450 acres of Tisbury and Fonthill Gifford land from Farquhar, plus the 504 acres within the wall of Fonthill Abbey grounds, the timber, the trees, the mansion house and lands at Fonthill Gifford, the advowson at Fonthill Gifford, and the remains of the Abbey (stone, timber, metal, fittings etc). At the same time Farquhar sells 1400 acres of land, some of which is at Fonthill Bishop, to Henry King, Benett's old friend at Chilmark.[6]

However, due to financial constraints and also to the difficulties caused by the death of Mr Farquhar in 1826, plus a dispute amongst the beneficiaries of Farquhar's will, Benett does not actually complete his purchase until much later – in 1838 in fact. Although he is not yet the legal owner of this land, he treats it as if he has paid for it, instructing John Peniston, his architect friend from Salisbury, to create a survey of the property and value its materials. Peniston is given the task of selling off the construction materials of the Abbey and the letters between Benett and Peniston provide a fascinating glimpse into the way Benett was able to make money from the stone, timber, metal and even the glass from the damaged windows.[7]

At the same time James Morrison, a wealthy haberdasher from London (although originally an innkeeper's son from Middle Wallop in Hampshire), is buying some of the Farquhar land and the mansion, partly demolished by Beckford earlier, of Fonthill Splendens.

By 1830 Benett has built a new farmhouse and barns at Pythouse, with a threshing machine installed, driven by six horses. At Linley he also builds a new farmhouse and provides a water powered threshing machine and sawmill. He keeps large flocks of Merino sheep, recommending this breed as suitable for rearing in Wiltshire.[8] Because of his introduction of the threshing machines he is disliked by local agricultural labourers, who need the money they always earned in winter from flailing and threshing by hand. They say the machines cause unemployment which they certainly do during the starving winter months. His support for the Corn Laws, they feel, contribute towards the high costs of bread and the understanding amongst the poor is that the tenant farmers too are unhappy with the status quo and will support them. In addition there is uncertainty about the ownership of the estates and almost certainly unhappiness at the thought of Benett becoming the landowner and ultimate employer in Fonthill Gifford and even more in Tisbury. Their wages are already amongst the lowest in Wiltshire at 7s. per week – so what will they have to lose by making their views felt?

As a result it is hardly surprising the events of 25th November 1830 involve the workers and farms at Fonthill Gifford, Fonthill Bishop and Tisbury. Given Benett's predisposition to involving himself in disputes, his part in the failure to quell the rioting is equally understandable. His is not an heroic performance. It is certainly a performance of some importance – he sees himself as a beleaguered hero, trying to calm the ferocious mob, and his subsequent recitals of his efforts tend to show how brave he feels he was on the day, but history is unconvinced. Henry Hunt's version of the events of that day are equally unconvincing. The eyewitness reports which have survived are those from John Brickell, Benett's carter, and the young William Turner – both recalling in much later life the exciting events of the day, but those reports need to be taken in the context of Brickell being

Benett's employee, and the young William's recall of thrilling events of his childhood.

Afterwards Benett expends a great deal of energy in rounding up those he identified as rioters and taking statements from his witnesses. Most of these witnesses are Benett's employees, the statements are taken by him and the employees are subsequently rewarded.

Hunt accuses him of selecting men who Benett considered to be troublemakers. In response Benett admits that, 'selection did take place, when so many persons were concerned in the riots, it was natural that we should select only the worst characters for trial and should not be influenced by the previous good character of men'.

These activities can only have made him even less popular than before and Cobbett amongst others goes for him in practically every issue of his Political Register periodical, quoting Benett's 'gallon loaf' comments.[9]

Cobbett is subsequently tried for seditious libel for these and other comments he has made and published, but overturns the court's views completely. Benett, present at that trial, is said to be 'a spectre of vengeance'. He was called at the time 'one of the most hated men in the county'.[10]

In April 1831 he compounds local displeasure by commencing an Action in the courts against:

> the Inhabitants of the Hundred of Dunworth in the Division of Hindon in the County of Wilts. 'to recover compensation for the Damages which he has sustained by reason of the destruction, or part destruction of certain Barns and Outhouses, together with divers Fixtures, Goods and Chattels there, the property of the said John Benett at the parish of Tisbury by a riotous and tumultuous assembly on the twenty-fifth of November last'.

This is reported by the *Salisbury & Winchester Journal* on Monday 25th April but there is no further report as to the result of the Action, or that it is heard.

In August of the following year Benett tries to improve his image a little by letting over 50 lots of land for field gardens 'to poor persons of the parishes of Tisbury and Semley at 3d. per lug. (A lug is an old word and relates to an area of land of around 40 sq.m. – five lugs giving an allotment size of 200 sq.m. This measurement is still used in Pewsey in Wiltshire. Allotments are usually measured in rods/poles and measure around 250 sq.m.) Mr Benett's generosity is reported, rather curiously, by the *Worcester Herald* rather than the *Salisbury & Winchester Journal*.

Benett's part in the sad events of November and December 1830, including his position as Foreman of the Grand Jury at the special commission which tried the rioters, has an effect upon the rest of his public life. Punishment of the rioters is achieved quickly and by the early part of February 1831 they are on their way to Van Diemen's Land. He hopes the whole matter will be settled, forgotten and he can proceed with his life. His financial position however, is very insecure and he has still not managed to scrape up or borrow enough money to complete his purchase of the Fonthill lands. The state of his finances preclude him from being honoured with the knighthood he craves, unlike his fellow MP John Astley. His independent and noisily professed views count against him.

In one particular instance – when the Marquis of Bath dies Benett fully expects to be appointed Lt. Col. Commandant of the Royal Wiltshire Yeomanry, but he is passed over in favour of a younger man – G W F Earl Bruce. As a result of this he writes a very hurt letter to Lord Lansdowne, the Lord Lt. of Wiltshire and resigns his commission from the Regiment.

Further parliamentary elections deplete his capital and in 1838 he is eventually requested to complete his purchase of the Fonthill Abbey estate. He tries to borrow the immense sum of £90,000 from his new bank, Coutts & Co. and immediately puts the Abbey ruins and Fonthill Gifford village up for sale. No buyer is found. By 1841 his debt with Coutts has risen to £124,000 (this includes previous borrowings from them) but now he lists the value of his properties and assets, including the timber, the value of Fonthill Gifford's advowson, his Pythouse mansion and garden, his Norton Bavant mansion and garden and estimates that he is worth some £296,400.00.

The Tithe map and Apportionment Awards of 1842 give a good picture of his holdings in the area – Fonthill Gifford, Tisbury and Semley 4,672 acres in hand, farmed by him; 358 of the adjoining Hatch estate; 1416 acres at Norton Bavant and 640 at Boyton and Sherrington. Coutts have now lent him £12,500 on mortgaging Hatch, and a further huge mortgage of £136,500 equivalent to around six million pounds today[11]. The interest these loans incur is crippling. No doubt Benett would agree with E. P Thompson, the social historian, that 'land remained the index of influence, the plinth on which power was erected.' Those who own the land can dictate the lifestyle of those who do not and to this day considerable power is still invested in the ownership of land. If you are fenced off from the countryside which surrounds you, you cannot control or have any say in what happens on it. Land becomes a commodity, it is bought and sold, cut off from the mass of the people by fences and hedges which imply Keep Out, Private Property,

Trespassers will be Prosecuted. But trespassing, if no damage has occurred during the trespass, is not punishable by law. If you resist after being told to leave a property, the owner can call the police however, and the trespasser can be prosecuted for a breach of the peace. And some of the rioters were in fact prosecuted for this.

Around this time Benett is accused of interfering with the administration of Poor Law Relief in Tisbury union workhouse, but the relevant Minute Book record of 1838-39 is missing although curiously those for 1835-7 and 1840-3 survive.[12]

It is not until 1844 that he finally finds a purchaser for the Fonthill lands – Richard, Earl Grosvenor – who pays £89,500 for it, including the Fonthill Gifford advowson. The following year, Earl Grosvenor (now the 2nd Marquis of Westminster) buys more land from Benett and Benett's loan from Coutts & Co. is reduced to a more manageable £70,000. Benett confidently asserts:

> In my time I have been enabled by circumstances which occurred to others to increase the estate around Pythouse very considerably. Confidence in my own judgement as to the value of land has enabled me to do this by giving me boldness and decision in transacting the business of purchasing and selling land.[13]

It is quite difficult to agree that his impulsive purchase of the Fonthill Abbey lands and ruin was a successful business decision. He had spent an enormous amount of energy (as had his agent Peniston) in trying to sell the materials and he failed to make a profit on the sale of the whole property. However, Benett was never less than supremely confident in his own abilities.

His last years are rather sad. He had lost his wife, Lucy, in February 1827 when she was only 42 years old. In 1845 he is 71. Just after the Christmas of 1844 he hears that his son and heir John has died. On the 9th January his sister, Etheldred dies. He himself suffers from 'flu in February and then hears that his daughter Lucy, married to Arthur Fane, is very ill in Torquay and not expected to live. His grand-daughters come to live at Pythouse where Fanny, his youngest daughter, is to look after them. He records the deaths of two of his oldest employees – James Grey and John Ford. Daughter Lucy dies on the 6th April and his oldest friend Philip Miles also dies, as does his sister in law Ellen. A tragic year for him. He had been a good husband, brother and father, and to some extent a caring employer.

By 1846 Benett has mellowed considerably and after selling off some of his assets and finally disposing of Fonthill, he indulges his daughter Fanny by building a School House in the nearby hamlet of Newtown, close to Pythouse. Teaching is to be on the principles set out by the Church of England, services can be held in the schoolroom and the school is to be run by Fanny under the exclusive control of a Board of Trustees, of whom one is to be Fanny and another the Marquis of Westminster. That same year he gives £100 towards the cost of repairs to the church of St John the Baptist in Tisbury. He had already bought elegant gates for the churchyard there and paid for the rebuilding and renovating of the family church at Norton Bavant.[14]

Benett does not give up his London life entirely. He still attends Parliament from time to time, speaking on various subjects including the Irish question. He sells more farms to the Marquis of Westminster, reducing his Coutts loan to just over £50,000. Now his attendances in London are reduced and he eventually retires as a Member of Parliament.

On 29th September 1852 'Long' John Benett suffers a 'severe fit of apoplexy' – probably a stroke – and dies.

He has, in many ways, and particularly in his own opinion, served Wiltshire well as an MP, saying at his last election:

> you might find an abler man to serve you; but you will never have a Representative more devoted to our County's interests, or more anxious to maintain the prosperity and honour of the County of Wilts, than myself.

but his personality precluded him from being liked and respected. His actions during the rioting were unfortunate and his version of events and justifications for the way he behaved did not endear him to local people, either his tenants, his employees, or indeed the rest of the county. He cared deeply about the countryside and agriculture, and the responsibilities of land ownership, playing an important part in its reform and management. He left an incredibly elegant mansion and parkland, newly built beautiful farmhouses and well kept land. He was a good family man and caring about his long term employees both in the house and on his farms. His habit of falling out with people was unfortunate and his manner with his poorer labourers was patronising and unfeeling. Cobbett regarded him as a bitter enemy of the labouring class, and Henry Hunt was even more against him, although Hunt's comments should not be regarded as the complete truth.

As far as the rioters of November 25th 1830 are concerned, Benett was part of the cause of their problems, the tangible face of their poverty, the commander of the yeomanry by which they were attacked and taken prisoner, and a very visible instrument in court of their punishment and transportation.

14
Planned or spontaneous?

LOOKING AT THE list of the names of the men who were arrested and tried for the offences of riotous assembly and machine breaking, it is impossible to detect which of them, if any, acted as an organiser or leader. They come from various parts of the Tisbury area, Ansty, Tisbury Row and Ridge to the east, Church Street and court Street in the village itself, Fonthill Gifford, Fonthill Bishop, Hindon to the north and west, Hatch and Wardour to the south. Somehow the information that there was to be a demonstration/gathering on the morning of the 25th November at Fonthill Gifford, has been disseminated throughout the Tisbury area.

This information had to be by word of mouth, face to face, – there was no other way of communicating. Additionally, how did they all know so quickly that there had been rioting to the east of Tisbury, in Andover, Salisbury and Wilton? Some sort of organised communication must have rapidly evolved which is not mentioned in the trial reports.

A Mr Alford, an Arundell tenant farmer, is suggested a possible leader, but he quickly removes himself from the riot. He is said to be absent from his farm, Withyslade, from Friday or Saturday and has been seen in the region of Ringwood in Hampshire. A warrant for the arrest of Richard Alford is issued but he is not found or arrested.

Which Mr Alford is this? He is referred to in Lt. Col. Mair's warrant for his arrest as Richard Alford, but he is more likely to have been Samuel Alford, aged about 50, who was indeed in 1830 the tenant of Lord Arundell's property Withyslade Farm, paying an annual rent of £200. Samuel was a prominent member of the dissenting church in Tisbury and in his Will, proved in 1832 (by which time he had returned home and died) he arranges for payment of the annual rent for the 'Independent Church and

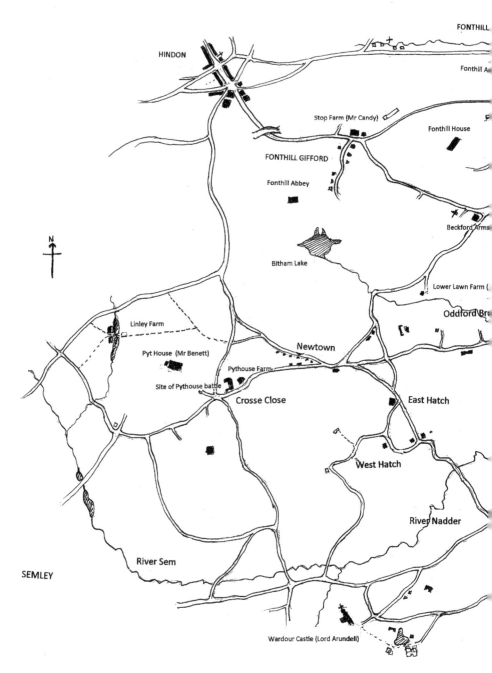

Map of the parishes of Tisbury, Fonthill Bish

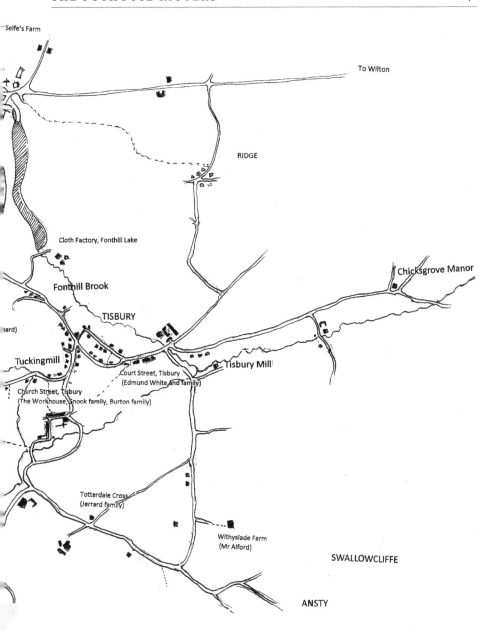

TISBURY AREA IN THE EARLY 1800's

hill Gifford showing the sites of rioting and the farms concerned

Congregation assembly in The Old Meeting House in Tisbury'. Samuel fits the description given by Lt. Col. Mair – 50 years of age, stout – he weighs 16 stone – grey haired. Joseph Alford is much younger, the nephew of Samuel and he takes over the Withyslade Farm in 1832 – he is only 35 in 1841.[1]

Samuel is certainly concerned about his workers, apparently encouraging them to attend a vestry meeting immediately before the rioting, where wages were to be discussed. Certainly some men would have found out at this meeting that there was unrest in the area, if, in fact it was to be held, as was suggested, on the morning of the 25th November 1830.

From 16th century meetings were held in church vestries in each parish. These meetings represented a form of local government in that they raised money from parishioners (those who owned land or houses) for the purpose of maintaining the structure of the church and for the support of the poor people in the parish. The meetings were normally held once a month, on the first Sunday, after the evening service, chaired by the vicar in the vestry room and attended by the main householders and employers in the parish though not the really large landowners. They were 'open' meetings so in theory anyone could attend and if the vestry became too crowded (the vestry room space in St John's is not very large) the company would move to the nearest inn – in Tisbury's case, the crown on the edge of the churchyard. An annual meeting held on Easter Monday was an opportnity for the parish clerk to present the accounts and for the meeting to elect new churchwardens. One churchwarden was called the Vicar's Warden and he was responsible for ensuring that the fabric of the church was kept in good repair. The other, the People's Warden was voted in annually by the householders of the parish. Both received a small stipend for their troubles.

Eventually the management of poor relief became the most exacting part of the vestry meetings duties and in the late 16th century an overseer for the poor was a necessity in the parish. This post replaced the lesser post of Alms Collector. The three men (most often they were men) were responsible for raising the money via the Poor Rate. Accounts of how this tax money was spent were kept carefully and give a picture of each parish. Sometimes a poor parishioner received a small weekly amount and sometimes a small sum for a specific need, such as a fee for laying out a dead person, a payment for fuel for a poor widow, but mostly it would be payment of rent or money for food, to supplement the low wages earned in the area.

So there was some concern at the vestry meetings in Tisbury at the rate of poverty in the parish – increasing sums had to be raised as tax from the householders to cover the needs of the agricultural labourers because wages were so low. It was a vicious circle, the lower the wages, the more householders and landowners had to pay to the vestry to keep the labourers and their families from starvation, so less money was available from the farmers, householders and landowners to pay wages.

It is quite understandable therefore that Mr Benett, on hearing the rumour that there was to be a vestry meeting early in the morning on Thursday 25th November, became suspicious and formed the opinion that there was a conspiracy in Tisbury. It was rumoured that the labourers were encouraged to attend to hear something about increasing their wages. Of course, Mr Benett knew that vestry meetings were not held on Thursday mornings. As a result he came to the conclusion that the overseer of the poor had called the meeting to assemble as many men together as possible in order to start the rioting. He makes this point very clearly in the debate which followed the rioting, in the House of Commons on 8th February 1831.[2] Unfortunately his point cannot be substantiated properly because the vestry records during that period are not available. If Samuel Alford was involved in this vestry meeting it was probably because he really did care about his workers. Lord Arundell, in defending his tenant in his letter of 6th December 1830 to the Home Secretary, speaks of Alford's kindness to the poor, and his 'willingness to come into measures for bettering their condition'. Arundell is also convinced that the pressure to arrest Alford is also due to his being a dissenter, and that both dissenters and Roman Catholics alike are blamed for the disruptions occurring in the area.

Alford however, sensibly leaves the rioters just after he dissuades some of them from attacking and destroying the cloth factory at Fonthill Lake. Perhaps he realises he is not going to be able to control the violence and as a respectable tenant farmer and elder of the Congregational Church, he has much to lose.

So if Alford is not the planner, organiser and leader, who is responsible? Young Charles Jerrard speaks up at Fonthill Gifford, and takes a prominent part in the machine breaking, but is never accused of being a ringleader. His father, also Charles Jerrard, prudently leaves the riot.

So if there is no outstanding candidate for leadership, how was the riot organised? It is not difficult to imagine that there might have been a small nucleus of men who instigated the riot but who were never brought to justice. Had they been meeting at the crown in Church Street, or in the Boot in the High Street, or at the Beckford Arms in Fonthill Gifford? How were all those mostly illiterate men persuaded to meet up in Fonthill Gifford on that bleak November morning? On their various routes to the hamlet they collected men who did not really want to join in, they broke up machinery in specific barns, they decided where they would meet up, where they would attack machinery and where they would end up – Pythouse. They acted together. By the time they had reached Fonthill Gifford the mob was said to be 500 strong. No-one ever accused any specific member of the arrested men as an organiser or leader, but some of them must have known where they were intending to go and what they intended to do.

Discussions amongst them may have taken place during the week before. Where would they have been able to meet up and talk? Perhaps after church or chapel on the Sunday. Perhaps some of them went with their employers to Salisbury Market on the Tuesday, where the talk in the town was of the rioting in the immediate area. They would have returned to Tisbury to do more talking, in the pubs and inns, in the ale houses.

There was certainly a strong tradition of drinking because hard work was compensated by hard drinking – there was no other way of relaxation for the manual labourer. During the harvest period labourers in the fields drank almost continuously and expected to do so. Their houses were small, squalid and uncomfortable – the ale house at least held out the possibility of chairs, conversation and the pleasure of getting drunk. William Hone wrote

> put an Englishman behind a pipe and a full pot and he will sit on until he cannot stand. At first he is silent, but as his liquor get towards the bottom he inclines to conversation. As he replenishes, his coldness thaws and he is conversational. The oftener he calls to fill again the more talkative he becomes; and when thoroughly liquefied, his loquacity is deluging.[3]

Those who did not drink were considered unmanly.

The pressure on them was considerable, they had no way of improving their financial situation and it must have seemed after exchanging views in the ale houses that this was the only way forward. In addition many of them were under the impression that the farmers themselves were in favour of machine breaking and an improvement in wages, together with perhaps, a reduction in farm rentals for farmers themselves. Mr Alford certainly gave this impression, and other farmers had already broken up their threshing machines before the mob arrived, such as Mr Selfe, Henry King's tenant at Fonthill Bishop, or moved them to a different place – for example Mr Lampard at Lower Lawn. They too were aware of the possibility of rioting in the area.

None of this seems to have been followed up by the authorities who were only intent upon arresting known 'trouble makers' or easy targets. It is noticeable that none of those blamed each other or spoke of any leader or organisers, but it would have been amazing if 500 men had spontaneously decided to gather together one a cold winter's morning had they not been persuaded to do so.

The pressure to do something grew in intensity, the workers returning home from the market or the pub calling on their friends and neighbours and fellow workmen on the way home – it's going to be Thursday morning, at Fonthill Gifford, you have to be there, we will make a success of this, it's our only chance.

15
The Garden of Eden?

THE *ELIZA*, HAVING rounded the Cape of Good Hope and crossed the southern Ocean, dropped anchor in the Derwent River off Hobart Town in Van Diemen's Land on the 29th May 1831. The ship's Captain, John Groves, together with the ship's Surgeon Dr William Anderson were no doubt highly relieved to be able to deliver their cargo of 224 convicts healthy and alive. The Hobart Town Courier announced:

> Saturday 4th June 1831 arrived on Sunday 29th May, the transport ship *Eliza*, 538 tons, J. J. Groves esq. commander from Portsmouth 8th Feb. with 224 male prisoners, consisting chiefly of rioters, incendiaries, and machine breakers, lately convicted under the special commissions at Winchester and elsewhere, the greater proportion of whom are said to be able-bodied, hard-working countrymen. Surgeon Superintendent W. Anderson, esq., R.N. The guard consists of Captain Moore, Lieut. Lewin, 2 serjeants, 2 corporals and 35 privates of the Royal Marines, who proceed to India by the first opportunity to join HMS Southampton on the India station, or some think the Southampton will come down here to embark them and two other detachments which are daily expected in the succeeding transport ships. This is a very economical plan of Government instead of sending them out direct to India by a transport expressly taken up for the purpose.[1]

So what sort of land were these hard-working, sturdy countrymen expecting to find? Having left Portsmouth in winter weather, they had arrived at the beginning of the southern winter, when temperatures were likely to be in the region of 3-11°C during the daytime and colder at night – 5-6°C. However, one of Van Diemens Land's advantages is that the climate is temperate – its latitude, south of SE Australia is 42.82 0S, 147.33 0E – in comparison Wiltshire is 51.35 0N, 199 0W, – so not too different as far as distance from the Equator is concerned. The rainfall is high in the western part of the island, varying across the island from an annual amount of 2,400mm in the west to 626mm around Hobart Town. This rainfall ensures that the rainforest is always damp, the river and lakes are full and clear and there is always fresh water easily available, an unheard of luxury for many of the settlers on the island. It ensures that crops grow easily and prolifically and that the native grasslands renew themselves easily without completely drying out. The summer heat is bearable, averaging 22-24°C, falling at night to around 12°C, unlike conditions in the Australian colony to the north of Van Diemen's Land.

In 1642 a Dutchman, Abel Tasman, landed at what became known as Blackman Bay, on the Forestier Peninsula, and named the newly found, heart shaped island on the southern tip of the Australian continent Van Diemen's Land, after the Governor of the Dutch East Indies. Settlement was slow however, and initially the land was used mainly as a refuge for explorers needing safe harbour, fuel, fresh water and fresh meat. Britain, however, fearing that a French expedition led by Nicolas Baudin had come to claim the island as a French possession, decided in the early 1800s to mount a small expedition and stake its own claim to the island. In 1803 therefore, the then Governor of Australia, Philip King, established a small military outpost on the Derwent River near to the present site of Hobart Town. This was under the command of a young man by the name of John Bowen, a 23 year old officer in the New South Wales Corps, who had just arrived in the colony. Three different parties made up of convicts, soldiers, civil and military officers and a few free settlers established two settlements, one in the north of the island and one in the south.[2]

In 1805 Marine and former judge Advocate David Collins was appointed Lt. Governor and was sent from London with a much larger expedition to the southern hemisphere. The convicts on the ship *Calcutta* were hand picked, with all sorts of trades being represented – sawyers, carpenters, shoemakers, fishermen. Some were from the East End of London, one was Polish, another German, seven of them were Jewish, two were Dutch and one was a French confectioner. Lastly there was an Afro-

American violin player – an interesting addition to the motley crew selected to establish the new British colony. The party included one convict who was very rich. Seventeen wives travelled with their convict husbands and some children. The free settlers who opted to travel with this mixed group also brought their wives and children. Lt. Gov. Collins brought his hunting staghounds.[3]

Unfortunately, they initially decided to settle, not in Van Diemens Land, but at Port Philip in southern Australia, where they met with a lack of fresh food availability, and aboriginal opposition. Twenty-one convicts attempted to escape, one died and the other 20 returned. After five months there, Collins moved on to Van Diemen's Land where the party arrived in the River Derwent in February 1804, not far from young Bowen's existing settlement with his New South Wales Corps. Here they found fresh mussels and oysters, kangaroos and emus. Black swans in abundance provided poultry meat as good as goose to eat and the expedition settled itself on the western side of the Derwent River at Sullivan's Cove, where the party's relationships with the aboriginal tribes on the eastern side remained cordial, mostly due to Collins' experience and knowledge of aboriginal customs drawn from his experiences in New South Wales earlier in his career. He was particularly keen to ensure that no diseases, such as smallpox, were transferred to the indigenous natives and above all, no violence took place.

Van Diemen's Land (now Tasmania) is not huge. In area it is about 26,410 square miles – 226 miles north to south, and 190 miles across from west to east. About the size of Ireland or Switzerland. Like Switzerland it has mountain ranges, which are mainly in the west, a high plateau with grassland plains to the north of Hobart Town, lush and green, all well supplied with rivers and streams of fresh water. The grasslands resemble English cultivated parkland with great grassy stretches, its park-like appearance enhanced by the beauty of its mature trees. In the temperate rain forest grow mosses, liverwort, lichens, fungi and the lower mountain areas are heathland, with strange spiky palm-like pandani plants. There are huge old pines, the Huon pine, slow growing, (some are over 2,000 years old) in the west and the central plateau. These would provide timber for settlers' huts; the Huon pine has a high oil-content, making it impossible for insects to bore into and also enabling the wood to be bent, carved and sculpted without splitting. It is ideal for boats, furniture making, timber walls for dwellings and for roof shingles. Deciduous beech trees grow in abundance too, and the native acacia, or silver wattle tree, haunts the forests with its distinctive peeling silvery strips of bark.

The grasslands had been managed for centuries by the indigenous population of aboriginal people who used controlled burning to encourage the new growth of grass every two to three years. They supplied themselves with fire-sticks, keeping a flame going all the time as they moved around. This enabled them to ensure that the land was always well stocked with herbivorous game; the native forester kangaroo, the nocturnal wombat, wallabies, possums, the curious spotted quoll, emus and the particularly beautiful black swan. There were predators – the thylacine (Tasmanian tiger), a carnivore but a slow moving and comparatively small one, the Tasmanian Devil (so called because of its unearthly shrieking at night when mating), the wedge-tailed eagle and of course snakes, including the tiger snake, but until the advent of immigrant settlers and convicts, the balance of nature worked very well. The aboriginals knew how to keep fire going, to cook in concealed underground pits and to move around in small tribal groups, hunter gatherers, never over-hunting any specific area, and successfully 'fire-stick' cultivating. They had no need to plant crops, there were plenty of berries and greenstuffs to eat in addition to their meat diet. By the 1818 census there were estimated to be around 7,000 aboriginals still alive to a white population of 3240, but by 1835 this had been reduced to 700 aboriginals.[4]

On islands to the north and north-east of Van Diemen's Land lived the seal colonies, where runaway convicts from NSW had partially settled, working as seal hunters or whalers. They ate the seal meat and sold the seal skins. There were no aborigines on these islands and lonely white men lived in comparative freedom, although on expeditions to the mainland they kidnapped aboriginal women, by whom they produced children. The sale of the skins was mostly handled by Sydney business men and was very unofficial. Emus and wombats were also killed and soon the fauna of the islands was threatened.

This was an incredibly beautiful, bountiful land which early settlers were able to enjoy, but soon exploited. The first settlers found that the land was amazingly fertile and extremely fruitful – crops grew quickly and the new farmers found a wonderful supply of fresh clean water, fish, kangaroo meat and enough timber easily accessible to build huts. The land was originally designated as crown property and although the settlers aspired to ownership, land was in such plentiful supply that it operated rather like the old commons system in England before the Enclosures Acts had taken the use of the commons away from the poor. This enabled settlers to run sheep on the magnificent grasslands, unfenced. Cattle too, and the stock numbers increased rapidly, from 489 cattle and 1091 sheep in May 1809 (the figures come from a Derwent muster report) to 3894 cattle and 24,691 sheep by 1813. By 1820 there were 182,000 sheep on the grassland plains of Van Diemen's Land. These animals were allowed free grazing anywhere they wandered – they were hardy breeds, bred for meat, self sufficient and with rough wool. Later changes in breeding by adding merinos produced a better wool but these were less hardy and prone to being scabby and gradually reducing in size. The meat from the animals was exported to NSW where the land was less sympathetic to pastoral husbandry.

An Irish Wolfhound – Stig, photograph courtesy of Dee Palmer

Initially a penal colony and an overspill for NSW transported convicts, by 1810 the first batch of convicts with seven-year sentences had completed their punishment and were free, although not to travel back to Britain. Fewer convict ships were arriving now because of the Napoleonic Wars with France and by 1817 only 16% of the Van Diemen's Land population were serving convicts. Later the proportion increased (between 1818 and 1856, when transportation ceased, serving convicts formed at least 30% of the population). Before 1820 though, the freed convicts were entitled to apply for a small land grant where they could live and work in freedom, without leaving the colony. Many of the newer arrivals were free immigrants, but some were also ex convicts from Norfolk Island.

During the Napoleonic War period no supplies were sent from Britain, clothing materials ran out and kangaroo skin became essential for garment making – splendid jackets, trousers, shoes, knapsacks, and hats. Now the imported hunting dogs, the large, fast deerhounds brought in by civil and military officers proved to be invaluable for hunting the kangaroos. The officers of the penal authority in particular kept and bred deerhounds. The kangaroos were considered to be crown property, and as in England, there were Game Laws enacted. These restricted hunting to those with an annual income of £100 from a freehold estate so only civil and military officers or their 'gamekeepers' could hunt legally. The 'gamekeepers' worked after completing the convict working hours. They were paid in skins and meat. Only officers could eat swans. This was a country where there were no natural 'dogs', and the deerhounds were naturally faster than the kangaroos and efficient killers. Firearms, such as there were, were not easily available and were inaccurate anyway. Ownership of a pair of deerhounds was a sign of a gentleman hunter and these became extremely valuable. The land was open, the hunting easy and in the abundant grasslands kangaroos were easy targets.

By 1805 however, in both north and south settlements the monopoly on the ownership and use of hunting dogs was broken; dogs had been stolen and used for breeding purposes and for sale, enabling convicts to live independently in the bush, hunting the kangaroos, selling their meat to the government or to private buyers, clothe themselves and becoming known as bushrangers. They built rudimentary huts on the crown lands and managed to survive even during the winters.[5]

In the meantime settlers continued with their pastoral agriculture – animal husbandry with stockmen (some ex convicts) living in austere wooden huts, thatched initially but later the roofs were covered in wooden shingles which were less susceptible to burning attacks by aboriginals. These stockmen only required a minimum amount of cultivated land on which to grow their own vegetables and corn crops, food for themselves and their families only. Nearer to Hobart Town and Launceston, the next largest settlement, there was more crop growing, but since the land was mostly unfenced, it was impossible to keep out the sheep, cattle and kangaroos. Most ex convicts were not naturally countrymen either, so agricultural labourers were needed and valued. Settlers nearer the developing towns cultivated the land immediately around their dwellings, renting a portion of land for a sheep run further afield, with a stockman housed on the sheep run. This system enriched some of the marine and civil officials.

In the towns however, the settlers were beginning to suffer from hunger, not famine because they could nearly always obtain protein from kangaroo meat, but from the lack of daily bread, tea, sugar and alcohol, plus all the other necessities of life such as soap, clothing materials, nails, etc. due to the absence of the supply ships during the Napoleonic Wars.

In 1810 Lt. Governor Collins died and Thomas Davey was appointed to the post. Collins' government had seen an increase in the value of the economy and a certain freedom for convicts and ex convicts. His humanity had been appreciated by most, though not all, settlers. His replacements, Lt. Gov. Edward and then Lt. Gov. Thomas Davey, lacked Collins' experience, administrative skills and wisdom according to Governor Lachlan Macquarie in Sydney.

By 1813 the bushrangers were almost in control of the colony. Macquarie declared a pardon for all bushrangers whether their conviction had expired or not, if they surrendered by 1 December 1814. This measure failed miserably and in April 1815 Lt. Gov. Davey declared martial law, banning all traffic in kangaroo meat and skins and ordering the destruction of the hunting dogs. But the bushrangers now turned their attentions to domestic livestock, stealing sheep and cattle and selling these. Small farmers faced ruin and it was not until 1818, under a new Lt. Gov. William Sorell, that a surrender was achieved and the grasslands were brought under the control of the colony's government, with an annual fee payable for land and a ticket or licence renewable annually.[6]

The next problem for the embryo colony was that the native aboriginal groups began to resist the encroachment of settlers and bushrangers across their traditional hunting grounds. This was not a new phenomenon, but it had gradually increased, with the white settlers, ex convicts and bushrangers equally being attacked, occasionally speared and in countering these attacks the settlers killed more aboriginals. The Rev. Knopwood, a chaplain who kept a detailed diary of his years in Van Diemen's Land, writes that, 'convicts killing aboriginals to protect the interests of their masters was tacitly accepted by the government'.[7]

There was little or no military protection provided by the government, the number of white settlers requiring meat from hunting had increased, and despite a growing resistance by the native population, their numbers were gradually decreasing. The government encouraged the convict kangaroo hunters to extend their hunting northwards out from Hobart Town into the midlands area of the island in order to provide enough meat for the population which needed sustenance during the Napoleonic period. Sadly the native population had begun to succumb to European diseases, although compared with the deaths from this cause in New South Wales, this was negligible. Hunting dogs were traded by the settlers in exchange for access to good hunting grounds; the British learning better hunting methods from the aboriginals. There seems to have been comparatively little direct violence during the period 1808-1820 despite the increase in cattle and sheep numbers on the aboriginals' traditional hunting grounds, which had become one huge 'common'.

To help pay for 'managing' these vast herds and flocks, the stockmen were often given ownership of one-third of the animals they managed, this paying for their labour. This guaranteed them a return on their work and the possibility of making real money by looking after the owners' animals in remote areas, defending them from robbery by ex convicts or by aboriginals. This was known as the 'thirds system' and by 1817 46% of cattle and 52% of the sheep were owned by freed convicts and run on land which the ex convicts did not own.

The towns in Van Diemen's Land were now growing and prospering but with a great divide between the free settlers and the bushrangers, ex convicts and convicts. Hobart Town by the 1820s had a thriving High Street and according to a Mrs Prinsep who arrived a little later in 1829 there were shops, cottages, expensive houses and gardens. The houses were modernised with roofs safely shingled, there was even a library. There were, unfortunately also about 50 shops selling liquor.[8] However, there were still many self made shacks and huts housing the poor.

In 1824 a huge change occurred in the form of the newly appointed Lt. Governor, George Arthur, an evangelical Calvinist who hailed from Plymouth in Devon. The number of convicts had risen again following the end of the wars with the French and transportation had resumed – some 2,000 each year from 17.7% in 1817 to around 40-50% of the population by the early 1820s. It was therefore essential, in Arthur's view, that this large part of the population should come under more strict controls and that their only means of salvation and a better life would be through hard work and self improvement. He now developed an efficient system of punishment or reward, building on Sorell's original but more humane system; the weekly muster for each convict, punishment for offences during the period of conviction and rewards for good behaviour. Convict labour would be withdrawn from any settler who aided illegal bushrangers.

Arthur's reforms were however, tougher. Van Diemen's

George Arthur, Lt Gov of Van Diemen's Land

*Mr Robinson's house on the Derwent River VDL c 1838 by John Glover, oil on canvas
National Gallery of Australia*

Land achieved its independence as a separate colony from New South Wales in 1825 and began to be known as Tasmania, although the name was not officially changed until the 1850s. Arthur's word was now law, and the only matter preventing him from immediate implementation of his proposed reforms was the military backing he needed. In 1826 he managed to get a full regiment posted to the island (607 rank and file soldiers plus NCO's and Officers). Now the new flocks of expensively bred imported merino sheep could be protected and their wool would become a most important part of the island's economy.

The last of the marauding bushranger gangs, led by Matthew Brady was finally confronted by the authorities and Brady captured. He was executed in 1826.[9]

Now Arthur could enforce discipline. Crimes against property ranked with murder and merited the death penalty (this of course included sheep stealing or receiving stolen goods). The seven-layer penal punishment system came into law; at worst if necessary convicts could be chained and worked in road gangs to improve the infrastructure of the island; a few days on the treadmill was a slightly lesser punishment; isolation in a tiny dark cell for repeat offenders; flogging; female 'factories' for recalcitrant female convicts;, loss of freedom for convicts after dark; and the permanent threat of the horrible prison at Port Arthur, from which escape was well nigh impossible. This establishment was situated on a peninsula connected to the mainland by a narrow isthmus of land which was successfully guarded by a continuous line of dogs and soldiers. It was surrounded by shark infested waters. The whole point was deterrence from reoffending, and to get the prisoners assigned to a master, with weekly muster attendances, no drunkenness or thieving and hard work rewarded by better conditions leading to a ticket of leave and freedom (though not to a permit to leave the island).[10]

To help achieve his aims Arthur set up a control system by dividing the settled areas of the island into four districts, each under a police magistrate. At the same time Arthur worked energetically to encourage more respectable free settlers, promising them land and free convict labour, but also enticing a number of women – some were selected by Mrs Elizabeth Fry from the London Female Penitentiary – who would become wives to freed convicts.

Arthur was also desperate to provide more agricultural labourers, not only for the settlers' farms, but also because he was being pressured by the newly formed Van Diemen's Land Company to provide it with ex convict labour. This company, set up in 1824 at the instigation of a group of English woollen mill owners, wool merchants, bankers and investors, was formed to provide better quality wool for the newly industrialised manufacturers in England, particularly in the midlands at a cheaper price than the expensive imported wool from the Continent. The company was encouraged by ex Lt. Gov. Sorell, and a Mr Edward Curr, who had recently come back to England from New South Wales. The new company was granted 250,000 acres to start with, where they intended to build roads, farmsteads, bridges, wharves and produce wool from the extraordinary merino sheep they would bring to Van Diemen's Land. It was granted a royal charter in 1824 by George IV, and eventually obtained six parcels of land amounting to 350,000 acres in the north-west of the island.

In 1826 Edward Curr, now appointed Chief Agent, accompanied by his newly appointed officials, Superintendent Stephen Adey, Alexander Goldie agriculturalist, Henry Hellyer, surveyor and architect, and two further surveyors, Joseph Fossey and Clement Lorymer, arrived in Hobart in March to begin work on the land granted to the company. They travelled north and chose land in the Surrey and Hampshire Hills south of Birnie; Woolnorth on Cape Grim and as a base site Circular Head, where they built a property to be known as Highfield House.

Also aboard the ship *Tranmere* which arrived in May 1826 were farm labourers from Britain, cargo and livestock. There were not many people, by 1832 the company of 62 men with 7 women and 10 children settled in the Surrey and Hampshire Hills, with a store at Emu Bay; at Woolnorth there were 24 men with 11 women and 25 children and at Circular Head 45

Van Diemen's Land 1837 and by 1852 Tasmania-dower-1837

men, 11 women and 25 children. The company also had 35 convicts by 1827 and was in desperate need of more. Some of the labourers were indentured and apparently badly treated. In addition, because they were all remote settlements, they were vulnerable to aboriginal attacks and the company encouraged counter measures, including spring-loaded guns and man traps placed in huts which it was stated were continually being plundered. In return for the killing of two white men, 36 aboriginals were killed. The rest were ejected from land they had hunted over for centuries. Eventually the number of natives fell from 600-700 in number in the area to only 100.

The land they had chosen was not conducive to pastoral farming. It was necessary to clear the trees, and the traditional method of cutting down and digging out roots was time consuming and expensive so the company chose to ring bark, as had been done in America. It was still not good grazing land, unsuitable for the expensive merino sheep, too exposed and subject to the westerly winds and too much rain. The sheep got scabby and lost their size, unfortunately dying in droves. The company decided to turn its attention to developing the land, letting it out in small allotment areas to settlers and encouraging them to do the clearance work. If they could not pay the rent at the requested time, they were turned off the land and dispossessed. The cleared land could then be let at a higher rent to other settlers. It is said that the labourers had no idea that the seasons in Van Diemen's Land were in reverse to those in England, and this compounded the errors made. The company kept requesting special consideration, more agricultural labourers, preferably with experience and it was certainly suggested they should take some of the transported Swing rioters who arrived in May 1831, as assigned convicts to the company.[11]

16
'Servants of the crown'.

AT DAWN ON the morning of 29 May 1831 the prisoners aboard the *Eliza* mustered on deck for the last time. It is not recorded whether they were still shackled or not. Certainly 224 leg irons are listed as 'cargo' in the ship's manifest and it is recorded that the chains had been 'used during the voyage'. On the *Eliza*'s sister ship *Proteus* the humane surgeon Thomas Logan had removed the convicts' leg irons on the grounds of damage to prisoners by accidents and the embarrassment they caused the wearers.[1] Dr William Anderson on the *Eliza* may have followed the same precept – after all, a most important part of the surgeon's remit was to ensure that the convicts arrived in Van Diemen's Land in good health, able to start work straight away.

Eliza was a fast ship – in 1820 she had achieved a record time in reaching Port Jackson from England – 90 days. However fast she was, it was still a terribly long voyage for these young men from rural Wiltshire and Hampshire. They had probably never even seen the sea before boarding the prison hulk in Portsmouth Harbour and can have had no idea of the vastness of the oceans they were to cross. Neither could they have been aware as they left the dreary English winter behind and sailed south that by the time they reached Hobart it would be the start of the southern winter. So no summer weather on arrival.

The men were disembarked in small boats and marched up to the Hobart Town Prisoners' Barracks, a walled complex of buildings with a central long courtyard, built in 1822. Entering through the gate between two hexagonal office buildings, they were lined up again and reviewed by a group of Van Diemen's Land officials – their own ship's surgeon William Anderson, the shipmaster Captain Groves, the Chief Police magistrate, the muster master (Comptroller General of Convicts), the Superintendent of the Prisoners' Barracks Josiah Spode and the Lt. Governor George Arthur. Arthur liked to be present at the convicts' first muster and to speak to them personally. According to a Quaker missionary James Backhouse:

> He alluded to the degraded state into which they had brought themselves by their crimes, this he justly compared to a state of slavery . . . that their conduct would be narrowly watched, and if it should be bad, they would be severely punished, put to work in a chain-gang, or sent to a penal settlement, where they would be under very severe discipline; or their career might be terminated on the scaffold. That, on the contrary, if they behaved well, they would in the course of a proper time be indulged with a ticket-of-leave . . . that if they should still persevere in doing well, they would then become eligible for a conditional pardon, which would give them the liberty of the colony and that a further continuance in good conduct would open the way for a free pardon, which would liberate them to return to their native land.[2]

From now on they would be subject to a game of snakes and ladders – up the ladder to a ticket of leave and freedom, down the snake via labour on the roads, work on a chain gang, banishment to a penal colony and worst of all, labour on a penal settlement and in chains. They would need to behave immaculately for four years to obtain a ticket of leave if the sentence was for 7-years, longer of course for longer sentences. Arthur was in favour of reform for prisoners, strict but never vindictive in punishing.

Each prisoner now received clothing stencilled PB (Prisoners' Barracks), after which individual statements were taken and physical details recorded. The prisoners were then grouped into one of seven classes:

Skilled labourers who were to be assigned outside the barracks
Skilled labourers assigned to work in the barracks
Road gangs or quarry work
Chain gangs
Isolated chain gangs in remote areas (the interior)
Penal colonies
Hard labour in penal colonies

The men from Tisbury were in a comparatively fortunate situation. Van Diemen's Land desperately needed experienced agricultural labourers and Arthur had worked hard at influencing the Home Office in London to ensure that these men convicted as a result of the Swing Riots were sent to him at Hobart, in order to assist in the development of his island colony, whilst Sydney on the Australian mainland received 'Irish offenders and London pickpockets'. Arthur denied using his influence but his letters to Viscount Howick (Under Secretary of State for War and the Colonies and eldest son of Prime Minister Grey) confirm his requests. On 4th June 1831 Arthur was able to write to Viscount Howick at the Colonial Office that 30 of the men from the *Eliza* had been retained by government departments for service as craftsmen, 25 sent to Launceston to the Van Diemen's Land Company, three to the VDL Establishment Norfolk and the rest had been assigned to farmers, landowners and other private settlers.[3]

The government of Van Diemen's Land had received a specific request from the Van Diemen's Land Company that they should receive some 50 men from the machine breakers, as they were considered to be skilled agricultural labourers. It had requested carpenters, blacksmiths etc. and received ploughmen and grooms. As the company had very little agricultural machinery available, due to difficulties with repairs and spares etc. the agricultural labourers were of great use to the company but there was dissatisfaction at the company not receiving the 50 men it had requested. In the event the 25 allocated, which ones being decided by Josiah Spode the Superintendent of Convicts, only ten from the *Eliza* were amongst those names specifically requested by the Company.[4] These were disembarked at Hobart and the Company was left to arrange their transfer to Launceston. Arthur refused to agree to the *Eliza* being used to transport them round the colony to the north-west. There were other difficulties with *Eliza* – no arrangements had been made in London for the Royal Marine guard of 39 men and two officers who were due in Singapore and *Eliza* was kept in demurrage whilst the dispute between the Master, Groves and Arthur was settled. Finally the *Eliza* was released but the Master had to pay for the transfer of the Marines to Sydney on another vessel. Arthur wrote to tell Howick of the decisions made and reiterated his pleasure that his Lordship had not allowed the particular selection of men by the Company which had been made in London.

The local newspaper, the *Tasmanian*, on 4th June 1831, praised the decision made with regard to the number of men to be allocated to the Company following its request that their Directors in England, Pearce and Cripps, be able to select the 50 men they wanted from their offices in London. This decision, stated the paper, 'had enabled Mr Spode to assign to almost every agricultural applicant, one ploughman. This is as it should be and entitles the Local Government to the highest praise'.

Incidentally, the next two ship loads of convicts, from the *Proteus* and the *Argyle* were treated in the same way – the allocations requested by the VDL Company were halved each time. It ended up with 50 men allocated to it in total. The local government was not going to be told how to run its assignment system by a bunch of MPs, JPs and directors in London. Arthur wanted his convicts to have a chance to be reformed and become useful citizens, not free slave labour for rich mens' investments. None of the men from Tisbury were assigned to the Van Diemen's Land Co.

Arthur kept an eye on his machine breakers from the *Eliza* throughout their sentences including requesting information about them if they had to be admitted to hospital at any time. He was concerned to find that many of them were thoroughly dejected, miserable and ashamed of being there, and that some indeed died, according to the Colonial Surgeon 'from diseases to which they had been predisposed by despair'. Thirteen men from the *Eliza* died during their sentences, six by the end of 1831, only one of these being as a result of a confirmed industrial accident.

The Pythouse rioters therefore were mostly assigned to farmers – 'free settlers of good character' who were, in the main, the recipients of grants of land. These settlers were retired military men, civil officers, doctors, lawyers, clergymen, a diarist (GTW Boyes) and an artist (John Glover).

The Public Works Department however needed skilled labour. The Department was in the process of building the infrastructure of the island colony and were looking for experienced craftsmen in the building trade.

Thomas Burt from Fonthill was a 'top sawyer' by trade and therefore a natural assignment to the Public Works Department. Thomas, who was 26 years old, had probably been working since he was 12 or 13 since he would have had little or no education. He lived in Fonthill so it seems very likely that he would have worked at the old sawmill on the Fonthill estate (which is not far from Beckford's Fonthill Abbey). William Beckford was still the owner at Fonthill until 1822 and during his ownership there must have been plenty of work on the estate for a good sawyer – Beckford spent a great deal of money on clearing trees, creating rides and open glades, and timber was always being prepared, either for sale or for necessary use on the estate. After the sale of the Abbey to John Farquhar there may have been less regular work and by 1830 when John Benett was in the process of trying to raise the money to finalise his purchase it is unlikely that Thomas was able to obtain regular work at Fonthill sawpit. Hence his comment at his trial that he was out looking for work on the day of the rioting and, perhaps, his

A top sawyer at work – woodcut print showing two men cutting a log into planks; Latrobe Photographic Collection National Trust Tasmania 1800's

resentment that his former employment was now really threatened, just as he had reached the position of 'top dog'-an infinitely preferable position to 'bottom dog' in a sawpit.

At his initial examination Thomas was recorded as being 26 years old and his surname was alternatively spelt Birt or Burke. Some of these alternative names being recorded may be due to the strong Wiltshire accent that the men probably had – in addition they themselves varied the spelling if they could in fact write their own name.

Thomas Burt's offence is recorded as:[5]

> charged on the oaths of John Uphill and others, with having together with other persons riotously assembled and destroyed a thrashing machine, and part of a barn, the property of John Benett esq. at Tisbury. – Warrant dated Dec.22 1830.

Thomas also had two previous convictions – one for poaching and one for stealing wood for which offences he had received three months' imprisonment each time. Unfortunately he was just the sort of worker who had incurred the displeasure of Mr Benett – hence his being taken into custody later (22nd December) on the oath of John Uphill, shepherd, an employee of John Benett, rather than being detained on the day of the rioting, 25th November 1830.

Thomas is recorded as being 5ft. 6ins. in height, with a sallow complexion, brown hair and eyebrows, reddish brown whiskers and grey eyes. He had a long nose, high sloping back forehead, moles on his left arm and a small scar on his left hand near to his little finger – unsurprisingly, since he was a sawyer by trade. He stated that he was married to Ann (formerly Stevens, from Hindon) and had two children.

Thomas, upon being assigned to the Public Works Department, remained with this Department for the full term of his conviction.

Thomas Abree was also assigned to the Public Works Department. He was the skilled stonemason who, according to Lord Arundell, had been hauled up the spire of Salisbury Cathedral in a basket to work on repairs to the stonework. As a skilled stonemason it seems unlikely he would have been assigned to the quarries. His skills would have been more appreciated in the techniques of building and dressing stone and in Van Diemen's Land much construction was proceeding.

An interesting example is the wonderful bridge at Ross, a small town nearly equidistant between Hobart and Launceston, the design of which is credited to the government civil engineer, John Lee Archer. However, it was built by convicts and completed within 58 weeks of commencing the work. The work was slow in getting started as it was discovered by Gov. Arthur that the sandstone, quarried locally and the prepared timber intended for the bridge, had been used to build a number of houses at Ross first. The work commenced in 1833, and the two convicts whose names are primarily mentioned, are Daniel Herbert and James Colbeck. Daniel Herbert, from Taunton in Somerset, was a convicted highway robber, but a brilliant stonemason. James Colbeck was another experienced stonemason – he had worked on the construction of Buckingham Palace but, tired of living in London without his family, had returned to his native town of Dewsbury and resorted to burglary. He too was convicted and sent to VDL, in 1828. However, there were obviously other stonemasons and builders involved and as Thomas Abree was working for the Engineer's Department, it is tempting to speculate that he was involved in the building of Ross Bridge. Certainly the Department must have been pleased to receive another skilled stonemason. The bridge is beautifully and meticulously put together with three symmetrical arches, a curved stone staircase at each end of the bridge leading down to the river and chain linked stone pillars leading on to the bridge from each side. Each arch is decorated and carved on both sides with

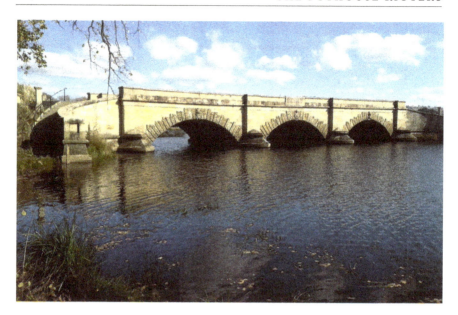

Ross Bridge Van Diemen's Land – ourtasmania.com.au/Launceston/ross-bridge.

icons of animal and human figures, which seem to be of Celtic origin and of the heads of known people in Tasmania, including Gov. Arthur. There is a theme of death and oppression, followed by birth and renewal of life, one which the convicts would well have understood. The centre arch features a lion (Britain) gripping a lamb in its claws. Dogs appear, as does a stag, bales of wool and sheaves of corn.[6] It is quite wonderful and a memorial to the convicts who built it, and the carvings have an almost religious appearance. It would be good to think that Thomas Abree's skilled stonemasonry helped with such elegant work.

Thomas was 5ft. 9¼ins. in height, tall for the period. He was blind in one eye, which looked white, the remaining eye being brown. He had dark brown hair and whiskers, and a brown complexion. His visage, it is stated, was large and masculine, his forehead had perpendicular wrinkles and his nose was large. He too had several moles on his left arm.[7]

Alternative spelling of his surname is written as Abery or Albury or Abrey. This was the man who had been recommended for a pardon by Lord Arundell (which failed to

Ross Bridge keystone: the royal lion holding a lamb in its claws -ourtasmania as above

materialise). His wife was Mary (Roberts), a widow who he had married in 1827; she had two children who Thomas loved and was bringing up as his own. He was reported in an application for mercy submitted to the king, as having 'a general quietness of his demeanour, his character as an affectionate husband, and a kind relation, having brought up the infant orphan of his departed brother, all combine to influence this application for the extension of mercy'. The petition was turned down.

Where Thomas Burt and Thomas Abree were posted to is not recorded – the Public Works Department may have been based in Hobart but of course the work could be anywhere in the colony.

It is clear that Thomas Burt was not always working directly for the Public Works Department. In October 1832 he is recorded as being 'loaned' to Captain D'arcy Wentworth, then Commandant of the barracks at Bothwell. Captain Wentworth sounds as if he ought to be a hero of a Jane Austen novel, and he is indeed at this time commencing building a palatial mansion. This is to be called Inverhall to start with but becomes known as Wentworth House. It is recorded that he used convict labour on the building work, which cost £560. As Thomas Burt was a competent sawyer, he was probably temporarily loaned to work, perhaps, on the big structural beams necessary for the new property. In any event, in October of that year Thomas is fined 5/- for being drunk. Perhaps Captain Wentworth gave his convict workers bonuses, either in the form of cash, or notes entitling them to buy rum, which was the spirit available at that time. It is worth mentioning that Samuel Barrett is also at Bothwell – perhaps they managed to get together for a drink?

Thomas Burt now musters under a Mr Parsons for 1832 and 1833. But on 23rd February 1835 Thomas is found to be 'absent without leave until late at night', for which he is reprimanded. By this time he is with a Mr Fenton, a politician and a Captain in the Army. Perhaps he has been loaned out again. It seems that the Public Works Department loans out its convict labour to individual landowners probably for specific jobs.

On 10 October 1835 Thomas Burt is absent from the monthly muster and is ordered to muster for the next six Sundays.

Burt and Abree stayed with the Department until granted their tickets of leave in 1835 and free pardons in early 1836. The Ticket of Leave for Thomas Burt is however, in the name of Thomas Burke.

Abree, working for the Engineers' Department, was reprimanded for working unofficially for a Mr C Hanagan contrary to orders, in March 1833 (was this, perhaps on one of the unofficially built houses in Ross?)

and on 5 May 1834 he was given a quick dose of solitary confinement for three consecutive Saturdays after being found drunk. Thomas Abree kept in contact with Thomas Vinen during his time in Van Diemen's Land, being mentioned in two letters to Thomas from Vinen's sister Elizabeth Martin. As late as 24 July 1849 she is still writing to her brother to give them news of the family in Tisbury. She tells him that Martin was pleased to have news that 'Thomas Ebery (sic) is well, please give his best respects to him when you see him and tell him that our old Landlady Mrs Snow is dead'. In August 1851 she tells her brother that if he should chance to see Thomas Abrey (sic) to send kind love to Thomas and his daughters from John Snow who would like to have a letter from Thomas.[8] Has Thomas remarried and had daughters? His wife Mary Roberts has sadly died, in 1836, and perhaps Elizabeth has mentioned this in one of her letters to her brother, although it does not appear in any of the published correspondence.

There is no record of a new marriage, but after he receives his certificate of freedom on the 27th December 1837, he goes into partnership with one Joseph Lewis as Licensed Victuallers at O'Brien Bridge in Glenorchy which is about five miles north of Hobart. They trade under the name of Abery and Lewis and are running an inn named The Dusty Miller. The name Joseph Lewis does not appear amongst the Wiltshire Swing rioters. The partnership does not last long as in March 1845 it is dissolved and Thomas takes over the firm, receiving the debts owed to it and becoming responsible to its creditors. On the 2nd September of that year he receives the Licence to run The Dusty Miller at O'Brien's Bridge on his own account.[9]

The inn is part of the early settlement of Glenorchy and is situated close to the Houghton Mill and Tannery, a site which is now in the industrial and commercial centre of the city of Glenorchy. The inn becomes an important stop for carriers – Cooley's Omnibus stops there about eight times a day, taking passengers to and from Hobart centre. Other carriers also use it as a stop, and passengers can travel from there to Oatlands and as far north as Launceston. No doubt the travellers were glad to refresh themselves at The Dusty Miller.

The bridge, built by convict labour, spans the Humphreys Rivulet and the inn is on the Main Road, between the Post Office and the Council Chambers. The buildings are still there in 1946, minus the stables, but by 2017 the site is empty and under consideration for rebuilding although it is classed, according to the Glenorchy Planning Authority as a 'Place of Archaeological Interest'. Sadly there does not seem to be a photograph of the frontage.

Thomas evidently makes a success of running The Dusty Miller and moves on to run The Kensington Inn 'on the corner of Argyle and Bathurst Streets'. This is now known as the Racecourse Hotel. It would be good to think that he is a happier man, now free and remarried with children. He is recorded as having died the year after Elizabeth was writing to her brother, on the 13th August 1852, at his residence The Kensington Inn. His death is reported in the *Hobarton Guardian* on the 25th August 1852, so it would seem he dies a respected member of the community.

The machine breakers as a whole benefitted from being part of family, friends and village groups, some even being related to one another – there were several pairs of brothers on board Eliza, although not from Tisbury. They had spent a great deal of time in close proximity on the voyage out, and they developed a sense of group identity – they began to all describe themselves as 'machine breakers', rather than stating the exact offence for which they were being punished – for example Samuel Barrett for riotous assembly. They saw themselves as a special class of convicts, with perhaps a greater sense of grievance at their treatment in England. Although this closeness was to be dissipated, the habits of drinking together in ale houses continued and thus quite a number of men were convicted for drunkenness – but what else were they to do when they did have time off? There was in addition the traditional element of ale drinking by agricultural workers – the ale house was a place for social contact, finding out any news or gossip in the village and in most instances in England it was within easy walking distance from their homes. In Van Diemen's Land the distance to an ale house was considerably greater, and so when they did get there, intensive drinking bouts occurred i.e. binge drinking – an occupation which still occurs, and one which in fact became a characteristic of the Australian rural scene. Some thieving of alcohol from their masters also occurred and was severely punished.[10]

Thomas Burt had asked for and received an assisted passage for his wife and three children to go to Van Diemen's Land but they did not arrive. There are no further records for Thomas Burt in VDL, other than receiving his pardon in February 1836. The assumption is that he left the colony but he did not return to England. He may have travelled to Australia, as many of the released convicts did.

In the UK the census Return for Fonthill Gifford in 1841 lists Thomas' father, another Thomas Burt, as being 65 years old, an agricultural labourer. Ann, Thomas' wife, is now 30, Martha, 25 and another Ann 30 (his sisters?) plus Thomas' children Mary, 14 and John, 10. In 1844 on the 18th

February the elder Thomas Burt died.

By 1851 Thomas' daughter Mary is 24 and is recorded as being in Tisbury union workhouse. Listed after her name is Margaret Burt aged 1, presumably Mary's illegitimate daughter. There is no record of either of them after this, except for a Mary Ann Burt, aged 72 dying in Tisbury on 6th November 1899. This Mary Ann would be the right age to be Thomas' daughter, but there were two or more other branches of the Burt family in the area.

Thomas' son John becomes a policeman and in the 1861 census for the UK he is listed as a Police Sergeant, living at 8 Summer Grove, Lambeth with his wife Ann, son George 7 and daughters Sarah, Maria and friendly soc, 4, 2 and a baby of one month respectively. 10 His father would have been proud of him.

17
Roped to the plough

The very day we landed upon the fatal shore
The planters they stood around us full twenty score or more;
They ranked us up like horses and sold us out of hand,
They roped us to the plough, brave boys, to plough Van Diemen's Land'1

IN FACT, THE evil reputation of Van Diemen's Land as a convict hell was beginning to change, mainly due to Governor Arthur's tactics of the system of control by rewards or punishments. This was to be reinforced by a supply of troops and by appointments to the colony's young police force. It was becoming safe for free settlers to invest their money in land. The Pythouse rioters were among the first convicts to benefit from these changes – they were that desirable commodity – skilled agricultural workers, and what is more, from the settlers' point of view, they were free labour.

Under the Governor's new system the island's economy was growing. Wool, wheat, real estate, money lending, the import and sales of spirits, roads, bridges, public buildings – all these contributed to a growing sense of satisfaction amongst the settlers. Profits could be made from the improvement in infrastructure – land granted to a settler which might be needed for roads or bridges for example, could be sold at a considerable profit, particularly if such infrastructure was needed to provide access to previously undeveloped land, or for a budding new settlement. In 1824 when Arthur was appointed Governor, the white population numbered 12,000 but by 1836 it had grown to 40,000.

The mild climate and incredibly fertile soil of Van Diemen's Land initially produced abundant crops with no effort by the settlers – no fencing, no hedging, no ploughing. Sheep (and kangaroos) roamed at will over the rich native grasslands. Sown ground, in spite of the animals' depredation, produced an average of 35 bushels of wheat per acre, the process being known as 'chipping in', on uncleared, unploughed, unfenced and unmanured grassland. Farms of only 30-60 acres could support a family but in order to create a proper farming business, the settlers needed to sell a surplus to the official commissariat – this controlled the main cash market. Most farms were too far away from Hobart for the farmer to get his crop to the market easily and on time, so crops often had to be sacrificed at less than the market price, causing losses to small farmers. Properties were sometimes confiscated because of debt, and the family would be cleared out. The land could then be granted to a settler with more capital available to spend on it. Most then, aimed for self-sufficiency rather than expecting to make a profit. This had been the way of life until the advent of Governor George Arthur.

On Arthur's arrival the government policy changed, to encourage greater capital investment by granting bigger acreages to those who declared that they had considerable capital available to enable them to run a greater acreage economically and efficiently, producing more wheat and running much bigger flocks of sheep, both for wool and for meat. Labour, therefore, would be essential and needed to be of a quality that was tough and experienced. Hence the Governor's welcome to the men on the *Eliza* and the *Proteus* – the Swing rioters – mainly agricultural labourers from Hampshire and Wiltshire.

Now Arthur could make bigger land grants – between January and July 1831 he granted 250,000 acres of crown land to new settlers (this included the 100,000 acres of the some of the best agricultural land on the island, situated around Ross).

Subsequently small land grants became quite difficult to obtain – they were not an economical proposition. In particular, ex-convicts, even if reformed, found it difficult to obtain land at all for themselves. A minimum amount of £500 capital was required for free settlers, so ex-convicts were very unlikely to benefit from land grants. Indeed some who had settled (or squatted) on land for years after their convictions were spent, were dispossessed and evicted as they had no legal status and stood in the way of a new, rich settler being granted a larger stretch of acreage, on which the ex-convict's small holding might be sited.[2]

Plans were now made for building small towns between Hobart and Launceston – Perth, Campbell Town, Ross, Oatlands, Brighton. Roads

John Glover: A view of the artists house and garden in Mills Plains, Deddington VDL 1835 Oil on canvas Art Gallery of S. Australia, Adelaide

and bridges would be built to connect these new towns. The Public Works Department, as we have seen, was kept busy.

Many of the new, better off settlers brought letters of approval obtained from the London government giving permission for them to be granted land. However, it also meant that whilst they should, of course, farm it properly, they were able to sell it immediately for a quick profit, sight unseen, or leave it to go to waste pending an increase in its value. To gain more land, unscrupulous settlers boasted of having more capital available than they actually had. Apparently, 'some 50% of 'the entire land granted in Van Diemen's Land to 1830 was obtained by evasion of the law'.

This is confirmed by letters written by settlers – one Hamilton Wallace wrote to his father in 1825: 'I was only entitled to 500 acres however I managed to get 1280' (for which he was offered £700 straight away).

William Williamson, who 'sought to do my duty to all as a truly honest man' then boasted that he had 'given in a fictitious capital' to receive his grant of 1,000 acres.

Attempts were made by Chief Justice Pedder to stop this practice and to dispossess those who had lied, but the matter was soon dropped and legislation passed which confirmed the status quo.3

Arthur was determined, with the consent of Lord Howick at the Colonial Office in London that the land should be granted on condition that it would be farmed economically and although Howick advised the use of immigrant unemployed labour imported from England, Arthur wanted to use his convict labourers as part of his rewards and control system and now, with the advent of the Swing rioters, this plan could be implemented.

The plans of the 'get rich quick' land grantees were thwarted. Some had seen land grants and their subsequent sale at a quick profit a way to make enough money to return home and buy farms in England. Arthur ensured that this was not an option and most stayed, eventually finding the beauty of the landscape, the fertility and the climate worth the loss of living at home in England. Moreover, beautiful gardens could be created in spite of the differences in plants, trees and of course, animals.

And labour came free in the form of the convicts. This did create other problems, however. The free settlers considered themselves to be of a vastly different, superior social class to the convicts, even the ex-convicts who were now, in theory at least, free. There could be no socialising. William Williamson, who considered himself to be a truly honest man, wrote home:
'the inhabitants are like a set of vultures . . . defacing one of the finest countries in the world'4

Accusations of 'moral turpitude', 'degrading character' amongst the convict and ex-convict class encouraged settlers in petty snobbery, and an obsession with status – Edward Lord, a Hobart merchant, divorced his ex-convict wife and George Meredith insisted upon his wife, an ex-governess of his children, remaining on his property at Oyster Bay, not allowing her to accompany him to Hobart Town. No vault could be erected over the graves of convicts or ex-convicts, and Mrs Pedder, the wife of the Chief Justice, was forbidden to write to a woman whose grandfather had been a convict.

In New South Wales there was less class divide – the freed men, the conditionally pardoned class, were able to amass money and means there, whilst in Van Diemen's Land this had not been encouraged. David Burn, who wrote widely about early Van Diemen's Land settlement, comments about 'the tide of emigration which set up in 1820 having thrown all the power into the hands of the free people of Van Diemen's Land'.

In the northern part of the territory the settlers were not quite so snobbish; civilisation had arrived more slowly in the Launceston area. Gradually the free settlers everywhere were introducing better furnishings for their newly built stone or brick houses, they were able to wear better clothing copied from recently imported items and made locally by tailors or dressmakers and by 1832 Arthur was able to express his satisfaction at the fact that Hobart Town now presented as a properly civilised place, in contrast to its appearance as a rough settlement in a wilderness only 30 years previously.

Even as recently as 1820 when George Thomas Lloyd arrived in Van Diemen's Land he had found Hobart Town to have only 15 to 20 buildings worthy of the name of dwelling house – the rest of the dwellings (about 250 at that time) had been made of various rough materials, logs, split palings, wickerwork strengthened with clay daubs and turf roofs. In Launceston the buildings had been described by the Superintendent of the Van Diemen's Land Co., as 'hovels'. Progress was now producing stone and brick architecture in the colony. However, the convicts had to live either in barracks, or in rough hovels erected by them, or for them, on the settlers' land. They would have to wait for pardons and the ability to earn money before they could aspire to proper housing.

The second problem for the settlers was the indigenous aboriginal population, which had been dispossessed of its traditional, hereditary hunting grounds by the land grants to the new settler population, an area which had provided them, for centuries, with their food supply, their body coverings and their way of life.

Arthur was keen to solve this problem too, this time by a system – he always had a proposed system- of partition of Van Diemen's Land. He would give the aboriginal tribes the north-east coastal area (which was not the best agricultural land). He was keen to settle the matter before it became unresolvable, with the skirmishes between aboriginals and settlers turning into outright war. Unfortunately, although the suggested partition officially allowed aboriginals to travel across inhabited, settler occupied lands, the settlers took the whole idea of partition much more seriously and started to prevent the travelling aboriginals from crossing their lands, treating any who attempted to do so as criminals.

A proclamation in 1828 stated, or advised, that: 'the coloured population should be induced by peaceful means to depart, or should otherwise be expelled by force from all the settled districts therein'.

In spite of Chief Justice Pedder's attempts to ameliorate the situation by removing the words 'by force' from the proclamation, it resulted in the assumption by the settlers that any aboriginal could be legally killed for simply crossing an unmarked, undefined border.

Rather than settling the matter peacefully, this situation inevitably led to war with the indigenous population, the eventual outcome being the total annihilation of the Van Diemen's Land aboriginals. Arthur enlists ex-convicts to fight alongside his police and troops and although the whole

Proclamation issued by Lt Gov Arthur 1830 (incorrectly attributed to Lt Gov Davey 1816) oil painting on Huon pine board (libapp.sl.nsw.gov)

matter dragged on through the governorship of many other Governors, it ended in disaster for the aboriginals. In 1881 it was still a contentious situation and a 6,000 acre reserve on Cape Barren Island was made available for the then remaining natives, which continued as a centre for aboriginal culture until at last, in 2005 they were actually granted ownership of the reserve.

The arrival of the ships *Proteus* and *Eliza* provided the settlers with extra labour and defence against the 'aboriginal threat'. The Swing rioters were to be unfree labour, assigned but still owned and under the control of the crown. Arthur would successfully implement his system of controls and rewards. He would improve the economy, the lives of the convicts but at the same time the value of the crown lands. Hence the term 'servants of the crown'.

His system worked well; it provided labour on the farms, benefitting the settlers and it gave the assigned convicts a comparatively secure way of life until they could qualify for a ticket of leave and, eventually, a pardon. Richard Dillingham, a convict assigned under this system, wrote to his parents in 1836:

> As to my living, I find it better than ever I expected. Thank God I want for nothing in that respect. As for tea and sugar I almost could swim in it. I am allowed two pound of sugar and quarter pound of tea a week and plenty of tobacco and good white bread and sometimes beef, sometimes mutton, sometimes pork. This I have every day. Plenty of fruit in the season of all sorts ... and I want for nothing but my liberty but though I am thus situated it is not the case with all that come ... For some through their misconduct get into road partys and some into chain gangs and live a miserable life.[5]

Now churches were being built, both Church of England and Catholic for the free settlers and, more popular with the convicts, Methodist chapels. Schools and the press came under government control as did a Poor Relief System. A school for orphans was established in 1825, which concentrated on producing reliable workers – and a little education – many of the pupils being the illegitimate offspring of white men and aboriginal women.[6]

This society then was one which fortunately welcomed the comparatively well behaved Swing rioters, who described themselves as machine breakers, but were nearly all poor but respectable agricultural workers with very few previous convictions – and those were for minor offences such as poaching. The men who were not assigned to the Public Works Department or to the Van Diemen's Land Co. were sent to work for free settlers, many on large estates where the owners enjoyed a high standard of living in beautiful surroundings. There was very little machinery used at that time, but that was no problem for the Wiltshire and Hampshire lads – machinery had been one of the causes of their downfall at home. They had worked as ploughmen, stockmen, shepherds, carters, hedgers, foresters, grooms, gardeners, and were perfectly able to turn their hands to any agricultural tasks. Their main punishment would be the terrible separation from their families, friends and familiar community and a sense of despair at their inability to change this. Not all would be well received or well treated and their living conditions would be spartan and work hard, but eventually they knew they would be freed and the sensible among them worked towards this goal, making the best of having drawn the short straws.

18
Brave boys

BOTH JAMES MOULD and Samuel Banstone (Macey) were assigned to William Gunn, the Superintendent of the Prisoners' Barracks in Hobart. Samuel had originally been assigned to a Lt. Thomas Burgh RN, a farmer and horse breeder living in Inverary, but quite soon he was reassigned to William Gunn. His behaviour may have had an effect upon his assignment, as on 11th October 1831, only five months into his arrival, Samuel was convicted of disobedience and neglect of duty and sentenced to the treadmill for seven days.

This horrific machine was based in the Hobart Town Prisoners' Barracks. It was situated in a large building, taking up the whole length of a big room, with a dividing partition between a small area of treadmill used for punishing the militia and/or the general public, and a much larger area for the punishment of convicts. The wheel was 2 m. in diameter, each step being 17 cm in depth. The wheel's axle ran through one end wall into a mill room where it was connected to large grindstones. A big clock on the wall behind the backs of the prisoners counted the hours of stepping up to turn the wheel and regulated the treadmill. After each three hour shift, a bell would ring and the prisoners could step off the treadmill and rest, swapping shifts with the next batch of prisoners. After each four minutes of the three hour period the man at the left hand end of the mill stepped down and everyone moved one space to the left. During rest periods the convicts sat on benches around the room, awaiting their next turn to rejoin the treadmill.

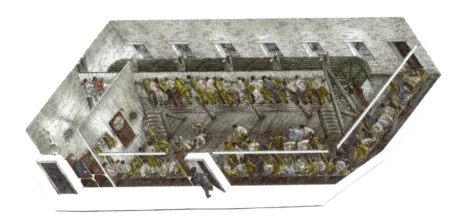

Treadmill at Hobart Gaol

Apparently the treadmill and its grindstones produced a grinding rate of three and a half bushels of wheat per hour. [1]

A spell on the treadmill was a considerable deterrent to disobedience and neglect of duty. It was possibly as a result of Samuel's disobedience that he was transferred to William Gunn's authority. Samuel already had a number of previous convictions before his machine breaking – aged 18 he committed an offence against the game laws which resulted in a sentence of three months in prison and twice more he received three months imprisonment for poaching. In 1826 he, together with Thomas Banstone (possibly Samuel's brother) and Charles Lovett, had been charged with stealing a purse of monies from John Turner at Fonthill Gifford. It seemed inevitable that he would be amongst those accused of 'riotous and tumultuous assembly' and breaking John Benett's threshing machine in November 1830, receiving a sentence of seven years' transportation. Samuel, now a 41 year old, married to Charlotte Macey and living at Fonthill Gifford had eight children. He was a small, probably tough looking man, just over 5'2 in height, with brown hair and whiskers. His brown hair was going grey, he had blue eyes and a long straight nose. There was a mole on his right arm above his elbow and the thumb joint of his left hand was described as 'crippled'.

Lt. William Gunn, his assignment master, was 31 years old and having started his career as a second lieutenant in the Bourbon Regiment as a 15 year old, he was placed on half pay the following year (probably because of the end of the Napoleonic Wars). In 1822 he had managed to obtain a letter of recommendation from the Colonial Office enabling him to settle in NSW in Australia until he could rejoin the Army. His ship however, docked at Hobart Town on the 24th December and William was able to attend church on Christmas Day where he was recognised by the then Lt. Governor, William Sorell, who persuaded him to remain in Van Diemen's Land, granting him 400 acres as an inducement. The land was in the Sorell district where William Gunn named it Bourbon, after his regiment.

William Gunn went on to have an exciting career, fighting against the bushrangers and losing his right arm after he was shot by a member of the notorious bushranger Brady gang. A public subscription for him raised £341 to compensate for his 'patriotic exertions' and he was granted, in addition, a pension of £70. In early 1826 William was appointed Superintendent of the Prisoner's Barracks and in 1832 he was also in charge of the Male House of Correction. In spite of wishing to remain in the Hobart area, he was moved in 1850 to Launceston where he became Police magistrate whilst also being responsible for the convict establishments.

William Gunn was considered to be a brave, clear thinking and honest man, completely unafraid of saying and doing what he felt to be right. He worshipped at St Andrew's Church in Hobart where he became an elder and later at Chalmers Church in Launceston. He was also an enthusiastic member of the Van Diemen's Land Missionary Society, donating land and money to both Anglican and Congregational Churches in Van Diemen's Land. A keen gardener, his rose garden in his home in Launceston was apparently the most beautiful in the whole of Australia. He and his wife Frances had six daughters and three sons.

So Samuel Banstone remained with William Gunn at Old Beach, where the Bourbon estate was situated, until given his ticket of leave in June 1835, whereupon shortly afterwards, on 20 July 1835 Samuel was quickly convicted of being drunk and imprisoned for six days. He was probably celebrating his ticket of leave! Eventually Samuel managed to obtain his free pardon, in 1836, whereupon his record in Van Diemen Land comes to an end.

In 1832 Samuel had applied for permission for his wife Charlotte and the eight children to join him in Van Diemen's Land, but they did not go. Probably they could not afford to do so, or perhaps they did not want to leave the comparative security of a home in Fonthill Gifford for the great unknown, frightening, foreign land so far away. But in Fonthill Gifford Charlotte and the children are having a hard time. She is recorded as in receipt of parish funding – for the month of December 1834 she received £1 11s 2d. Their youngest child, Henry had been just under one year old when Samuel boarded the *Eliza*. By 1851 Charlotte is described in the census Return as a widow and an agricultural labourer aged 61. A very hard life –

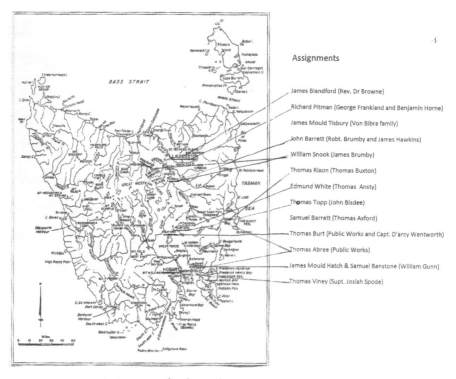

Assignments for the Pythouse rioters – the author

did she think she was a widow by then or was it just one way of facing her situation? Henry, 21 in 1851, was still living with his mother in Fonthill Gifford.

The census of 1871 reveals a big surprise – poor Charlotte has now died but Samuel has managed to return home – he is living with his brother John Macey, aged 78. They are both listed as labourers, although it is difficult to imagine that they were still actually working. They are old by the standards of the day – a couple of tough old men. Samuel eventual dies at Fonthill Gifford aged 86 three years later in 1874.

Another of the Pythouse rioters, James Mould from Hatch, is also assigned to William Gunn at Old Beach. James too is quite mature when he is transported, aged 39, a married man with five children. Two of his children had contracted typhus a few days after he was arrested for machine breaking and one of them, nine year old Eliza, died on the 9th December, whilst her father was in Fisherton Gaol awaiting trial. His wife Elizabeth (formerly Mullins) was left to bury her little daughter and come to terms with bringing up their remaining four children on her own at East Hatch. And no apparent income.

Curiously Wiltshire & Swindon Archives (WSA 413/23) holds a list of men at work at Hatch Farm on the 25th November 1830. This paper records that all these men and boys 'were in their work during the whole day of the 25th November 1830 for John Turner of Hatch Farm'.

Thomas Turner, James Sanger, William Woods, James Mould, Henry Turner, John Trobdige (sic) and Thomas Woods. The boys are Charles Collons, William Collons, John Turner, Thomas Mullins, William Combes and . . . King. In addition there are Farmer King's men listed as Job Ford, Jonathan Ford and Alexander Turner, with boys Thomas, George and David King, and Joseph Combes.

However, both William Woods and John Ford are amongst those men rewarded for informing and identifying many of the convicted labourers including their own colleague and co-worker at Hatch Farm, James Mould of Hatch. Woods receives £102 and Ford £34. James could write and had obviously had a little education. Before his banishment to Van Diemen's Land he wrote in appeal to John Benett:

> Mr John Benett esqr.
> James Mould of Hatch
>
> Took The Liberty to rit to your oner to say that all the mersheens was broke all to pieces and the hors house all the postes was cut of before I went into the yard your oner I had not ax in my hand all the day and I ham not gilty of the crime as I was charged with. I hope your oner will tak a little pity on me. You can no the rest of it from John Turner of hatch and mister henry.[3]

Mr Benett however had not taken pity on James Mould, who received a sentence of seven years' transportation, which he spent assigned to Lt. William Gunn at Old Beach. He received his ticket of leave in 1835, but had already been appointed a constable in 1834, so had clearly behaved himself very well. His free pardon is dated 3rd February 1836 and as for many of the others, there his record in Van Diemen's Land ends.

On his arrival he is described as nearly 5ft. 10ins. which is tall for the period. He has brown hair and whiskers and blue eyes. He has 'perpendicular wrinkles on his forehead, a long straight nose and a large mouth, very large ears and very hairy arms' He is a ploughman by trade. No doubt his height and good behaviour recommended him as a constable, plus his literary ability, unusual for his time.

It is not known precisely what duties James Mould or Samuel Banstone had at Old Beach. They were perfectly capable of turning their hands to any hard work, from gardening (Lt Gunn's main hobby) sheep rearing, ploughing or any pastoral activity. It would be good to think that both of them were able to socialise together sometimes and that they were provided with reasonable accommodation. These labourers were a valuable commodity in their own right, tremendously useful to the settlers and so worth looking after and feeding well. Both James and Samuel survived their punishment very well, and although it is not known what happened to James Mould, the fact that he had been appointed a constable boded well for his future in the colony.

To this day there are members of both families still living in the Tisbury area, the names Mould and Macey being very well known.

The Brumby family in Van Diemen's Land is also very well known, although not in Tisbury. Two of the Pythouse men were initially assigned to members of this clan, John Barrett to Robert Brumby, and William Snook to James Brumby. The Brumby family gave its name to the wild horses of Australia known as Brumbies. Apparently the first James Brumby, who had been a private in the NSW Corps, arriving in Australia with Lt. Col. Patterson in 1791 aboard the *Britannia* (a ship of the second convict fleet), left Australia in 1804 to found a settlement at Port Dalrymple on the Tamar River in Van Diemen's Land. He left some of his horses behind in Australia, thus the Brumbies.[4]

James Brumby remained in Van Diemen's Land after the Corps returned to NSW, being discharged from the Army in 1808. He married and had three sons, the third son, another James, being born in 1811. The family received a number of land grants in the Norfolk Plains district of Van Diemen's Land and at one time owned nearly all the land on which the town of Cressy is situated. James Brumby became a District Chief Constable and a co-tenant with James Hortle of a property in the Norfolk Plains where Cressy is situated. It is a prosperous and successful farming area, and labour was very much needed there.

William Snook, the young ploughman from Church Street in the parish of Tisbury, whose parents were Henry and Lavinia Snook, was 22 years old when he arrived in the colony. He had been convicted of riotous assembly and destroying a threshing machine, the property of John Benett of Pythouse. He received a sentence of seven years' transportation. On arrival he states that his offence was 'machine breaking'. William is nearly 5'4' tall, with a fair complexion, brown hair, whiskers and eyebrows and grey/hazel eyes. A full round visage and a long chin completes the physical description. He is assigned to James Brumby in 1832 and is still there in

1833. William remained with the Brumby family as an assigned convict worker until he received his ticket of leave in June 1835. On 3rd February 1836 he received his free pardon, after which he stayed in northern Van Diemen's Land working as a labourer.

In October 1841 William, now a free man, marries a young 16 yearold, Louisa Gilman, whose father was an ex convict. Louisa and her five siblings had arrived on a free passage on the ship *Harmony* to Van Diemen's Land in 1829. Her father Thomas had been convicted of smuggling and was transported for life but was able to apply for his wife and six children to join him.

Louisa and William Snook live initially at Longford where they have two children and then move to a house owned by the Rev. Bishton, in Westbury, near Launceston. The Rev. Bishton is a kind man, an idealist. In 1840 he had bought eight acres of land and in 1841 a further seven acres, which he proceeded to divide into smaller lots. Each lot could be purchased by ticket of leave holders. This would, reasoned the generous reverend, give them the chance of a fresh start as a free citizen of the colony. William and Louisa are able to settle there where they have two more children. On 19 July 1852 William dies of an inflammation of the lungs, at Westbury. Sadly Louisa, probably worn out with being pregnant and looking after four small children, had died before her husband. She was only 22 when she contracted a fever and died.

In 1848 the Van Diemen's Land census had reported that William is employed, still living in the house at Westbury owned by the Rev. Bishton. The house, the census says, is built of wood and is properly completed. There is a note that William is actually absent on the night the census was taken and so only his wife and his children are recorded – they are all under seven. Louisa states that they are Church of England believers and because of course Louisa is not working and William is away, the section on employment is left blank. [5] Their children are another William, born 1841, James Richard born 1842, a daughter born in 1844 who dies in January 1848 (perhaps at the same time as her mother, or perhaps just before) and Thomas Edward, born 1847. Young William, James and Thomas, all grow up and marry in turn.

William Snook never returns to Church Street, Tisbury where his parents, Henry and Lavinia, are according to the census report, still living with a young lad, also William. Henry was a tailor and although James Turner, an employee of John Benett's had reported Henry as being seen breaking a threshing machine at Lawn Farm and also at Mr Benett's at Pythouse, Henry was not taken into custody, although his son William was. According to Elizabeth Martin, writing to her brother Thomas Viney in August 1851, the Snook family 'is all broke to pieces' and Charles Snook, William's younger brother, born in 1806, is said to be

> the worst scamp there is in Tisbury and as bad off as anyone there he would be glad now to drive a horse much more ride on one in the Cavalry. I do not think there is one in the place that pities them in their downfall' [6]

Charles Snook, or Charly, had been listed as a private in the Hindon troop for the year April 1830 to March 1831 and had presumably been amongst those who fought and arrested the Pythouse rioters in November 1830, including his own brother. He was clearly very unpopular in the village. He lives in Course Street, (now court Street), Tisbury in 1841 with his wife Anna and his children. The young boy William, born 1826 and living with Henry and Lavinia, probably his grandparents, in Church Street in 1841, seems likely to be the son of the third sibling, Lavinia. Young William, is, by 1851 living in London – a painter, lodging at 2 Charles Street, Kensington. The Snook family were clearly severely affected by what had happened that November day at Pythouse. Family rifts from the arrests were certainly affecting the village. Members of the Snook family still live in Tisbury.

Another Tisbury family affected by the riots was the Barretts. Two brothers, John and Samuel are both transported for seven years, which must have been terrible for their family – John's wife, his children and also John and Samuel's parents.

Back in Van Diemen's Land the Brumby family properties had expanded. John Barrett is assigned to Robert Brumby, who had bought Harwick Hill, a large estate at Cressy, from his uncle, the elder James Brumby. This is presumably not too far away from William Snook at James Brumby's, but in 1832 John Barrett is reassigned, to Lieutenant Hawkins at Little Swan Port, being mustered there in 1832, 1833 and finally in 1835. Little Swan Port is a small village on the Swan River inlet of the eastern coast of Van Diemen's Land at the mouth of Oyster Bay. It is known for its excellent fishing and Lt. Hawkins, who had been an officer on the Maria Island Penal Colony, had been granted land there. John managed not to commit any offences whilst in Van Diemen's Land and after working hard, he received his ticket of leave and his free pardon and finally was able somehow to save up enough money to pay for a passage to return home to Tisbury in 1836, working at home to start with, as a labourer and then as a blacksmith.

Convicts at work in VDL gathering the harvest – 'My Harvest Home' John Glover 1835

He returns to his wife Eliza and they produce four more children. John had been a 24 year old ploughman when he was sentenced to seven years' transportation; already married to Eliza, they had one child. He had already been accused of stealing beef from a house in Hatch in January 1825. He is described on arrival as having brown hair, brown complexion with blue eyes, a small nose but a large chin. His wife had been Eliza Mould before her marriage and was probably related to James Mould from Hatch.

John's brother Samuel, aged 30 when committed, was a single man, still living with his father Edward a farmer, in Tisbury Row. He too had been accused of the beef stealing at Hatch and it would appear that the two brothers were subsequently acquitted of this offence, but Samuel had also been caught stealing turnips. He was sentenced to one month in gaol. These two accusations give a clear picture of the poverty which the family was suffering. Samuel's transportation offence was for 'riotous and tumultuously assembly' and attacking the Hindon troop of Wiltshire Yeomanry Cavalry. On his physical examination on arrival in Hobart Samuel too has blue eyes, brown hair, high cheekbones and a wrinkled forehead. Initially he is assigned to the Public Works Department and then in 1833 to Mr Thomas Axford.

Mr Axford had arrived in Hobart Town in November 1822 and in 1823 he built a watermill at Bothwell, on land he had been granted, and which he named Thorpe Farm (probably about 800 acres), just north of Hobart. Thomas Axford had brought with him his wife Martha (nee Slade) and their family. The mill and farm were named for his wife's home village of Upthorpe in Berkshire. Thorpe Mill ground wheat for flour and Mrs Axford's diary records daily bread making, catching eels in the millpond and having a one-armed convict working for them. This was not Samuel. Mr and Mrs Axford ran their farm, raising sheep and milling flour until 1865, when, sadly, he was murdered by a bushranger 'Rocky' Whelan. Axford's son carried on for a while but then sold the property to the Chamberlen family, Mrs Chamberlen being Thomas Axford's daughter, a Mrs H. J. Chamberlen. This mill has, in 2022, now been restored by the current owners, the Bignalls.[7]

Samuel stayed assigned and working for the Axfords until he obtained his ticket of leave in 1835 and his free pardon on 25 May 1837 (later than some of his compatriots). Perhaps he had misbehaved in some way during his period at the Public Works Dept and received an extra few months, but this does not seem to be recorded. Nevertheless, his free pardon is later in being granted than his brother's. By the date of the UK 1841 census he is back home in Tisbury, living once again with his father at Tisbury Row. Perhaps he had earned enough at the Axfords after receiving his free pardon, to pay for his passage home with his brother John, in 1839.

John and Samuel Barrett arrive home in 1839, John reuniting with his wife Eliza and his son, also John, who is now nine years old and has probably forgotten all about his father, since he was only a baby when his father left. By 1841 the census records them living at East Tisbury with their new child, William, who is now two. By 1851 they are living in The Quarry at Tisbury, an enclave of small houses that were originally built for quarry workers, just off the top of the High Street. It was a very crowded little area at the time, with a large number of people living in each small house. By now John and Eliza's son young John is 20, his brother William is 10 and there are three new siblings, James, 7, Martha 5 and baby Lucy who is only one month old.[8]

In the same year Samuel, now married to Sarah Gerrard, (probably from the Jerrard family at Farm) but still living in Tisbury Row, has a little daughter, Martha and is working with his brother John.

However, according to our prolific letter writer Elizabeth Martin, wife of Charles Martin (who was found not guilty of machine breaking) the two brothers started to work as agricultural labourers but took up blacksmithing together. Elizabeth, writing to her brother Thomas Viney on 27th August 1851, tells him amongst all the other Tisbury news:

both John and Samuel is carrying on the blacksmith together they cant agree together they have been to fight and Samuel as knockt out one of Johns eyes and so I think they soon be as bad as Charles Snook so my dear brother there is no prospect by them.[9]

John Barrett dies in 1852 and his brother Samuel in 1864, both still in Tisbury. Did poor John die as a result of having his 'eye knockt out'? Any infection that resulted would have been hard to shake of and impossible to cure. People died from infection from small cuts, let alone having an eye 'knockt out'. He had had a hard life, and it is sad to think he only had a few years at home before he died.

By 1861, Eliza Barrett is living at Chilmark. She is a washerwoman, and has a 'boarder' living there, Charles Barrett aged 6 . On the night of the census she has two visitors at home with her, William Barrett now 21, an agricultural labourer and Mary Ann 16, a house servant. This is probably the child named Martha in the 1851 census, being about the right age. [10]

Another family hit hard by the results of the riot, which certainly did not improve the financial status of the Barretts.

19
'gallant poachers'.

YOUNG THOMAS TOPP travels, probably on foot, to Hutton Park, White Hills, Jericho, to be assigned to John Bisdee, Governor of the Hobart Town Gaol, Keeper of the Hobart Pound and Chief Constable for the Murray district. Bisdee retired as Governor of the Gaol in 1833 and lived at his home, Hutton Park, until 1835 when he returned to England, coming back to VDL in 1840. By that date his land extended to some 10,000 acres where he raised Merino sheep for their wool and for meat. Whilst in England Bisdee had advised a select committee of the House of Lords that the assignment system was more humane and successful in rehabilitating convicts than the probation system, but pointed out that there were insufficient suitable men to appoint as overseers and said that more men should be sent out to the colony to work with the convicts. At Hutton Park Bisdee ran his estate like an English aristocratic park, planted English trees, imported a herd of fallow deer and raised pheasants – presumably for his friends to shoot in the traditional English way.[1] He kept a pack of beagles, known as the Hutton Park Beagles, whose exploits were frequently the subject of local newspaper reports.

At the time that Thomas Topp is assigned to Hutton Park, it is actually to John Bisdee's brother Edward, who is managing the estate and the farming of the merino sheep. Thomas Topp is very young, only 20, but he has already received two previous convictions in England – one for poaching and the other for vagrancy; he served one month's imprisonment for each sentence. Thomas is unusual amongst the Pythouse and Tisbury men – he has red hair, red eyebrows and a pale complexion. His small eyes are dark grey and he is recorded as having a large head with a small mouth. His hands are small but he is 'stout made'. Probably quite tough as he is a ploughman . He is said to be from 'Fundle Bishop', which gives a flavour of the way he speaks – 'Fundle' being, of course, Fonthill. [2]

Thomas has been sentenced to seven years' transportation at the special commission in Salisbury, for 'riotous and tumultuous assembly' destroying John Benett's threshing machines and for assaulting John Benett by 'striking him with a stone'. In addition he is charged with destroying James Self's threshing machine at Fonthill Bishop. Quite a number of charges and convictions but Thomas does not offend again whilst in VDL and receives his Ticket of Leave on 1st June 1835, followed by his free pardon on 3rd February 1836. On 13th December of that year Thomas boards the ship '*Henry*', leaving VDL and disembarking at Port Philip, where there is a 'vast, cheap and fertile acreage' to be farmed. Presumably he makes an adequate living in Australia, (even if he doesn't get really rich from the gold rush which occurs a few years later), as in 1840, now nearly 30 years old, Thomas marries Mary Watson with whom he has six children most of whom are born in Belfast (Port Fairy) a town on the coast of Victoria, to the west of the new Australian city of Melbourne. Thomas dies in Victoria at the grand old age of 80, in 1891. The bad news is that in 1875 a Thomas Topp was convicted of breaking into a dwelling with intent to commit larceny. This was at Aararat near Melbourne. Thomas would have been about 65 by then, so it is to be hoped that it was not him. However, it could perhaps have been his son? [3]

Both Thomas Topp and his brother Jeremiah, sons of Mary Topp, were born illegitimately. Jeremiah too, 23 at the time of the riots, was also apprehended for riotous assembly and of breaking Mr Self's threshing machine. Jeremiah was lucky in being found not guilty of these crimes and by 1841 is living with his wife Ann (formerly Ingram) and his children Henry, Elizabeth and John, still in Fonthill Bishop. By 1851 he is a widower and living on his own. However, by the time of the 1861 census Jeremiah has married again and is living with his new wife Elizabeth – he is still an agricultural labourer. In the same house, at Fonthill Bishop, is James Topp and his wife Charlotte (formerly Coombes) who may possibly be his cousin. James is 52 years old, also an agricultural labourer. The family is obviously still just about managing.

Mary, the mother of Thomas and Jeremiah is not so lucky. She does finally get married, to James Trimby, a widower from Fonthill Bishop. The ceremony is witnessed by Charlotte Topp and everyone makes their mark including the witnesses, so none of them are even able to write their own names. This marriage is in February 1837, but by 1851 Mary Trimby is a widow, living in the Tisbury union workhouse at Monmouth Hill in Tisbury. She dies there in September 1855. A miserable end.[4]

The rioting had been of no help to this family's circumstances. But perhaps at least Thomas in Australia with his six children managed some happiness.

Richard Pitman had lived in Hindon, with his wife Mary and his six children. She works as a laundress and he is a kitchen gardener and sometimes a groom. He is apprehended for the same offences as the others, riotous and tumultuous assembly and machine breaking. But Richard already has already notched up one conviction, in England, for poaching – no doubt it has been difficult to feed his large family. There is also a record of him being convicted of larceny at the Lent Assizes in 1824. He is described on arrival in VDL as having brown hair and grey eyes. He is aged 30, he is 'stout made' and has a tattoo of an anchor and PR on his left arm.

Very soon after his assignment to George Frankland, the charismatic, English, Surveyor of Van Diemen's Land, Richard receives a reprimand for being drunk and disorderly on a Saturday night in January 1832. Unfortunately he is found drunk and disorderly again on the 24th March and this time he is sentenced to a spell on the dreaded treadmill 'until Monday next week to be discharged at 6 a.m.'

This is however his last recorded offence in VDL and at the end of 1833 he is transferred, now being assigned to Mr Benjamin Horne at 'Chiswick', near Launceston, where Mr Horne runs 1000 sheep. Chiswick is a substantial stone property with several outbuildings also constructed in stone. Mr Horne had been granted 2000 acres having come to VDL in 1823, from Hamburg, where he had been a merchant and shipowner presumably declaring himself to be in possession of a sufficiently large amount of capital to justify his generous land grant. Mr Horne is appointed a magistrate at Ross.

Richard behaves himself very well with Mr Horne and receives his Ticket of Leave in August 1835 and his free pardon on 3rd February 1836. There is no further mention of him in the VDL records, nor does he appear to have been able to return home to Wiltshire.

Back in England in 1841 Richard's mother and father, Richard and Ann, are still living in Hindon, aged 70, the older Richard still working as a gardener. Brother Thomas and his wife are in the village too, with a number of children, seven in all. He is an agricultural labourer. In 1845 father Richard dies and is buried in the churchyard at Hindon. There is no record of Mary Pitman and the six children Richard left behind when he was transported. [5] Did she change her name, obtain employment somewhere else and take the children with her? There is no record of her remarrying, and indeed she had no way of knowing whether she was a widow or not. She does not appear in the workhouse records either, so it is to be hoped that she found satisfactory employment and a way of living with the loss of her husband.

Richard obviously enjoys a drink on a Saturday night in Launceston, so it would be good to think that he is able to meet up with a fellow Pythouse rioter, James Blandford, the one man in the group to be convicted for a 14-year stretch. James is a 28-year-old ploughman from Duck Street in Tisbury. He is a widower, having lost his young wife Mary only a couple of years after they married. They had one child, William. James had been accused of being involved in destroying three threshing machines on 25th November 1830 – one belonging to John Benett at Linley Farm, one to James Lampard at Lawn Farm and the third to James Self (Henry Selfe) at Fonthill Bishop. In addition he has 'assembled riotously and tumultuously with others, and attacked the Hindon troop'. It could not have been more calamitous, as James has a previous conviction, for larceny, for which he has already served one year in gaol.

At his trial in Salisbury in early January, he attempts a defence, bravely cross-examining John Uphill, Benett's shepherd, saying

'Did you not say when the mob entered the yard 'That's it my lads, down with it my lads; I should like to see it down' Is that not what you said?'.

Uphill denies saying this, responding 'that his master Benett had set him to watch the yard'.

Blandford tells him

'John! John! You are a false swearer'.

Unfortunately William Woods too swears that he has seen James Blandford at Pythouse breaking the machine with a hammer.

James tells the court

'I am very sorry, my Lords, that I was there, but I was forced to go'.

This first trial sets a pattern for James. On being charged with attacking the water driven threshing machine at Linley Farm, he denies being in the barn, telling the witness Woods

'You never saw me. I do know there were a number of frocks like mine. You must have had very good eyes to have seen me. I was not in the barn at the time you mention '.

But Charles Wilkins also says he saw James with a sledger hammer, breaking down some of the wheels.

The following morning, January 4th, sees James in court again with some of the others, to be sentenced. Mr Baron Vaughan, the presiding judge, states that James had acted as ringleader and was therefore to be transported for 14 years. [6] No-one has spoken up for him in the form of a character reference. Presumably this is because of his previous conviction – for having 'feloniously stolen from the person of Henry Lambert a canvas purse, containing fourteen pounds in gold and silver and one pound promissory note, Lambert's property at Fonthill Gifford.'[7]

This seems a great deal of money and so it is surprising that at the time James received a sentence of only one year in gaol, with hard labour, but coming as it did shortly after the death of his young wife, it must have been a hard blow.

James is not convicted for the attack on Henry Selfe's machine at Fonthill Bishop, as he has already been 'capitally convicted'. Now he has to join his friends on board the hulk '*York*' in Portsmouth Harbour, from where the Eliza leaves for VDL.

On arrival in Hobart Town James musters with the rest of his friends. He is recorded as being 5'7' tall, with brown hair and grey eyes. His ears are large and his face is wrinkled and on his right little finger he has a scar. He is assigned to the Rev. Dr Browne at Launceston, an Irish born clergyman who had studied to become a doctor but changed his mind and became a priest instead. Browne wants to become an official of the church and soon he has acquired his LL.D and is appointed a colonial chaplain, sailing from Cork in southern Ireland and arriving in Hobart Town in October 1828.

The following month sees the Rev. Dr Browne gazetted to St John's Church, Launceston, responsible for a large parish which covers Launceston, Campbell Town, George Town to the north and Longford on the east coast. He holds six services a week, including those at the gaol, the prisoners' barracks and the house of correction. He reaches the remote parts of his parish on horseback although he does have a bad fall which causes him to take leave during 1828 to 1830. He is a true Evangelist, suspicious of High Church tendencies and 'new' rituals. A keen supporter of education for everyone, he founds a small school in Launceston and then a much larger Grammar School. He is a serious, community minded man, campaigning for such projects as bank facilities at rural post offices.[8]

St John's Anglican Church; Colonial Gothic style 1824; tower added 1830

This was probably a good assignment for James Blandford, but he is not with the Rev. for very long although Browne sounds a kind, caring individual and James must have appreciated that. Sadly, the young man becomes very ill, is transferred to Launceston Hospital and dies there on 23rd February 1833, having spent less than two years in VDL. He is buried in St John's churchyard at Launceston, the record stating that he is 'the assigned servant to the Rev. Dr Browne'. Dr Browne himself conducts James' burial service.[9]

Launceston High Street in the 1860's – St John's Church on the right

James is 29 years old at the date of his death. His little boy, William Blandford, is now eight and living in Duck Street with his grandfather, Samuel, another agricultural labourer. James' own grandfather, another Samuel Blandford, had died in 1813 when James was only three. He had been a dairyman, although illiterate, and had owned and lived in a house with an orchard in Duck Street, Tisbury. In his Will, which is very explicit as to the disposal of his assets, James' father is left with the eastern half of the house in Duck Street with its orchard, his brother Edward receiving the western end. The family remain there until James' father dies in 1856. He is by then described as a pauper and has a 'housekeeper/pauper', Ellen Turner, living at the cottage.[10]

So had young James Blandford survived his transportation and received his pardon, he might have been able to return to the family home in Duck Street, with its orchard. His life was short and sad, losing his young wife Mary shortly after their first and only child was born, committing a stupid and probably impulsive theft of a purse, joining in too enthusiastically with the mob, receiving the longest sentence of them all, then tragically becoming ill and dying far away from home at an early age. A hard life but a wasted one. His son William goes on to grow up, get married and have a son, Henry, living in Hindon Lane and then in the Quarry.

In Little Swan Port, Oyster Bay, Thomas Rixon (or Rixen) has been assigned to Thomas Buxton. Buxton had been a Lt. in the Royal Navy and hailed from Mayfield in Derbyshire, arriving in VDL in 1821 aboard the ship *Westmoreland*. He had no capital to speak of and therefore received no land grant. Initially Thomas Buxton went to work as an overseer for a Mr William Talbot at Belmont, until he was able to save up and receive a land grant, in June 1823, of 500 acres at Little Swan Port, where he built himself a small house from 'sods', which he was soon able to replace with a large stone house with outbuildings – Mayfield. This was built with the aid of free convict labour. There he developed an orchard and a garden and where he lived with his wife and his family. In 1828 he became Division Constable and Pund Keeper at Little Swan Port. That same year he received a further grant of land of 780 acres which, it was reported at the time, he received because he had entertained Governor Arthur to dinner.

Mayfield had been attacked by aboriginals and the new house had large cellars with a separate water supply where the family could take refuge at night if necessary. An alternative hiding place was provided in the attic, with access through a concealed doorway. In 1836 Mr Buxton added a flour mill to his estate and although Thomas Rixon may have worked on the building, he never saw this completed.[11]

At Little Swan Port Thomas Rixon is living not far from Samuel Barrett, assigned in the same small town. Thomas is a married man, he and his wife Elizabeth have five children. His offences for transportation are for riotous assembly, machine breaking and assaulting the Hindon troop of the Wiltshire Yeomanry Cavalry. He too receives a seven year sentence, and he too has a previous conviction for poaching. Thomas is already going grey, his eyebrows are bushy and overhanging, he has grey eyes, a large oval head and a 'furrowed visage' with a long nose. His arms are unusually hairy.

Whilst with Mr Buxton, Thomas Rixon behaves himself well, he has no convictions for drunkenness or misbehaviour and he obtains his ticket of leave on 1 June 1835. But sadly a letter dated 6 July 1835 from a Mr A Mackenzie states that Thomas Rixon has died, so he never receives his free pardon and never returns to England to Elizabeth and the children. His period of near freedom is very brief.

At home in Tisbury Thomas' family are thriving – his son William is married at the time of the 1841 census and has six children of his own. The family are members of the Zion Hill Independent Church (Congregationalists). Thomas' grand-daughter works as a house servant in Hibberd's emporium at the top of the High Street and marries John Foyle a cordwainer.[12] (A cordwainer makes new shoes from new leather as opposed

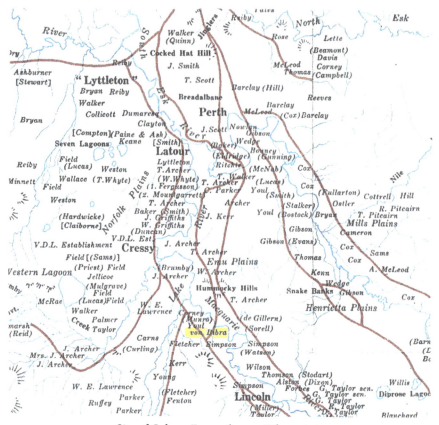

Site of Coburg Farm, the von Bibra estate

to a cobbler who repairs old shoes). They live in the High Street next door to Hibberds. The Rixon name is still very well known in Tisbury, as one member of the family was responsible for all the carved stone heads which can still be seen on various cottages in the village.

The other James Mould, stated to be from Tisbury, is 23 years old and he too has received the sentence of seven years' transportation for 'having riotously and tumultuously assembled ... and broke and destroyed the threshing machines of John Benett esq' and also with having assaulted the Hindon troop. Like so many of the Pythouse rioters, he is described as having brown hair and blue eyes. He has a large oval head, a long straight thin nose and a small chin. James is assigned to the von Bibra family at an estate called Coburg, near Cressy, on the Macquarie River.

The father of this old aristocratic German family, Lt. Franz Ludwig von Bibra, had sadly drowned in the Macquarie River in 1823, leaving his wife Elizabeth to bring up their nine children and to run the estate on her own. A neighbour's son, Sam Lucas, a young man in his twenties, had offered to help and fell in love with the youngest daughter, Maria who was still really only a child. Sam Lucas and Maria got married, in spite of her very young age. By 1830 Elizabeth had become disillusioned with life in VDL and decided to leave the colony and return to England. The estate would be left in the care of her eldest sons, Benedict, 20 and Frederick 18, together with daughter Maria who was now 16 and still with Sam Lucas. The idea was that the younger children would be able to be properly educated in England and Charles and Francis, two of the sons, would eventually return to help run the huge estate. But by 1835 when the boys, now nearly grown up, returned they found that their eldest brother Benedict had sold the estate. His father had not made a Will so Benedict had inherited the whole estate under the eldest son rules. He then moved to Western Australia and his brother Francis had gone to NSW.[13]

James Mould therefore is actually assigned, in 1832, to the young von Bibra brothers at Coburg near Cressy presumably not far from John Barrett and William Snook. By 1833 his assignment is altered to the son in law Sam Lucas. On 17 June 1835 James receives his Ticket of Leave, which probably follows the sale of the estate and on 3 February 1836, his free pardon. There are no more records in VDL for James Mould of Tisbury – he may have left the colony – perhaps to go to work for one of the older von Bibra boys to Australia. There is no record of him returning to Tisbury.

Accurate details of James Mould's family in Tisbury are difficult to determine. There were a large number of members of the Mould family, in Tisbury, in Hatch and in Fonthill. There would appear to be no record of a James Mould being baptised into the Church of England in about 1806, and his parents may have been members of a dissenting order, such as the Zion Hill chapel. There is a William Mould who might well have been his brother listed in the 1841 census returns, married to Elizabeth (Moxam), with three daughters. Again, there is no record of William's birth being registered, so it is difficult to find his parents' names. He died in the union workhouse aged 73 in April 1877, but although he seems a likely candidate to be James' brother, it is not certain.[14] Certainly the Mould family went on living in Tisbury until quite recently and one of the very early and enthusiastic members of the Tisbury History Society in the 1980s was the late Kathy Mould, whose considerable store of photographs of the village and its people is now in the Society's archive.

20 – the Intrepid Jerrards

YOUNG CHARLES JERRARD and his father, also Charles, were assumed to be the ringleaders of the body of labourers numbering around 400, who assembled at Fonthill Gifford on the morning of Thursday 30th November 1830.

Father and son lived at Totterdale Cross, a cottage just at the top of the steep road known as Jobbers' Lane which leads out of Tisbury towards Ansty and Swallowcliffe. They lived in a cottage on the left side of the road opposite the drive up to Totterdale Farm. There a small lane known as Browns Lane led down across the fields to Tisbury Row. Ann, Charles' sister was there too and Mary, his mother. Presumably the men worked for Richard Rebbeck the farmer at Totterdale at the time, who owned 190 acres. Charles the son is a carter and his father a labourer. The Jerrard family had, some time previously, owned a small farm of about 59 acres, known as Jerrards, at Fonthill Gifford, but this had long since been lost by the Jerrard family, since by the 1780s it was left in the Will of Joseph Lane, the grotto builder, to his daughter.[1] The Jerrards had been reduced to the labouring, landless class and may have felt some residuary resentment about this.

On Thursday 30th November young Charles is distinguished from the rest of the mob by the fact that he is wearing a coloured sash around his body. This coloured sash attracts the attention of Mr John Benett, for whom such an adornment can only signify one thing – Revolution. Revolution, in fact, of the sort that the French aristocracy had suffered. He immediately calls out to Charles that wearing that sash will hang him – to which the young man bravely but rashly replies, 'I don't care about hanging. I don't care'.[2]

Young Charles goes on with the mob to help destroy Benett's threshing machine at Pythouse Farm and to damage part of a barn, but he is remembered. He is arrested after the rioting, and no doubt his words to Benett do not help his defence at the special commission, when Mr Benett gives evidence against him. He pleads not guilty to the charges, but Mr Benett's carter John Brickell is also a witness and testifies that he saw Charles Jerrard with his sash on taking part in the damage, as does John Jay, Benett's Bailiff, and two others, both Benett employees.

Charles defends himself manfully:

The mob came to my house that morning before I was out of bed, and they swore they would pull me out if I did not go. The sash the witnesses spoke of was a handkerchief, which I tied round my waist as I was very warm.[3]

Unsurprisingly this cuts no ice with the jury led by Mr Benett. Charles Jerrard junior, in spite of a good character witness statement from William Jeffery who says that Charles is very honest, is found guilty.

On Tuesday 4th January 1831 Charles, together with Samuel Banstone (Macey), the two Barretts, both James Moulds, Richard Pitman, Thomas Rixon, William Snook, Thomas Abree, Thomas Topp, Thomas Vining and Edmund White are sentenced to seven years' transportation. Although he leaves Fisherton Gaol to board the prison hulk *York* with all the others, he is separated from his friends and is not transported on the *Eliza* when she leaves for Van Diemen's Land. He is reported as having suffered from pneumonia on the voyage, but perhaps he contracted this on board the *York*, and was kept back for a week or so. Instead he is put aboard the *Eleanor*, a 301 ton barque built in Calcutta in 1824 and often used for transportation of convicts to Australia. The ship has a crew of 24 sailors, the Master is Robert Cock and the Surgeon Superintendent John Stephenson. There are 133 convicts on this trip, all of them Swing rioters from Wiltshire, Berkshire, Hampshire and Dorset, the youngest being only 17. They would be on board for 126 days, guarded by Lt. Stuart of the 4th Regiment, four non-commissioned officers and 24 privates. In addition there are six women and ten children aboard.

The *Eleanor* departs from Portsmouth on the 15th February 1831, calling in to various islands and then to the Cape of Good Hope where three more convicts are added to the cargo, not agricultural rioters, Thomas

Davis, George Smith and Pierre Tuite. This call at Cape Town is a good opportunity to load the ship with fresh meat, fish, vegetables and fruit (plus wine for the officers), all of which helps the health of everyone on board. In addition, the crew, officers and military are allowed to go ashore for a brief period, but not, of course, the convicts. The Surgeon Superintendent makes a great effort to keep his cargo in good health since payment to the ship owner is dependent upon each man arriving in good health and ready to work. Generally the convicts' health aboard the *Eleanor* is nothing to worry about, only 11 of them being ill during the voyage. Perhaps Charles is included in this number, as he has had very little time to recover from his pneumonia if he became ill whilst aboard the *York*. Even amongst those who were recorded as ill, says the Surgeon's log, some need not really have been included on that sick list. The soldiers, women and children suffer from very minor complaints – catarrh, tonsillitis and one case of rheumatism.

However, the poor Captain has a very bad trip. According to the medical log, he has severe urethral strictures, causing frequent retention of urine, so bad that the Surgeon Superintendent, in trying to relieve the stricture, is fearful of puncturing the bladder. The trip must have been a nightmare for the Captain, whose name, in the circumstances, seems too unfortunate.[4]

The *Eleanor* has a number of sets of brothers on board including the articulate Mason brothers from Bullington in Hampshire, the four members of the Shergold family (two brothers and their cousins), and the Bulpitt brothers. These men are the radical element of the Swing rioters and the Mason brothers write home frequently, managing to get their letters sent from various ports en route.

The weather on the way to the Cape is reported as 'in general very favourable, the heat at no time excessive, the thermometer never rising above 84'. After leaving the Cape though, the weather is less clement, gales succeeded by light airs and dense fogs with frequent rain. However, often it is cold with a strong breeze and the ship has a tendency to labour, taking on water so that the hatches have to be battened down for two or three days at a time. This means that strict rules for the lower decks have to be observed, with cleanliness, dryness and ventilation undertaken for the benefit of the prisoners.

Surgeon Superintendent Stephenson is glad to be able to report the good health of the ship's company on its arrival at Port Jackson, NSW on 26th June 1831. At anchor in the harbour there is unfortunately a 'disturbance on board and two prisoners were shot and killed in the resulting chaos'. The

Sydney Gazette however is enthusiastic about the arrival of these men and reports that: 'As fine a body of men as ever set foot on Australian shores from a convict ship and were nearly all assigned to individuals up the country'.

And on 18th July 1831 the *Sydney Herald* reports that it had been agreed by the government that the Swing rioters would only be assigned to 'respectable' men. They were, the paper commented 'fine healthy men, agriculturalists and a valuable acquisition to the colony'. This would have been encouraging for the convicts had they been able to obtain copies of the newspapers, or to read them.

On 1st July a muster is held on board by the Colonial Secretary, when full details of each convict are recorded – name, age, education if any, religion, marital status, family, native place, trade, offence, when and where tried, sentence, any previous convictions and physical description. The notes also record to whom the prisoner is to be assigned.

In ordinary circumstances the convicts arriving in Sydney would be issued with new prison clothes, since the ones they had travelled in, issued in England, were of such poor quality that they mostly fell apart on the journey. However, the Swing rioters aboard the *Eleanor* are allowed to disembark in their own clothes. This is considered to be a great privilege.

Now the convicts are divided up and rowed ashore in small boats to a point near the site of the present Sydney Opera House. Four abreast, they march to the convict barracks at Hyde Park where another muster is

Hyde Park Barracks, Sydney, NSW Australia – watercolour by Robert Russell 1836
Rex Nana Kivell Collection National Library of Australia

held before they are sent to their quarters. At this stage they receive some exceptionally sensible advice – do not communicate or attempt to make friends with the resident convicts, who had been transported to Australia for 'normal' criminal offences, many of whom were old lags, eager to relieve these 'new chums' of anything they could take from them. Luckily the Swing rioters do not have to stay in barracks for very long and are soon moved on to their assigned masters.

Young Charles' occupation is as a carter and he is assigned to Thomas Barker, an ambitious 32 year old mill owner, who in 1824 left his former employer John Dickson and his steam engine and set up in business on his own account as a miller, in the Darling Harbour region of Sydney. In 1826 Barker, in partnership with John Smith, builds a windmill at Darlinghurst (then known as Elizabeth Point). This business prospers and in 1827 Barker is able to buy out Cooper & Levey's steam mill which is sited next door to Barker's new house on the corner of Sussex Street and Bathurst Street in Sydney, paying £6,000 for the 'building, steam engine and other machinery and apparatus for the purpose of grinding corn'. Of this, £5,000 is left on mortgage to Cooper & Levey. By now Barker has 26 employees, including two carters.[5]

During 1829 Thomas Barker continues to expand his business interests, buying land to the west of his property and more in 1831, which gives him a site of around six acres in a prime area of Sydney, Woolloomoolo. Sussex Street was the main thoroughfare for this busy district, running between the wharfs, warehouses, flour mills, shipbuilding yards and factories on the east side of Darling Harbour and including no fewer than eight working flour mills.

Barker's mills were steam driven, sited in two long rectangular buildings, about 95' in length and 30' wide, with smaller buildings adjacent, one probably housing the boilers. The main buildings were five storeys in height. Two mill ponds were fed by a stream running east to west under Sussex Street. At this period (up to 1834) Barker and his family and servants live in the house next door to the mill.[6]

So this is where Charles Jerrard is going to work, possibly still as a carter, but Charles is a bright and bold young man, clearly one with enthusiasm, energy and a desire to improve himself. He will be able to learn about the 'new fangled' steam engine and its potential for the future. He is officially assigned to 'Thomas Barker Steam Engine', so it is possible he actually works in the steam engine shed.

Charles is described in the muster as being 21, single, a carter. He

Barker's Steam Mill, Sydney – Casey & Lowe, cross city tunnel project 2004 study

is 5'51/2' tall, ruddy, with a 'much pockpitted complexion', hazel/grey eyes, brown hair and has received no education. He has a horizontal scar over his left eye, and another on the forefinger of his right hand.[7]

It is not recorded whether Charles is housed somewhere on the mill site, or whether he has to stay in the convict barracks, Hyde Park, sited nearby. Normally the convicts assigned to the Australian government are housed in the barracks, but as Charles is privately assigned, it is more likely he is housed and fed by Mr Barker's company somewhere on site with the other employees.

In 1833 Barker builds a palatial new house for himself and his family, at Darling Point. This was Roslyn Hall, close to the site of his original windmills and to there he retires in 1835, still a young man, and keen to go travelling. He keeps on a number of community responsibilities but takes his family to England and the Cape. He leases the mill business in Sussex Street to his brother James and Mr Ambrose Hallen, the architect of Roslyn Hall. They add a new mill, steam engine and boiler house to the site which is, by now, a considerable enterprise. They pay Barker the magnificent sum of £2000 p.a. for the lease.

On 1st February 1838 Charles Jerrard is pardoned and receives his Certificate of Freedom to work as a labourer. He does not return to Tisbury, so by now he has presumably decided to remain in Australia, or perhaps he

View of part of Wooloomooloo and Mr Barker's house and mills with Bradleys Point: George Edwards Peacock State Library of NSW

just never manages to save up enough to pay for his fare home. He behaves himself in New South Wales – there is no record of any conviction.

As he is uneducated he is unable to write home to his parents Charles and Mary, who are still at Totterdale with their daughter Ann. Charles senior is 65 by 1841, Mary is 60 and Ann 20. Charles and Mary have another son, Joshua born 1804, baptised in Tisbury and so Charles' older brother. Joshua is not at Totterdale on the night of the 1841 census but he appears in the 1851 census, by which time their father Charles has presumably died, because Mary is listed as a pauper and Joshua as an agricultural labourer, now living back at Totterdale with his own son of 18, William.

Also in the cottage at Totterdale are Andrew Barrett and his wife Ann nee Jerrard, who is Charles' and Joshua's sister. Andrew and Ann have two small children, Henry, aged 2 and baby Elizabeth 6 months old. Interestingly their neighbours are James and Elizabeth Viney (of which family more later).[8] Presumably all the men work for Richard Rebbeck at Totterdale Farm.

Joshua Jerrard has already had one conviction by now – for a burglary committed in 1850 for which he receives a sentence of 12 months' imprisonment. He must have just been released from prison at the time of the 1851 census. He is arrested again in 1852 but found not guilty of larceny at the Assizes in New Sarum in April of that year. By 1861 Joshua has moved from Totterdale to the Quarry in Tisbury and he and his wife Eliza have five children, William, Emma, Samuel, Ellen and Tom. Samuel, curiously, is baptised in the union workhouse in July 1849 – perhaps the family went through a difficult period as far as work was concerned, as this is just before Joshua is sent to prison. Joshua continues to be listed as an agricultural labourer until the 1881 census lists him as a stonemason – now back at Totterdale with his son Tom now 25 and Henry, his grandson of 32 (presumably William's son). In 1883 Joshua dies.

Charles Jerrard senior ingeniously managed never to be taken by the militia or the parish officers for his part in the Pythouse riots, disappearing for while until an amnesty is granted and only returning when the coast is clear. However, the family was always very wary and even after his return home, if any member of the militia or figure of authority was spotted approaching from Ansty or coming up from Tisbury, Charles senior would, according to his family, hide up the massive stone chimney, standing on the 'pot lug'. This is certainly a family legend confirmed by young William Turner when writing his account of the riots some 63 years later:

> Charles Jerrard a swashbuckler living at Toterdale Cross was sought for in vain by the civil and military authorities. Jerrard had a diligent daughter who closely watched the approaches of the four ways, giving timely warning to her father if a red coat or a parish officer came in sight (the Provincial Policeman was then unknown) when astute Charles like he of kingly race ascended and stood in safety on the Pot Lug until the fruitless search had ended. Charles and Mr Alford, a considerable holder under Lord Arundell of Wardour eventually left the neighbourhood and remained away till the amnesty.[9].

The family is understandably wary of authority.

Ann Jerrard, the diligent daughter, has a boyfriend by the name of Andrew Barrett, the son of Edward Barrett a small farm owner from Tisbury Row. The Barrett cottage is a short walk via Browns Lane over the fields to Totterdale Cross. Andrew was probably illegitimate, as his mother's name is not recorded, but he had two half siblings, Samuel Barrett who had been transported in 1831, and Sarah.

To add to the Jerrard family's woes, not long after Charles' departure for New South Wales, Andrew Barrett is charged with larceny (probably poaching on the Wardour estate), tried at the Lent Assizes in Salisbury in

1833 and also sentenced to seven years' transportation. The grief this must have caused Ann can only be imagined.

Andrew Barrett is duly transported on the 9th April 1834 on the convict transport ship Surrey, together with 260 other convicts, amongst whom are five of the men from the Dorset village of Tolpuddle, who became known as the Tolpuddle Martyrs. These men from Dorset are convicted, not for forming a trade union, because by this time it was not illegal for working men to combine for trade purposes, but for administering and being bound by secret and unlawful oaths under an act passed in 1797. The sixth member of the Tolpuddle men, George Loveless, had been ill and was kept back for a few days, being eventually sent off to Van Diemen's Land on a different convict ship.[10] Andrew arrives in Sydney on the 17th August 1834 and as before, the convicts are mustered and then marched four abreast to the Hyde Park Barracks in Sydney.

The records for Andrew are held in Australia, so it is not possible to record here where he was assigned. But it is quite extraordinary to think that he and Charles were within a stone's throw of each other, in the same city, in the same area, and even, possibly, in the same barracks. Did they meet? It is a tantalising thought. Andrew serves his time and receives his pardon. Incredibly he manages to return to Tisbury and marries his sweetheart Ann Jerrard, because there they are, recorded in the 1851 census Return, back at Totterdale Cross with their two small children Henry and Elizabeth. Did he have news of his brother-in-law Charles? We shall never know. Andrew and Ann are still together in 1871, now having two more children, Lucy and Frank. By 1891 the two of them are living on their own in Deptford in the Wylye Valley and Ann is still alive in 1901, a widow aged 81. A considerable achievement and an eventful life.[11]

Sadly for the Jerrard family the cottage at Totterdale Cross no longer exists, although Browns Lane is still visible, leading off Jobbers Lane and across the fields to Tisbury Row. It cannot have been much fun standing on the 'Pot Lug' waiting for the authorities to go past.

'Alright Dad, you can come down now!'

21
Successful Settlers

THE VINEN (OR Viney or Vining) family in Tisbury was a very large one – William Vinen and Sarah Singleton who marry in Donhead St Andrew in 1793 have ten children. One of their sons, Thomas Vinen, is born in 1810 and works as a ploughman, probably for the Wilkins family. This job requires a number of skills, working with horses, knowledge of working with some machinery, sowing seed (at that time by hand), harvesting the corn with a scythe in a co-ordinated team of men and women, stooking the corn stalks to dry out, loading wagons and carting the heavy corn stalks back to the farm, building ricks and thatching them and of course, threshing by hand in the winter. But it was good work, respectable and satisfying. What was not satisfying was being unable, in spite of all those skills, to earn enough to keep oneself well fed and certainly not enough to feed and house a family, without recourse to the public funds reluctantly provided by the parish.

So it is hardly surprising that young Thomas finds himself part of the group of farm workers who protest in November 1830. His sisters Harriet and Elizabeth are married to two of his friends, Robert Obourne and Charles Martin, who are also farm workers, all of them living in the Tisbury area. Robert already has a conviction, in April 1826 he is convicted of stealing one hammer from James Bracher of Tisbury and one pair of pincers from Thomas Jukes – for this demeanour he serves six months in gaol, with hard labour – rather expensive pincers and hammer. However, although he joins in the rioting in which his brother in law is to be convicted, Robert is found not guilty.

Thomas' other brother in law, Charles Martin, married to Elizabeth, is also found not guilty of machine breaking in spite of his previous conviction of having stolen James Bracher's chisel and other articles – he too has been to prison for that offence, but only for two months. He is acquitted on the machine breaking charge. Presumably the two young men had committed the tool stealing together.

Young Thomas Vinen is not so lucky. He is found guilty at the special commission of riotous and tumultuous assembly and of breaking John Benett's threshing machine. The carter, John Brickell testifies against him, as does John Jay, John Uphill, James Dogrell and Joseph Trim. They all agree that Thomas was breaking down the wall of the horse house 'with a very heavy sledge'. A written deposition by James Snow, taken at Pyt House on the 20th December 1830 by Mr Benett states that Thomas was 'beating down the stones under the posts of the said Horse House to throw it down'.

It should be recalled that each of these witnesses was a Benett employee. Their jobs probably depended upon them giving this evidence, and they received money for witnessing against their neighbours. It may have been a difficult choice for them.

In his defence, Thomas admits joining in but says:[1]

> 'I am very sorry that I was there. There was a great number of farmers there in the morning encouraging the people to go on, and if they did not give them that encouragement, or if they had told them not to go on, I do not believe they would have done any harm, or gone about. I am very sorry I was there but it is my first offence of any kind.

Of course this falls upon deaf ears in the court and Thomas is sentenced to the usual seven years' transportation, removed with the others to the prison hulk *York* and travels to Van Diemen's Land on the Eliza to serve his sentence. On arrival in Hobart his physical details are recorded at the muster – he is quite short in height, 5'4' (although this is not unusual for the period) and he has the usual brown hair with grey eyes, a large round head and a small nose. He is assigned to the Superintendent of Convicts, Josiah Spode.

Mr Spode is the grandson of the well known potter Josiah Spode of Stoke on Trent in Staffordshire, so is descended from a successful family and has financial expectations. He had served in the Navy as a midshipman and by 1809 he was a naval officer. On retiring, still young, from the Navy, probably because the Napoleonic Wars had come to an end, he went home

Oast house at Shooter's Hill, New Norfolk beside the Derwent River for Josiah Spode – John Redeker Oast Houses of Tasmania

to Stoke on Trent and ran the family business. However, the arrival of a male cousin meant that he was no longer the direct heir so he decided to leave England and seek his fortune elsewhere. He married very well, and with his wife he arrived in Hobart Town in 1821 with his considerable assets of over £800 in capital. This large sum enabled him to obtain grants of land, the first near Hamilton which he then exchanged for land at Macquarie Plains, adding a further land grant so that his property at Shooter's Hill, New Norfolk totalled over 1,000 acres.[2]

In the late 1820s, Spode, having built a homestead for himself and his family, added an oast house to his property. This is built in local wood, with a hexagonal tower and drying area several storeys in height. It is surrounded by huge poplar trees forming a screen against the prevailing winds. Tasmania's hop industry became one of the most important industries in the country, with the hop vines being tied to bush poles with reeds gathered from the marshes bordering the rivers. The conditions in the Derwent Valley were ideal, very similar to those the settlers had found in Kent.

Spode however, was keen to become an official in the colonial service and with his credentials from the Colonial Office, service record in the Navy and considerable assets, he was able to obtain the appointment of Muster Master and Police magistrate for Hobart in 1827, Coroner in 1828 and Principal Superintendent of Convicts in 1831. By 1839 Spode had been appointed Chief Police magistrate and had become a member of the

Legislative Council. Eventually he retired with an excellent colonial service pension, having enjoyed a very successful career in Van Diemen's Land.

Mr and Mrs Spode built themselves a house at New Town called, appropriately, Stoke Cottage and by retirement owned some 2137 acres of Van Diemen's Land. The family, with their two sons returned to England in 1854 and lived out the rest of their lives at Tring in Hertfordshire.

As Superintendent of Convicts he was acknowledged to be scrupulously honest and had a reputation for fairness in his assignment of the convicts to the free settlers. He kept extensive and very accurate records, keeping an eye on his convicts during their assignments so that his advice to Governor Arthur was of real use. He was, however, considered to be rather arrogant and had a singular lack of humour. He probably took himself very seriously indeed.

Thomas Vinen from Wiltshire Machine Breakers by Jill Chambers

So this was the man for whom young Thomas Vinen is to work and Thomas settles in well, remaining with Spode probably on the New Norfolk property, receiving his ticket of leave in June 1835 and his free pardon on 3rd February 1836. That same year Thomas gets married. His bride is Mary Burrows, a Scottish lass, who also has a convict record and is in fact, not yet free. Mary came from Edinburgh, where she had lived at Cant's Close, Cowgate. She is reputedly a widow and may well have had to leave a small child behind in Edinburgh when she is transported. Mary is unfortunately charged and convicted with 'uttering base coin' and her punishment is seven years' transportation. She was probably desperate as a widow with a small child.

Mary becomes a much loved and faithful wife for Thomas. This is very sad for Thomas' sweetheart in England, Sara Stevens, who had waited for him to return, saying that she would wait a further seven years if necessary, only to find that he had married in Van Diemen's Land and that by the time she found out about this, Thomas and Mary already had one son, born three weeks after they got married. They went on to have six more children and despite frequent pleas from Thomas's sister Elizabeth Martin, who actually offered to pay for him to return home, Thomas lives out his long and quite satisfactory life at New Norfolk. In one of her wonderful letters his sister Elizabeth Martin mentions that she is pleased he has been to the 'diggins' and hopes he finds plenty of gold. She mentions that there is a lot of gold in London but none seems to come their way. Mary dies on 29th January 1891 and is buried in the Wesleyan Section, Cornelian Bay Cemetery at Hobart.

Elizabeth Martin continues to write long loving letters to her brother, full of gossip about Tisbury and her life in London where she and Charles Martin, now a gardener, are living. She tells him about the Great Exhibition and the cost of attending it. The last letter available is written in July 1856. Charles and Elizabeth have built themselves a new house. Sister Mary unmarried, is living with them. Their brother Isaac has died leaving three girls and a boy. Robert and Harriet Obourne in Tisbury have had 17 children but sadly only six have survived.[3]

William Turner, the young boy who witnessed the rioting and machine breaking, writing in his old age, recalls sitting in the pub in Tisbury

> After an enforced absence of 50 years and believing Thomas Viney to be in Tasmania – I was after the manner of Falstaff taking mine ease in the private bar of The Boot when a stranger as bearded as the pard stood at the open door. I looked and was the first to speak saying 'You are the brother of Joseph Viney.[4]

Annoyingly, he does not go on to tell us whether the stranger was in fact Thomas or not, and whether he had returned, perhaps after the death of Mary, to see what had been happening in Tisbury during his many years in Tasmania. The bushy beard is good, but not really enough evidence to prove that it really was Thomas. However it does appear that William Turner is an educated man, able to quote from Shakespeare's As You Like It – 'bearded as the pard'. Certainly Thomas had a beard and a Thomas Viney is recorded as living in Fonthill Bishop in 1881 – he is a widower aged 69 (Thomas would now have been nearer 71) – recorded as a groom and gardener, where his brother Isaac lived.[5]

It would be good to think he came back for a visit to Tisbury and perhaps to his sisters in London, after Elizabeth's faithful attempts to keep in touch with her brother with her wonderful letter writing. The 1891 census returns for London record a Thomas Vinin aged 78, a widower, living at 4 Durnsford Road, Wimbledon. He is the uncle of Eliza Moxam, a widow of 58, head of the household. Eliza Moxam is the daughter of Thomas' brother Isaac and the widow of Morgan Moxam a stonemason from Tisbury. It does seem likely therefore that Thomas Vinen did return to England, possibly visited or lived in Fonthill Bishop for a while and then with his niece Eliza in Wimbledon. Eliza and her husband Morgan Moxam lived at Round Windows in Cuffs Lane Tisbury in 1871 before moving to London.

Thomas and Mary's son Henry dies in 1912 in Stephen Street, New Norfolk, and there are still Viney relatives in Tasmania, members of the Tasmanian Ancestry Society. There are also recently Vining family members in Tisbury. Some are Vinen, some Vining, some Viney, but it is clearly the same large family.

The Swing rioters who chose not to return to England, who could perhaps have done so, were mostly the skilled mechanics, or craftsmen such as carpenters or stonemasons. These were the men who could earn a reasonable wage after obtaining their freedom. From the total Swing rioters transported to VDL, around 300, about half remained in the colony for the rest of their lives. Some 40 or 50 men returned home, the rest (about one third of the total) leaving the colony in three waves following their grant of freedom, the first wave in 1836/7, another wave during the severe depression of the 1840s and the final wave left during the 1851 Gold Rush. They settled in New South Wales, Sydney and Victoria.

Many of the men who were not really craftsmen but basic agricultural workers such as ploughmen, and who stayed in VDL managed to save up just enough to lease very small but self sufficient blocks of land, build a basic cottage, marry, and remain working the land.

All the young men who remained in the colony tended to be in contact with either relatives transported at the same time, or men they had known from their own village, links which proved strong even after years of assignment to different parts of the colony. Once there was freedom to travel, they could find out where old friends were and reunite. These contacts can be found because they acted as witnesses at each other weddings, some intermarrying – the son of one machine breaker marrying the daughter of another machine breaker for example.[6] One family in Tasmania today has three machine breakers in its ancestry – the Parsons family of Sandy Bay have Arthur Hillier from Enford in Wiltshire, William Wadley from Oxfordshire and William Snook from Church Street Tisbury amongst its heritage. [7] Sometimes family members or village friends went into partnership on a small farm or embryo business venture and occasionally family members were able to join them from England. Their family and village based networks continued to exist for years and Elizabeth Martin's letters are a vivid record of some of these. She tells her brother Thomas Vinen about the return to Tisbury of the Barrett brothers; she is pleased to hear that Thomas has seen Thomas Abree and is able to let Abree's mother know that he is well. She thinks that Thomas Rixon and James Blandford may have returned but she has not had definite confirmation of this.

Not many of the Swing rioters however, in spite of their good behaviour and hard work, were able to make a financial success of their lives. One exception to this generalisation is Edmund White, the young blacksmith from Course (subsequently court) Street, Tisbury who had been shoeing the doctor's horse when his mates arrived on that fateful morning of 25th November 1830. His father John is elderly and ill and it is Edmund at 21 years old who is the only working member of his family, keeping his father, mother Fanny and the rest of the family.

Edmund is genuinely forced to join the mob, and as a result, finds himself in Fisherton Gaol, committed during the week ending 11th December, charged with having riotously assembled with others in the farmyard of John Benett Esq and destroyed a threshing machine and other implements. On 10th December Edmund writes a long letter to Mr Benett, which vividly describes what had happened to him:

Mr John Bennett esqr pyt house
Sir im sorry that I should offend you on this Occasion but I hope your honour will be favourable to me as it is the first offence And being forced possible to leave my work being pulled out of shop by 2 persons by the same of Samuel Ares & thomas hayter early on Thursday morning as the rioting began by which I said I was busy and would not go went to my work as Usual for the space of an hour or more till the mob returned as I was going to breakfast Rice Chivrel entered the door with a....sledge in his hand & said come thee must go with us which i answered I was busy & would not go & he pushed me to the door Where there stood William Snook of ansty water with a long ash bludgeon in his hand & said go on or I will make thee I went in to the shop & said I would not go for I was going to shoe the doctors horse by which several went out of the shop And Charles Gerred their Captain as he called himself said is not he coming by which the mob answered he is going to shoe the doctors horse which Answer Charles Gerred said damnation

sease the doctors horse make him come Or else beat the bugers damnation brains Out by which several entered the shop and pushed me for the space of 10 ... & said that if I offered to go back be damned if they would not kill me i am sir your Obedient and humble servant
Edmund White Tisbury from fisherton Gaol[8]

This apparently elicits no reply so Edmund tries again, writing on 20th December:

To Mr Bennett esq. dated Salisbury December 20th 1830
Your honour I have sent to beg your pardon and am very sorry that I should have went with the mob but I hope your honour will forgive me or I most humbly beg your pardon & was forced to go as my life was threatened by some of the ring leaders before it was light but as I Own my .... In a fault and do most humbly beg your pardon for to forgive me I still remain your Obedient and humble servant
Edmund White
I hope your honour will not be offended as I have write to you to ask pardon.

He could not have done more, but the letters had no effect upon the unforgiving recipient, although Mr Benett did endorse this letter 'I tried to save this man from transportation but without effect. He was a young Blacksmith with a good previous character but did much mischief'. In what way he attempted to save Edmund from transportation is not recorded and Edmund appears at the Guildhall on the morning 1st January 1831 with all his friends, where they plead not guilty. On this first appearance Edmund is found not guilty of the charge of destroying John Benett's threshing machine at Pythouse Farm.

However, the law is not finished with the young blacksmith. In the afternoon of 3rd January he is brought to the Guildhall again, with most of the same group of friends, charged with destroying John Benett's threshing machine at Linley Farm. He was apparently using a sledge hammer to destroy the cast iron rollers – which would require the strength of a powerful blacksmith to do. This time he is not so lucky and although none of the witnesses specifically identifies him and several people speak up as to his good character, including Matthew Coombes and John Gray, all the prisoners, including Edmund, are found guilty by Mr Justice Anderson. Edmund does get a recommendation for mercy, as does Thomas Abree, James Mould of Tisbury and John Barrett.

The recommendation for mercy is useless. They are sentenced the following day to seven years' transportation.

Clearly Edmund is a personable young man. On 13th January 1831, Charlotte Wyndham of Dinton House, (sister of Captain Wyndham of the Hindon troop) writes to her brother George Wyndham, a settler in New South Wales, Australia:

> The special Assizes took place at Salisbury last week before three judges, and a great many prisoners are sentenced to transportation. Two are to be hanged . . . I think these convicts will be most valuable servants to you and other settlers in New South Wales. I fancy they will not be inclined to quarrel with machines they will find there. . . . Papa has done his utmost to get one of the men's sentences mitigated, but he has not succeeded. Edmund White, a blacksmith, the most quiet and industrious young man in the parish. He was absolutely collared and taken out of his father's house by violence; but of course, when his spirit was up he was active enough, and being a blacksmith he well knew how to break the ploughs and rollers . . . I know there is hardly a chance of seeing poor Edmund White, but if you do, don't forget that Papa has interested himself on his behalf. He has seven years to spend at Botany Bay.[9]

George Wyndham based in NSW could not have helped Edmund White or the other Pythouse rioters (except for the younger Charles Jerrard) because they are bound for VDL.

Lord Arundell offers a few words on Edmund's behalf, writing to Colonel Mair from Wardour Castle on 13th January, and his recommendations are passed on to the Colonial office by the Colonel:

> This youth was forced from his Father's House in the morning of the 25th. He works for his father who is a very infirm man and has a large family. This his eldest son is now his only support in his Trade. The Jury recommended him to mercy.[10]

But the government wants to rid itself of these troublesome agricultural rioters, in its opinion radicals challenging the status quo. And so the Eliza is quickly filled and departs for VDL on 6th February 1831 before the matter can be debated in the House or an amnesty arranged.

On arrival in Hobart Town Edmund is mustered and his physical details recorded. He is nearly 5'8' tall, with a fresh complexion, brown hair

Edmund White, arrival details and death record ibid

and facial hair, grey eyes and a large head. His mouth is continuously open (perhaps he has breathing difficulties) and he has a short chin.

Edmund is assigned to Thomas Anstey Esq. a 54 year old free settler from Dulverton in Somerset. Mr Anstey was trained as a lawyer but did not follow this career – instead he travelled to London where he became a partner in a firm of fabric importers in Bond Street – they imported calico cottons from India. In 1811 he married Mary Turnbull, a young lady from Edinburgh. When his Bond Street company failed and was dissolved, he decided to emigrate with his family to become a farmer in the colonies. Mr and Mrs Anstey travelled in style, taking family, furniture, household goods and farm implements with them to VDL, plus sufficient capital, their assets totalling about £8,000. This satisfactory amount of assets enabled him in 1823, to apply for and obtain the maximum land grant available amounting to 2560 acres, which he selected himself, situated near Oatlands on a tributary of the River Jordan. Naturally enough he names his property Anstey Park and starts to build a stone house, square, unadorned but spacious which he calls Anstey Barton.

Thomas Anstey decides to specialize in sheep breeding and rearing so he imports 50 pure bred merinos from a flock owned by Sir Thomas Seabright. He now claims another maximum land grant, actually buying even more land (as opposed to receiving it as a grant) and finally owns some 20,000 acres. Understandably his great spread of land and his excellent sheep attract thieves, and sheep are stolen by both the aboriginals and by convict servants. In 1824 Thomas Anstey is appointed a Justice of the Peace and takes an active part in the ambush and capture of the notorious William Priest, a bushranger. In 1826 he is appointed coroner and Police magistrate for Oatlands and in fact is the person mainly responsible for the creation and building of the township at Oatlands.

He pursues stock thieves and marauding gangs with military enthusiasm and suggests to the Governor that all the aboriginals should be moved away from the central pastures to the south coast of the colony.

In 1827 he is appointed to the Legislative Council of Van Diemen's Land, continuing as a member until 1844. He is a founder and shareholder in the Bank of VDL, and a director of the Derwent Bank. He campaigns for nondenominational education by the state and supports the church. All in all, an outstanding man in Van Diemen's Land, admired for his wisdom, humour, and tough disciplinary attitude.[11] He is an excellent role model for the young blacksmith.

Edmund is one of many convict assignees at Anstey Park, but no doubt a very useful one. He remains with Mr Anstey until he receives his Ticket of Leave in July 1835.

The following month Edmund gets married. His new wife is Mary Smith a 'free woman', the daughter of Sergeant Major Smith, of the East India Company, Calcutta; but because he is not yet quite free Edmund has to apply for permission to marry Mary. They settle in the township of Oatlands and after Edmund receives his Free Pardon on 3rd February 1836, he continues to work as a blacksmith in the town, acquiring two acres of land, for which he pays £11, and then a further two acres for £8. where he starts to build a stone house for the two of them. The 1842 census return for VDL reports that Edmund White is living in an unfinished stone-built house in the High Street with his wife Mary, and two children. He describes himself as a 'mechanic or artificer'. By 1848 they have six children.[12]

But in 1846 Edmund makes a big change in his occupation – he takes on the licence for the City Hotel in Oatlands, running this until 1849. The following year he moves up a scale and becomes the licensee of the Wardour Castle Inn in Oatlands (which he presumably names to remind him of home). There the family run the business for 11 years, until in 1864 he is recorded as having taken on The White Horse Inn, Lake Tiberias where he remains for a year.

Edmund and his wife become very respectable members of the Oatlands community, running the businesses carefully, not putting up with

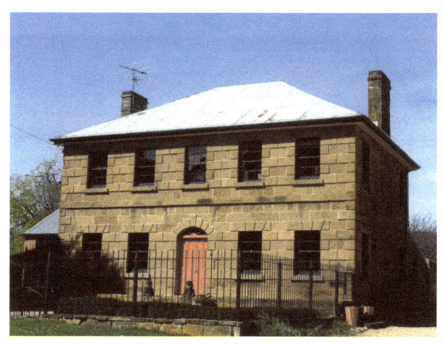

The Wardour Castle Inn at Oatlands

anyone who tries to take advantage of them. Perhaps he never forgets that he was himself unfairly treated and although he did commit the crimes for which he was convicted, he had not wanted to join in and had tried very hard in fact not to join the mob. No-one would be able to take advantage of his good nature again. So in September 1855 he prosecutes one George Liegers for stealing a watch valued at £7 and other articles. In 1861 he prosecutes William Thompson, an employee, for taking 'French Leave'. Thompson is fined 10s. In 1862 he takes one Alexander Denholme to court for 7s.6d and the cost of refreshments, for non-payment for admission etc. to a public ball which took place at the Wardour Castle. The defendant had attended the ball but failed to pay his admission charge and refreshment bill. Edmund writes twice to Denholme requesting settlement of the bill but nothing is forthcoming so he sues him. Mrs White gives evidence of non-payment for the refreshments. Denholme says he put enough money into the musicians' collection to cover his costs, but judgement is given against him.

In Oatlands Edmund impounds stray cattle, advertising this and inviting claimants to collect their cattle and pay for their keep. In 1864 he finds a 14-year-old scrumping in his orchard and breaking one of his greengage trees. This is not a new occurrence and Edmund eventually decides to take the young man to court to teach him and his friends a lesson.

The boy admits, tearfully, to having done the deed, is fined 2s, which he is able to produce from his pocket there and then and smartly leaves the court. Perhaps learning the lesson, or perhaps not.

Clearly Edmund has been finding times hard but in October of 1864 a meeting of his creditors is arranged at the court House in Hobart Town, to hear the matter of 'an application by the said insolvent for an order of discharge'. He had been declared insolvent in April 1842 when still working as a blacksmith and farrier, but was at last able to pay his debts and apply to be discharged from the insolvency order.

His last prosecution in 1867 is against one John Griffiths for trespass and breaking and entering Edmund's house, which is actually rented from John Griffiths. This trial took a little longer than the scrumping one and eventually the jury finds for Edmund, awarding him £20 damage.

These prosecutions seem to follow a pattern – does he bear a grudge all his life – to go to so much trouble to prosecute each time seem excessive but perhaps understandable. He never gives up working hard and trying to succeed.

He is thoroughly immersed in the social life of Oatlands, taking a booth at the Annual Ploughing Match, where no doubt all the locals prop up the bar and maybe even some of the Pythouse men are able to meet each other. Edmund is part of a Deputation of inhabitants of Oatlands who present a letter and 120 sovereigns to a Mr Whitefoord, chairman of the quarter sessions, when he retires. In addition Edmund's name appears on the electoral roll – a considerable achievement for an ex-convict.

In 1882 Edmund White, the most successful of the Pythouse rioters, becomes ill. On 17 April, still resident in Oatlands, he dies and is buried in St Paul's churchyard. where his simple tombstone is inscribed:

Edmund White Died 17 April 1882 in the 73rd year of his age.

Mary remains a widow until her death in 1902, on 13th June at 2 Nile Terrace, Elizabeth Street Oatlands. In 1891 Edmund's family place a Memoriam in the local newspaper: 'White – In memory of Edmund White, died at his residence, Oatlands, April 17 1882. The Eternal God is thy refuge, and underneath are thy everlasting arms.'[13]

22 – Habitat

Although Tasmania is a comparatively small island, comparable in size with Switzerland or Wales, it was, in 1831, short of horses for transport so the assigned convicts were forced to walk to their place of assignment. This could take a week or so if the assignment was in the north of the island.

The Swing rioters were treated with more care than the convicts who had been transported for the usual offences such as stealing, murder, assault or even poaching. These men would be a valuable asset to the colony and thus received better rations and better working conditions than the road gangs or the incarcerated prisoners. All convicts, however, if they had to be moved, would be marched in groups, guarded night and day by militia and, since tents were not only in short supply but heavy to carry, the convicts would be expected to build rough shelters for the overnight stops. Cooking an evening meal would, of course, be over an open fire and would consist of whatever they could find in the bush, from wild animals to stinging nettles. Flour had to be carried to make bread.

How to build a shelter for the night was a quickly acquired skill. Many of the Swing rioters were, fortunately, quite accustomed to working with wood and to thatching ricks or even cottages. The temporary huts were known as 'brush huts' or 'break winds' based on A-frames from straight tree branches used as poles, lashed together at the top and then thatched with long grasses. These were originally inspired by and based upon the temporary shelters built over the preceding centuries by the native aboriginal peoples. It was quite possible to make these water resistant if not completely watertight very speedily.

The evening meal would probably be damper – a bread made without yeast, in a pan over the fire, and some sort of meat, perhaps kangaroo, stew. The native kangaroo was still abundant in VDL although it became over-hunted later.

On arrival at the assignment estate, the men had to set to work again to build a less temporary shelter. This might take a little longer. Log huts were the most successful homes. A stringy bark tree would be cut down using an axe, and the straightest piece of 12 foot length chosen. This section could be moved to the chosen site by means of wooden levers or hand spikes, also cut from the nearby bush. The 12 foot section would now be divided and split with the help of wooden wedges into straight planks which were to be 8 – 12' wide and about 2' thick. The stringy bark wood split easily and accurately.

Four thick posts were shaped and driven into the ground, with narrower posts used to create door and to support window frames. Grooved, heavy logs were sunk into the ground and wall-plates laid along them. Now the men could insert and attach the planks to the uprights, ensuring that there was a watertight fit. Sometimes clay was daubed into any cracks to fill small gaps. At one gable end of the new building an enormous stone chimney would be built, with roughly cut stones. Tie beams held the top of the wall constructions together, and a basic upper floor could be laid. The roof beams were attached to the tie beams and the whole hut thatched, although with experience, wooden shingles were found to be better, safer and more fire resistant. Attacks by aboriginal people were frequently made upon the new huts, built as they were, on what was considered to be aboriginal land. Fire spears thrown at the thatch caught fire instantly. So wooden shingles became the norm, and proved to be more successful against fire spear throwing. Throughout the hut notches and pegs were used for fastening, not nails.

So even if there was no money available for building, these huts could be erected and become a very successful two room home.

Even in the towns in VDL, log huts were the acceptable form of homes until after the 1820s, and convicts, after receiving their freedom, were often given a small allotment of land, of about a quarter of an acre in a town, to build a hut for themselves and their family. These were known as 'skillings'. It was believed, probably correctly, that once an ex-convict had built himself a home, he was much more likely not to commit any more crimes, as his home would then be forfeited. [1]

Cottage for assigned convicts

These huts were not particularly tidy or elegant, but they were practical.

With more money being earned after a convict was pardoned had worked in the community and become acceptable, came the ability to build a better home, a stone or brick house. The free settlers, who brought money with them, liked their homes to be built of stone, in the traditional, simple Georgian style they had known in England. These were large, plain houses, of good proportions but few decorative features. The size and solidity of such a home reflected the settler's status in the community. Few of the ex-convicts aspired to these larger properties (except, among the Pythouse rioters, Edmund White) although one or two managed to build stone cottages, as the census recorded.

Clothes were a bit problematic. They needed to be hard wearing because life in the colony was one of physically hard labour with not much in the way of clothes washing facilities. Convicts were issued with uniforms of coarse cotton, clearly marked with arrows, but unsurprisingly they preferred their own old clothes. Shirts were of rough cotton, probably very old and worn, softened by washing, and trousers, waistcoats and good waterproof jackets could be fashioned from kangaroo skins, as could boots. Not much clothing of European design, quality and standard could be found in the colony until later.

Wallaby skins sewn together into seven foot squares were used as sleeping bags, half under the body and the other half on top. Knapsacks of kangaroo skin were useful. Skins were sewn together using the sinews from the leg of the kangaroo.

Military men kept their official uniforms for formal occasions and otherwise dressed in grey wool, trousers and fur trimmed jackets. Their caps were opossum fur trimmed, but made of kangaroo skin as were their cartouche boxes.

The Pythouse men and the other convicts did not suffer too much from hunger. The first settlers and convicts indeed had a very good diet, since VDL was very well stocked with edible wildlife – from shellfish, to swan, seal, emu, wallaby and kangaroo. After 1820 sheep and cattle provided even more protein. But of course they had to catch, kill, butcher and cook the fish or animal, so a large amount of time had to be spent in hunting and preparing food.

In the mid 1830s the government issued statutory diet requirements for convicts and the assigned men had to be very well provided for by their employers. The authorized Scale of Rations to Assigned Servants, issued on 4th November 1834 was as follows:

1lb fresh meat,
1 1/2lb bread and 1 lb vegetables or 1lb bread and 2lbs. vegetables. 1oz sugar, and 1 oz roasted wheat for coffee, or 2pints milk or 2 pints of table beer.
10oz. Salt pork or 1 lb of other salt meat, not to be issued oftener than twice a week in lieu of fresh meat.

However, the most useful meat continued to be kangaroo and one recipe was very popular. It was considered to be as delicious as venison – and prepared similarly to the traditional English dish of jugged hare (without the blood)

Kangaroo Steamer

Ingredients –
500gm kangaroo fillet, coarsely minced or finely chopped
400 gm speck (or bacon), finely diced
1 onion, finely chopped
250ml or 1 cup port wine or other red wine
2 teaspoons salt
1/2 teaspoon ground white pepper
½ teaspoon ground mace or nutmeg
½ teaspoon ground allspice
2 tablespoons thyme leaves

1 bay leaf

3 juniper berries

Place all the ingredients except the bay leaf and the juniper berries into a large, non-metallic bowl and using the hands, mix the ingredients together to form a slightly sticky, slightly sloppy mixture. Cool overnight if possible.

Pack the mixture into a 1 litre jar or tin to just below the top, as the mixture will expand during cooking. Using a knife, remove as many air pockets as possible and place the bay leaf and the juniper berries on the top. Seal the container tightly.

Put a trivet in the bottom of a large metal stockpot or saucepan. This will allow water to circulate below the container. Put it on top of the trivet and fill the saucepan with cold water to three quarters full. Bring the water to the boil, reduce the heat if possible (difficult over a fire), and simmer for three hours, keeping the water in the stockpot topped up.

Allow the water to cool a little before carefully removing from the container. Cool and serve cold, cut into slices.[2]

This recipe could be prepared before travelling, or in an evening whilst on the march, some being kept for the following day. It was eaten with a chunk of the 'damper' and greens from the bush such as boiled stinging nettles.

Damper was made with flour and baking powder – it rises a bit during the baking stage but requires very little kneading or preparation and a pan-full cooks in 45 minutes.

Not so nice was:

Slippery Bob: Take kangaroo brains and mix with flour and water. Make into a batter with pepper and salt, then pour a tablespoon at a time into an iron pot containing emu fat. Take them out when done.[3]

But 'Sticker up Kangaroo' – chunks of kangaroo flesh cooked on spikes close to the fire with a piece of pork fat or bacon at the top of the spike which dripped fat down onto the sizzling chunks, seems a good way to drum up a barbecue.

Still, probably the best thing to do with a large piece of kangaroo meat would be to roast it on a spit, turning slowly. A sort of jam, or chutney could be made from mangolds and carrots but later on settlers and ex-convicts planted fruit trees which provided fresh fruit both for eating and for jams and chutneys.

Hunting for food

Emu was considered to be as good as beef, and no doubt the men eventually had mutton from older sheep (probably not spring lamb however) and a little beef. Vegetables grew quickly – potatoes, onions, turnips and carrots gave way in spring to spinach and greens. Soup could be made using vegetables and stock from kangaroo tails. A young wombat roasted was 'as good as sucking pig' – but not so good if the wombat was mature – it was then only any good for soup apparently.

Salt was brought into the mainland colony from Kangaroo Island, although it was said to be blackish and gritty. Wheat for the damper was grown in the rich midlands soil, sown and harvested by hand, threshed by hand – the Swing rioters, ironically, were particularly useful in these tasks.

However, there was a definite absence of dairy foods, as there were few cows kept for milking. This was not good news for anyone who loved cheese (particularly the men from Wiltshire, – chalk and cheese country), or for babies.

Some indigenous plants were used, such as the cider gum tree – these would be tapped and the outflowing sap collected to make a slightly alcoholic drink. From the East Indies came sugar, which cost 4d./lb (as opposed to a shilling/lb in England) and tea was imported from India, both of these products being considered absolutely essential to everyone's well being morning and evening.

Fish and shellfish were abundant for the people lucky enough to be living near the coast or a river. There were large oysters, giant mussels and huge freshwater crayfish. Eggs were obtainable from ducks, emus, teal, quail or heron, but these wild delicacies gradually faded into Tasmanian food history as domesticated fowl were introduced and became more available to everyone.

When it was possible, everyone went to the pub, a tradition going back to the very early days of the colony, when there were shops which sold spirits and then pubs. The first free settlers, ex convicts soldiers and government officials all took part in drinking sessions. The liquor of choice (although there was not actually much choice about this) was rum, which dealers imported and by 1818 there were 11 pubs in Hobart Town alone. Later on the pubs (renamed inns), were less egalitarian but the quantity of rum which everyone drank was even greater. The excise duty was a useful source of income for the government. It was an easy way to make money for the local merchants. It also helped to ensure the happiness of the labour force – the local land commission reported: 'Wheat, the staff of life, is the standard for wages in other countries, here rum is the alpha and omega'.[4]

At the pub – and it was estimated that there was a pub for every 100 to 200 people in VDL – there was singing and dancing, sometimes to music played on the violin. It is said that the convicts, when in chains, would rattle their chains rhythmically to their singing. Rattle and hum? Men made up rude verses about the Governor, or the jailers, or the Army, and set them to the tunes of well known folk songs. One well known balladeer in the 1830s was Francis McNamara, or Frank the Poet. Singing was so popular that the crowds at hangings would sing together to support the condemned man in his last moments. A better way to go than the depressing sentiments of the local priest.

The liquor trade made a few men very well off indeed. One such entrepreneur was Anthony Fenn Kemp, an adventurer who arrived in Van Diemen's Land after a number of enterprises started by him had failed in various places, including France, Carolina and New South Wales. In 1800 he had returned to London with his girlfriend and their child Emily, going to Aldgate where his family had a profitable business trading in tobacco and rum. Kemp had originally inherited, as a very young man, a considerable sum of money in stock, cash and property but had spent this fortune in two years, hence his original departure to France. In France he had developed republican political views and from there he had travelled to America and on to New South Wales in Australia. By the time he was 22 he was a seasoned traveller, adventurer and a bit of a rogue. He knew the tobacco trade and also the spirits export business.

In New South Wales and also in Van Diemen's Land in the early years of the 19th century these commodities were in really high demand, the convicts being desperate for them, valuing them much more highly than they did sex or food.

Kemp now became Paymaster of the New South Wales Corps in Port Jackson. He knew the shipping agents in India, the Caribbean and Mauritius – Bengal rum was the most popular spirit and during his time as an officer at Port Jackson, he had used Regimental funds to buy goods and sell them on. He utilised the family business in London, Kemp & Potter (his father and brother in law), issuing promissory notes in the company's reputable name and the treasury bills which, as Corps Paymaster, he needed to pay the soldiers. The goods he bought were then sold on to his customers at enormous profit. He would also insist that the soldiers exchange their pay dockets for his goods rather than give them the cash due to them as pay.

In 1804 he arrived in Van Diemen's Land, having been appointed 2nd in Command to Colonel Paterson on board the Buffalo. Paterson's instructions were to settle the northern half of VDL and develop a town there. This was not a great success as the wrong site was selected, the community of 181 convicts and settlers suffering terrible hardships and illnesses and near starvation, many packing up and leaving. Kemp, after more adventures including bankruptcy, was still trying to make money and settle down.

Having at one point returned to London, he failed to patch up his difficulties with his father, who had not approved of his plan to marry his girlfriend, an ex convict named Judith Crawford. In a fit of pique he had abandoned the idea himself and departed to the other side of the world, leaving both Judith and his little daughter Emily to be cared for by his sister and her husband, the long suffering William Potter, his father's partner. He chose VDL, got married, had two more children and settled in Hobart Town, building a store in Macquarie Street. By 1820 Kemp controlled 80% of the liquor landed in Hobart, the duty producing half of the state's income. He supplied cognac brandy to the rich, rum to the poor and port wine to the cultured settlers, overcharging for all of them, and becoming a money lender as well, charging the astounding sum of 42% interest on a loan.

Now financially successful he became a magistrate, treating people he met with disdain (including Governor Davey – to whom he was so rude that on one occasion he was ejected summarily from Government House).

Back in London his father died and Mr William Potter, Kemp's brother in law, who had not received a penny back from Kemp's use of his promissory notes, or repayment of a loan he made to Kemp, removed the name Kemp from the business completely. In spite of his success in VDL, his family in England were glad to be rid of him. Later on, on a final visit to London he left his two new children in William Potter's care.

In VDL Kemp pursued a vendetta against the new Governor, Col.

William Sorell, an excellent, kindly man but 'married' to the beautiful Julia, who as Kemp discovered, was in fact the wife of a Lt. In the 21st Dragoons, and not 'married' to the Governor at all. Kemp, in spite of his own marital history and desertion of his first and second family, now turned into a Puritan, attacking the unfortunate couple as having 'Immoral Habits and pernicious example' He wrote to London requesting that Sorell be removed from office and in spite of Sorell's defence of himself and Julia, Sorell was actually recalled.

Kemp is an example of the sort of entrepreneur who could become successful in an embryo colony although of course not every entrepreneur behaves in quite so extravagant a manner. Kemp now metamorphosed into a country gentleman, improving the old cottage on the 800 acres he acquired at Kemp's Lakes. He built an elegant frontage to the house which he then renamed Mount Vernon. He bred merino sheep (bought with Potter's money) and extended his land to 3,400 acres. He bred racehorses which he ran on his own racecourse and Sambhur deer to enhance his pleasure grounds. The local town of Green Ponds renamed itself Kempton. 6

In all, Kemp fathered some 18 children and lived to a great age – 95, leaving his mark upon the island now officially called Tasmania, which happened in 1850s, the Tasmanian Constitution coming into effect with self-government in 1856. However, the name Tasmania for Van Diemen's Land had been in common use there since the 1820s. A guide to the island was published in 1823 – 'Godwin's Emigrant's Guide to Van Diemen's Land, More Properly Called Tasmania'. The free settlers preferred the term Tasmania, as Van Diemen's Land came to be associated with the stigma of convict transportation. The two terms co-existed until the 1856 constitution was established, after which everyone chose to relegate Van Diemen's Land to history.

There does not seem to be any direct contact by Kemp with the Pythouse rioters, except that Edmund White and Thomas Abree would have had to buy their supplies of spirits for the Wardour Castle Inn and The Dusty Miller from someone – and Kemp operated 80% of the imported spirits trade. It is to be hoped that Edmund, himself a wily operator and very well organised, would have negotiated a good price for his stock in trade.

Civilisation was becoming established on the island. For the children born to the settlers, the ex-convicts and the convicts, small schools were being set up in the colony. For the first few years convict and ex-convict teachers taught a small number of children, but in 1821 a new system evolved, with a superintendent of schools appointed. In 1825 Lord

Male and Female Orphan School at St John's Avenue, New Town 1833 designed by John Lee Archer

Bathurst of the British government, arranged for one seventh of all land grants to be made to the Church of England who were to use the income generated by this land, to provide religious and educational facilities for the colony.7 The English 'National' education system was introduced by the government and in each little township a state run school was established, very often with a close relationship to the church or chapel, but run on the state approved National system. In addition, under Governor Arthur an Orphan school was opened in 1825 to ensure that children did not follow in the footsteps of their convict parents or unmarried mothers. Many of these children were not, in fact, actually orphans at all, and the school was more like a Childrens' Home run by the state. The regime was a strict one, designed to produce good, honest domestic workers and labourers. If they did have a parent, visits were brief and rare being on the first Monday of every third month – January, April, July and October and from 11.00 am to 2.00 pm only. The visit had to be in the presence of the master or mistress. This was yet another of Governor Arthur's seemingly charitable attitudes towards the convicts in his care, but it could be called a form of social engineering, aimed at producing the type of worker the Colony needed.8

Religion too was becoming an important part of life in the colony. The free settlers tended to stick to the established Church of England, but many of the ex-convicts preferred the nonconformity of their rural English background. They were not interested in politics or radical thinking – what was most important for the ex-convicts, like those from Tisbury, was that they should earn enough money to build a home, to be able to afford for their family to eat, to provide education for their children and to have enough left over to be able to have a drink in the pub on a Saturday. Let others do the revolutionary thinking, it was enough to be free, healthy and comfortable and this is what the men wanted and why they worked. Which was, of course, what they had riotously assembled to achieve in the first place.

23
Red herrings and loose ends

WHEN THE NAPOLEONIC Wars came to an end, many of the officers (and men) in the armed services found themselves unemployed. One young man, a purser in the Royal Navy by the name of Francis Gerard Tabart, was one of these 'surplus to requirement' officers, retired on half pay. He had been born in 1789 to a Huguenot family and had served under the command of Francis Beaufort (the inventor of the Beaufort Scale of wind speed), although he had not, in spite of a family myth, been at the Battle of Trafalgar. He found work in the woollen industry at a weaving mill in Uley in Gloucestershire. However, this did not last as there was a depression in the clothing industry following the end of the Wars (far fewer uniforms now being required) and eventually Lt. Tabart decided to emigrate to Van Diemen's Land.1

Arriving there in 1830, by October 1832 thanks to his naval service record, Tabart found himself in receipt of a grant of land near what was to be called the town of Andover in the midlands area of VDL. Not part of the earliest settlements, this area is softly hilly wooded land in the eastern Marshes area, reminiscent of the land in Hampshire and Wiltshire and indeed many of the names of the settlements are from the south of England. They were not the most immediately desirable blocks of land in VDL which had already been taken up by earlier settlers, but Francis Tabart settled in happily, first pitching a tent and then building a basic cabin, which was swiftly followed by a substantial log house, with five rooms downstairs and

The restored log cabin at Fonthill VDL – photo Rediscover Tasmania

three more rooms in the roof. The walls are of solid logs and the hipped roof is of wooden shingles and this extends out over its porch/verandah. In October 1832 Tabart wrote to one of his daughters heading his letter from 'Fonthill'. This excellent cabin, now restored, provided very well for his family, but it was only the beginning.

He needed a larger home as he had married twice, once to Elizabeth Dulot and secondly to Emma Lewes – eventually there were 14 children from these marriages. So Lt. Tabart set to and arranged to have a large new house built and by 1843 he had a stone house on his land. He called this property 'Fonthill' and it has three steep gables on its front façade, a large hipped roof and unusually, ogee windows. The entrance which is to the side of the property, (not in the middle of the front as was normal in the Georgian style properties being built in VDL at the time) has an ogee shaped stone surround, with stone piers and double entrance doors. This is an unusual arrangement for VDL, where most of the larger houses are of standard Georgian design, front door sitting in the middle of symmetrically placed sash windows, entrance hall running front to back with rooms leading off the wide hall. Tabart's Fonthill has its main rooms running across the front with the grand entrance to the side. There is no curved central bay to the front either, since the steeply gabled 'Gothick' style required that the projecting central bay be squared off. The roof was originally shingled but is now in the vernacular corrugated iron, painted grey so that no rust colour appears.

The gallery at Fonthill Abbey – Graphical and literary illustrations of Fonthill Abbey Wiltshire 1823

Apparently the house was built with convict labour, 17 men, and may possibly have been designed by one of them, Andrew Bell, a competent but frequently drunk Scottish stonemason. The sandstone stonework is of good quality, and the window margins are said to be Scottish in style. Certainly there are Scottish baronial style indications but there are no conical towers, battlements or projecting carvings and the ogee windows and doors are not particularly Scottish in style. These, in fact have an uncanny resemblance to the windows in parts of William Beckford's Fonthill Abbey.

The banqueting house at Wardour Castle – photo by author

The interior of the house is properly plastered but Dr Eric Ratcliff mentions that the joinery, of New South Wales cedar resembling Honduras mahogany, is not of a particularly high standard and perhaps Tabart did not manage to find a good carpenter amongst his assigned convict labourers.

In the dining-room however there is a magnificent piece of carpentry, built in English oak, a revolving sideboard/dumb waiter decorated

Ogee windows at Stouts Hill Gloucestershire – Tasmanian Gothic Stuff by Elizabeth Barham

very simply and elegantly with ogee panelling. It is Regency in style and may have been part of a gift of furniture to Tabart by a previous Lt. Gov. of the colony – the Artic explorer Sir John Franklin, who, on leaving the colony in 1843, bequeathed to Tabart some furniture, including chairs, a settee and a card table. This too is apparently a family legend.2 Certainly the piece is by a sophisticated cabinet maker and is in English oak unlike the remainder of the joinery in the house.

The name he gave his new house – Fonthill – suggests that Tabart was well aware of the Gothick Fonthill Abbey built by William Beckford. This magnificent folly was put up for sale by Beckford in 1822 and bought by a Mr. John Farquhar – this being at a time when Francis

Ogee window in the dinning room at Fonthill VDL – ibid

Tabart had left the Navy and was employed at Uley in the cloth mill, between 1819 and 1825. It has been suggested that Tabart, out of work by 1825, heard of the woollen mill which had been created at Fonthill by George Mortimer, Farquhar's nephew, and visited, perhaps to seek employment, or even perhaps at Mortimer's suggestion to advise him3. The cloth mill, situated at the end of Fonthill lake, and close to the Beckford Arms, would have given Tabart the opportunity of visiting Fonthill Abbey and the interesting buildings in the immediate area, including Wardour Castle grounds. He would have seen the ogee windows in the Abbey, and also those in the Banqueting House at Wardour Castle. Fonthill Abbey itself was the epitome of Gothick fancy, although its exterior was more cathedral than castle.

Fonthill VDL and its main, side entrance – ibid

Lawn Lodge, Fonthill – author's photograph

If Tabart stayed locally, it is possible that he was at the Beckford Arms, Fonthill Gifford, which is on the crossroads close to the end of the lake where the Mortimer cloth mill and cottages were situated. There his host would have been Aaron Tabor.

The association between Fonthill in VDL and Fonthill Abbey is tenuous, but the really surprising aspect is the similarity in style between the colonial property and the gatehouses built on the Fonthill estate some 20 years later. Designed by William Burn, the Scottish architect, working for the Marquis of Westminster, whose purchase of the Fonthill Abbey estate from John Benett was finally concluded in 1838, these gatehouses were created after the new Fonthill Abbey was completed for the Marquis and his family. Mr Burn was commissioned to design two new lodges; Tisbury Lodge close to the Beckford Arms and Lawn Lodge on the Fonthill Gifford to Newtown road. 4 As may be seen these are uncannily reminiscent of Fonthill in VDL. Completely unlike the other new lodges at Fonthill Abbey for the Marquis which re of brick, stone and timber construction, these are simply elegant houses in the Scottish Baronial style, as is Fonthill in VDL.

However there appears to be no valid connection. If the dates were reversed i.e. the Fonthill Abbey lodges built first and Fonthill VDL later, it would seem much more logical.

The ogee windows at Fonthill could have been inspired by the gallery window at Beckford's Abbey although they are a very simplified version. Elizabeth Barsham suggests that Tabart might simply have seen pictures of Fonthill Abbey and been inspired to recreate his own Gothick folly.[5] K. Jane Evans suggests that the windows were inspired by Stouts hill – a Cotswold stone house or Owlpen Manor, another Cotswold property, both in the Uley area of Gloucestershire. Equally, Tabart might have seen the Gothick inspired Banqueting House at Wardour.

A last thought on Fonthill VDL – by the time it was being built in the early 1840s, both Thomas Burt and William Abree had received their pardons and were free men – how wonderful to think they might have worked there – Thomas on the sawmill or carpentry and William as one of the competent stonemasons. There is absolutely no proof for this speculation! Interestingly, the Hobart Press reports the death of William Beckford in 1844 – his name was clearly known to residents of VDL, amongst whom were, of course, the Pythouse rioters.[6]

At the time of the riots in November 1830, the landlord of the Beckford Arms in Fonthill Gifford was 38-year-old Aaron Tabor – a name rather similar to to Tabart – but apparently they were not related.

Perhaps they met when and if Francis Tabart visited George Mortimer at his cloth mill. The two properties were very close. Aaron, who came from Mere, a village not far away, was the son of Thomas Tabor and Aaron had married, in Gillingham just over the border in Dorset, Frances Jeanes on 11th April 1819. In September 1822 they had a son, John, followed by a daughter, Frances. John was a young boy at the time of the rioting, eight years old and no doubt knew young William Turner, who in turn became a frequent visitor to the Beckford Arms later on, recording his visit there years later when he saw, he thought, Thomas Vinen returned from VDL.

In 1850 John Tabor, aged 28, married Emily Alice Osmond, the niece of Edwin Osmund the then well known organist of St John's Church in Tisbury. Emily's brother(another Edwin) was also the organist for the church, (where there is a delightful stained glass window showing his choristers, installed in his memory in 1900). John and Emily ran the Beckford Arms in their turn since John's father Aaron had died in 1848. The 1851 census records the young couple living there, with William Burton as their ostler and Mary Parham as a female servant.[7]

However, in 1853 John and Emily decide to emigrate to VDL where they take on the Longley Arms Inn at Longley in the Huon region, south of Hobart. According to Peter Gregg, John Tabor's 2 X great grandson, John became a brewer and was heavily involved in the building and development of the region through his membership of the Longley Road Trust, the Huon Road Trust and the Victoria Road Trust.[8]

John and Emily had six children, four surviving into adulthood. John died in 1882 but Emily survived until 1919, including experiencing the terrible bush fire in 1897, which destroyed most of Longley including the hotel and the newly built Anglican church. The local newspaper reported that, 'Mrs Tabor a widow, was with difficulty rescued from her burning house by her sons and taken to the bridge'.[9]

A very unpleasant experience for a 70 year old widow. The newspaper report goes on to describe the terrible bush fire, including the fact that animals tethered in their stalls and sheds, were burnt alive. It is an area where bush fires are still common.

Would John and Emily have known any of the men involved in the Pythouse riots who had arrived in VDL 20 years before? By the time they reached VDL, the rioters had all been pardoned and moved on or settled in VDL. There must occasionally have been talk about the great riot and awareness of what had happened, particularly if it was known that John and Emily came from Fonthill Gifford. According to Peter Gregg, many of their descendants still live in the area.

The last red herring is a very small one. It is the name of a property in VDL – Malahide – which suggests a link between the Tisbury area and VDL.

The current Lord Arundell is John Tennant Arundell, the 11th Baron Talbot of Malahide, who was born in 1957 – the heir to the Malahide title is his son the Hon. John Richard Arundell, born 1998.

Malahide Castle, Fingal, Ireland – from A tale of two Malahides by James JHarvey and Keith Harvey for Tintean 2022

The title 'Lord High Admiral of Malahide and the Seas Adjoining' was awarded in 1475 by King Edward IV to a descendant of a Norman knight, Sir Richard de Talbot, who had arrived in Ireland in 1174 and who had received a grant of land around the village of Malahide, on the east coast of Ireland. The Talbot family had constructed a fortified dwelling there in the form of a motte and bailey and followed this original building with a substantial castle, which as a family they managed to retain and occupy for 800 years (except for a short period under Cromwell lasting from 1653-60, when they were banished to Connaught).

In 1831 the title Baron Talbot of Malahide was held by a woman, Margaret Talbot, the widow of one Richard Talbot. This was originally an Irish peerage title, but in 1856 her grandson was created Baron Talbot de Malahide, of Malahide in the county of Dublin under the English peerage. After passing through a number of inheritors – sons, younger brothers, even cousins and second cousins, the title passed to John Tennant Arundell, the 11th Baron Talbot of Malahide, who lives at Hook Manor, Donhead, close to the family seat of Wardour.

The wonderful Malahide Castle in the county of Fingal in Ireland is in the coastal village of Malahide, just north of Dublin. The oldest parts of the building are of 12th century origin but the main building has a

Malahide, Fingal, Tasmania in 1899 – ibid

distinctly Gothick flavour, crenellated and with ogee windows in the towers, so presumably largely rebuilt and enlarged in the early 19th century. The Talbots, despite fighting on the losing side, survived the Jacobite Rebellion but converted from Roman Catholicism whilst still managing to support Catholic emancipation and Irish rights. At the Battle of the Boyne it is said, 14 members of the family sat down to eat before the battle, and only one returned home afterwards. Malahide Castle still holds a wonderful collection of Jacobite Rebellion paintings. However, the Castle is no longer in the possession of the family. Death duties following the demise of Lord Milo Talbot in 1973 forced his sister Rose Talbot to sell the family's valuable possessions and the castle itself. The Irish state now owns the castle, the furniture being sold to private buyers and collectors. On Milo's death the English barony became extinct although the Irish barony of 1831 passed to his third cousin and then eventually to the current holder, Lord Arundell the 11th Baron Talbot of Malahide.

Rose Talbot, bereft of her family home, made the enormous decision to move to another Malahide – the property owned by the Talbot family in VDL. In 1820 a 36-year-old member of the family, William Talbot, had arrived in Hobart, proposing to settle. To obtain a grant of land, William had to travel to New South Wales in Australia where the then Governor, Lachlan Macquarie was able to grant him 2,000 acres and six convicts as personal servants. William and his assigned convicts travelled back to Hobart where Lt. Gov. Sorell granted him land. However, this particular block of land had already been granted to another settler and it was 1824 before William Talbot was offered alternative land. This time he obtained a grant for 3,000 acres sited in the north-east of the colony, to the east of the main road between Ross and Launceston, 70 miles south of Launceston. He named his new property Malahide after the family seat in Ireland and the nearby town was named Fingal. The land became a sheep station.

In 1830 another family member arrived – William's nephew Samuel Talbot. He had been granted land of his own but helped William to manage Malahide. On the death of the unmarried William, in 1845, Samuel inherited Malahide, passing it in turn to another of Williams' nephews, Richard Gilbert Talbot. The acreage by this time amount to 20,000 with 25,000 sheep and 1700 cattle running on it. The original timber house had burned down in 1835 and a larger house was built, retaining the old stables. Eventually the property had a number of buildings as well as the main house – a manager's house, cottages, stables, a coach house and barns.

Lord Milo Talbot visited VDL in 1951, arranged for some necessary restoration work to the house, collected Australian paintings and as a successful amateur botanist, collected plant specimens from VDL which he took back to Malahide in Ireland for his botanical garden there.

When Rose, his sister, arrived in VDL in 1976 she made alterations to the property and organised the thriving agricultural business, training her cousin a Naval Officer, Richard Talbot, in the management of the estate. The Talbot family still live there, in the now listed property, running a very successful agricultural business.[10]

A real red herring then – but the name Malahide is so unusual that a connection seemed inevitable. The connection is the tenuous one of the current Baron Talbot of Malahide being Lord Arundell and living close to Wardour and Tisbury. There is no evidence of any Pythouse rioters being assigned to a member of the Talbot family in 1831.

Just coincidences then – Tabart, Tabor, Talbot, Tisbury and Tasmania. Loose ends.

24
Aftermath

The God who took a little child
And set him in the midst,
And promised him His mercy mild,
As, by thy Son, Thou didst:
Look down upon our children dear,
So gaunt, so cold, so spare,
And let their images appear
Where lords and gentry are!
Charles Dickens: The Hymn of the Wiltshire Laborers: Verse 2 :
published 14th February 1846

THE EFFECTS OF the Swing Riots on the lives of the rioters' families in the south of England were catastrophic and Tisbury was no exception.

These young men, whose average age at transportation was only 29, had mostly married at a young age, which was typical for working agricultural labourers at the time and often had quite large families by the time they were 30. Many of them were related, some blood relatives, some by marriages in the small rural community. One example is the Viney/Vinen/Vining family; Thomas Viney's sister Elizabeth married Charles Martin, his sister Harriett married Robert Obourne. His sister Jean married George Moxham and their son Morgan Moxham married first Eliza Snook and subsequently Eliza Vinen, daughter of Thomas's brother Isaac. Robert

Barrett's wife Eliza came from the Mould family (two James Moulds were transported). The Jerrards were related to the Barretts, Charles Jerrard's sister marrying Andrew Barrett. Not only did the men literally disappear overnight, some never to be seen again by their families, there was no closure for the families – they were simply unable to find out where the men had gone, they did not know whether they would return, whether they were safe and well or even whether they were still alive. Few people could write (Elizabeth Martin was an exception) and when one or two did eventually manage to return it was not always a great success (the Barrett brothers, for example).

Financially the families were deprived of the income from the main breadwinner. Young mothers were forced to work in the fields as agricultural labourers, their income having to be made up from the parish relief system which was humiliating. For the month of December 1834, the Fonthill Gifford overseers' payments book records that Charlotte Macey (wife of Samuel, aged 43 with five children dependent upon her earnings) received £1.11s 2d from the parish. Of this 16s was for the family to live on, 2s was for the rent and a further 13s.2d was paid to her in cash – a sum which gave her about 4s. 3d. per week when bread was recorded in the overseers' book as costing 11d. per gallon. Charlotte died in 1851 aged 65, no doubt completely worn out.

Thomas Burt's wife Ann also received some money for Christmas that year from Fonthill Gifford's overseers – 19s.4d for the month for herself and three children. By 1854 Thomas and Ann's daughter Anna Maria is recorded as being in the Tisbury union workhouse. Eventually she married into the Viney family, taking her two illegitimate children Thomas and Emma. Perhaps these two offspring were why she had been confined to the workhouse. She and her husband William Viney, another agricultural labourer, went to live in Normanton hamlet at Durnford in Wiltshire, working for the Rawlings family farm. They had seven children of their own, but no doubt a crowded tied farm cottage on someone else's farm was better than being in the workhouse, or dependent upon the charity of the overseers. Thomas Burt's son John however is a success story – he leaves Wiltshire to join the Police force in London, living in Stockwell and then Brixton and he retires as a Police Sergeant in 1874 with a pension for himself and his wife Sarah of £65.17s. p.a. – or approximately £1.5s. per week – a respectable sum even in 1874.'

By 1841 Thomas Rixon's daughter Anna Maria is also in the workhouse aged 25, as is Mary Snook aged 85, and William Snook 15, Marie 12 and Martha 9. Mary and Charlotte Cheverill are there too.

Between 1847 and 1850 six of the offenders who were sent to gaol for minor offences had names with which the rioters would be familiar – James Viney, William Turner, Eliza Mould and James Martin all received short gaol sentences for 'misbehaviour in the union workhouse', James Viney being sent to the county gaol for three months, the others for less. Henry Snook and William Jerrard received one month and three weeks respectively for 'wearing away clothing belonging to the Tisbury union workhouse'.

By 1851 Anna Maria Rixon is sadly still there, and so is Eliza Jerrard aged 37. Thomas Topp's mother Mary who having had Thomas out of wedlock, married James Trimby in 1837, but he died in 1851, so Mary too is now in the workhouse.

Of course not all poverty can be blamed upon the absence of the Pythouse rioters – there were 97 people in the Tisbury union workhouse in 1851, including more members of the Mould and Moxham families. However, the lack of breadwinners clearly exacerbated the difficulties the families had to face.

Sadly, in 1836, Thomas Abree's wife Mary, living in Hindon, died during a night of 'Thunder and violent winds again', as recorded by the Hindon chaplain the Rev. Harbin. This storm however was not as severe as the 1831 storm in May when the *Salisbury & Winchester Journal* reported 'a dreadful storm of hail, thunder and lightning lasting nearly two hours. The hail was in some places three feet in depth. 'The deep muttering of the thunder and the oft succeeding flash glaring amid the hills, were distinctly seen and heard in the immediate neighbourhood of Salisbury. The appearance of the conflicting elements, looking towards Fonthill, was at once singular and awful.'

Life continued in Tisbury with the Tisbury Fair in May 1833 reported as being well supplied with stock. Cows and calves went off freely at advanced prices. And the yew tree in the churchyard was reported as now measuring in May 1833 '37 feet in circumference and the limbs are proportionally large. It is hollow and entered by means of a rustic gate and 17 persons lately breakfasted in its interior'. It was said to have been planted many generations ago by one of the Arundell family, but since it predates the 12th century church by a considerable margin this seems unlikely.

Some families were managing well – the Martins, Charles and Elizabeth, left for London, where he became gardener to a gentleman in a private residence. Charles had served his sentence of two months' hard labour in Devizes with his brother-in-law Robert Obourne and no further offences are recorded. In London the family thrived, eventually being able to buy a small new house for themselves. With them lived two nephews, George Andrews and James Obourne. Elizabeth's letters to her brother Thomas in Van Diemen's Land are full of interesting information about their lives in London, a visit to the Great Exhibition in 1851, visits to Tisbury to see parents, gossip about what was happening in Tisbury, who married who, who was prospering and who wasn't and the constant wish for Thomas to return to England. When she receives a letter from him telling her that he has now married, she is however wonderfully accepting of her sister-in-law and longs to see her new nephews and nieces who were born in VDL. She tells him that their parents have moved down to a cottage at Knapp, an area in Vicarage Road, Tisbury, which has a superb view out over the church and its surroundings. Their sister Mary comes to live with the Martins in the 1850s.

The Targett and Moxham families live on Common Lane, West Tisbury, which is the road running out of Tisbury towards Newtown and eventually Pythouse. They live next door to one another for many years, the Targetts with ten children and the Moxhams with eight. John is evidently chastened by his year's imprisonment in Devizes New Prison for his conviction for rioting and does not offend again, but Andrew Moxham, who was luckily not convicted in 1831, is committed to the New Prison at Devizes in November 1839, with Charles Stevens, for three months each for destroying game at West Tisbury.

In 1838 Edmund White's father John, also a blacksmith, dies aged 58.

Samuel Eyres is settled in Tisbury Row, with his wife and three children. At Totterdale Cross, up the track from Tisbury Row to Jobbers Lane, the Jerrard family keep a wary eye open for parish officials or the militia. Father Charles Jerrard, who was not arrested at the time of the riots, climbs up into the chimney, standing on the pot lug, until the intruders pass by. It is to be hoped that the fire is not burning at the time. By 1851 both he and his wife Mary have died, but their son Joshua, grandson William aged 18 plus Charles' daughter Ann and William Barrett with their small son Henry aged 3, are still living at Totterdale Cross cottage. Andrew's mother Elizabeth Barrett is with them. They are keen members of the Zion Hill Independent Church in Tisbury, as are a number of the rioters' families.[1] William Snook's sister for example, is still in Church Street, but now living with Mr and Mrs John Bevis – Mr Bevis is a tallow chandler (makes and sells candles), and they are members of Zion Hill Congregationalist chapel.

In December 1842 John Snook of Wardour, John Barrett and William Macey of West Tisbury are committed to the New Prison at Devizes for three months each, for destroying game in their respective parishes. John is from the Snook family in Church Street Tisbury. William is Charlotte and Samuel Macey/Banstone's son, now aged 21 and John Barrett having returned from VDL, is in trouble once more. In 1843 he is charged with stealing a sheep, the property of farmer Joseph Alford.

The same year William Turner and Robert Jerrett (sic) (probably Jerrard) receive three months each for destroying game and are committed to the New Prison at Devizes. William Turner is later convicted for assaulting John Tabor, the landlord of the Beckford Arms – who subsequently emigrates to VDL. William has to pay 2/- and costs. This no doubt upsets his very respectable family, who have been farming in the area for many generations.

The Rixons become very well known in the village as successful stonemasons and carvers, a descendant James Rixon being responsible for the intriguing carved heads which decorate many of Tisbury's old cottages. Thomas Rixon himself had died in VDL in 1835 before receiving his official pardon and it is said that his wife never knew whether she was a 'wife or a widow'. Most of the families are working as agricultural labourers on the minimum wage.

In the Tisbury area there was at least one other form of work – quarrying and stonemasonry. The main commercial centre for this was the adjacent village of Chilmark, which had provided the stone for Salisbury Cathedral and the stonemasons to work it. Tisbury and other villages in the immediate area had small family-run quarries. Otherwise the population was still dependent upon agriculture for its income.

The men who were acquitted in the rioting settled back into village life – William Scott in the Quarry, dying in 1885, and a neighbour of James Cheverill, who is there with his wife and three children. Robert Obourne and his wife Harriet (Viney) have a number of children, many of whom do not reach maturity and they live at Ridge, near Chilmark.

They are close-knit, these village families. In her monograph on the rioters, Dr Mary Dalton comments upon how alike the young men seem to be when they are mustered for examination in VDL. The tallest man measured 5ft 9' and the shortest 5ft 2'. This gave an average height of 5ft 6' which is in marked contrast, comments Dr Dalton, with present Britain, of 5ft 10 (in 1984). In 2021 this average height is still 5ft 10'.[2] All of them except one has brown hair and whiskers (one has red hair) and of the others two are going grey. None of them has brown eyes – this would be very unusual today – they all have blue, grey or 'grey to blue' eyes. It shows that the community of Tisbury was quite closed, with few brown eyed, blond or black haired incomers[3]. People at that time did not travel far so did not meet with many people from other counties or from larger towns or cities.

It would be wonderful to be able to report that the Pythouse riots contributed to a rise in agricultural labourer's wages, but this, in spite of John Benett's assurances to the House of Commons, was not true. Wiltshire labourers remained amongst the very lowest paid workers in England. In 1831 Henry Hunt spoke in the Commons about a landlord of his acquaintance whose estate had, 40 years previously, been let at £600 p.a. when the labourers weekly wage was 6s. per week. Now, said Hunt, the same gentleman's estate is let at £1,800 per annum but the labourer's weekly wage is still only 7s. The estate to which Hunt was referring was, of course, that of John Benett at Pythouse. Benett tried to explain this away by his purchase of £10,000 worth of tithes, but in the end both speakers were reprimanded for introducing personal matters into a Commons debate.[4]

However, it is apparent that Mr Benett felt he was doing his best for the poor of his neighbourhood as in 1839 the Morning Chronicle, a national newspaper, printed a contribution which stated that Mr Benett had allowed the poor people of Hindon a space in a plantation on his estate in which they could grow potatoes for their own use. They were allowed to 'grub up the brushwood to reclaim the soil' to do this. Next year Mr Benett would take the freshly cultivated land back and allow them a new area of scrub 'to break up'. The contributor reported that the potatoes grown this way were excellent. Normally pigs would have been used to do the grubbing up but no doubt this was an excellent way of killing two birds with one stone and appearing to be charitable at the same time. In January 1833 the *South Wilts Journal* reported that 'Mr Benett has as usual at this season distributed large quantities of fat beef and clothing amongst the poor in the neighbourhood of Tisbury'.

The year 1834, on the passing of the new Poor Law Act, finds Mr Benett writing to Colonel Charles A'court, the assistant poor law commissioner on the subject of poverty in the Tisbury area.

> You call this a 'sadly pauperized district'. – I know not from what you take your information on this point, but I do know from 40 years observation that the poor were never so well fed – house or cloathed – or more contented than they are now, and the Paymasters are equally well satisfied, and have only dreaded your operations.[5]

This new Poor Law Amendment Act, passed in 1834 as part of the 'reforming' current government, was derisively called the 'Poor Man's Robbery Bill'. Parishes had been forced into poor law unions, focussed entirely upon the workhouse. Wage subsidies, child allowances, the payment of rent and the provision of clothes and fuel stopped. Relief was only to be given, except under exceptional circumstances, by the poor law union.

By 1839 Benett is claiming, according to Colonel A'court, that he is paying 9s. a week, whilst other farmers in the area are paying only 7s or 8s a week. Thus, Benett claims, his employees would not be able to claim the 1s.6d. per week apparently available for every child above three in each family, due to the higher wage he is paying them. Colonel A'court considers that, 'in the Tisbury union …. they appear to me to do as badly, if not worse paid than in any other union in my inspection'.

It is perhaps worth mentioning that Mr Benett was not a guardian of the Tisbury union but felt he had the right to interfere with the way it was being run and that whilst the two Minute Books for the years 1835-6 and 1840-43 have survived, the Minute Book for 1838-39 is missing from the archive.[6]

By 1838 the state of the workhouse in Church Street in Tisbury, still in use, is recorded as appalling. It was a huge, old, decaying building, damp with water running down the inside walls, the floors having to be mopped three times a day. The water supply in the well was contaminated by seepage from the adjacent churchyard burial ground. The place was infested with mice, rats and bugs. It was known locally as the 'dead house' although the mortuary was actually sited in a small adjacent building. It was not until 1868 that the new Tisbury union workhouse was opened at the top of Monmouth Road.

In spite of Benett's assurances that he was paying better wages, a petition was presented to the Commons by Mr T Duncombe on behalf of six men from Fonthill Gifford parish – Nicholas Macey, Henry Lovett, William Gilbert, Samuel Neil, James Macey and John Hacker. The two Maceys were in fact Samuel's brothers. This was published in *The Times* on May 14th 1840. In the petition, the petitioners stated that they are employed at the rate of 9s. per week, that each of them has a wife and five or six children to support by his labour and that in consequence of the price of provisions they find it impossible to supply themselves with a sufficient quantity of barley and potatoes as their income is only 21/2d per day for each individual member of the family and this has to find them food, raiment, washing and house-rent, 'being a sum far less than the cost of keeping a dog'.

The petition goes on to state that the petitioners, having learned to read by the kindness of a now deceased clergyman, have found that the promised changes under the new Poor Law Act, rather than improving their standard of living, have in fact lowered the wage paid, that there are therefore more labourers available to work, especially single men who offer their labour for four or five shillings a week rather than go into the workhouse. Interestingly, they quote that before they learned to read they were in a state of ignorance and believed what they were told was true, but now they are enabled to know a 'hawk from a handsaw'. This quote is from Hamlet, so whoever wrote the petition was properly educated. Incidentally a 'handsaw' was a small hawk, or heronshaw.

Before the passing of the new Poor Law Act each family would have received, in addition to the wage of 9s. a week, a supplement from the vestry of 3s. 6d per week. i.e. the new Poor Law Act had reduced their income by more than a quarter. The petitioners had now heard that the overseers at Fonthill Gifford had obtained warrants to distrain upon the few remaining articles of furniture which the petitioners possess, owing to their inability to pay a poor-rate charged upon the cottages which they were renting. They therefore request that the Commons repeal the new Poor Law Act.[7] It does not do so, so presumably the families lost their remaining bits of furniture and continued to starve or were consigned to the workhouse.

In the meantime Mr Benett gives a dinner for the Hindon troop of the Wiltshire Yeomanry Cavalry to thank them for their support during the rioting and another for his own employees when an ox was killed and a gallon of 'real Wiltshire stingo' given to each man. No such generosity is shown towards the families of the transported labourers.

25
A Changing Society

THE 1830S SAW the end of the Georgian monarchy. Although the young Queen Victoria was related to the Georges and to William IV, she was distant enough to be a symbol of a brave new regime. With the help (from 1840) of her consort, Albert, she began to preside over a nation dominated by new industry, an emerging professional and middle classes, the spread of Britain's influence throughout the world and the creation of an empire which would have no rival.

Whilst Britain continued to extend its empire, Europe saw the spread of nationalism. The numbers of schoolchildren and university students rose sharply, being taught in their national language became the norm and this improved the rate of literacy, although even in the 1840s this was still only about 50% even in Britain and France. Most people still classed themselves by their religion and region rather than by the country of their birth, and many countries in Europe still had numerous patois-speaking groups rather than a national language.

Land, its tenure and methods of agriculture still dominated the way of life for the rural English workforce during the century preceding 1850, but now the increasing needs of industry dictated that change must happen. Traditionally the ownership of land had been through inheritance – to make changes for the common good it would have to become a commodity – i.e. easily bought and sold. These potential new buyers needed to be able to develop agriculture as a productive resource for the whole country and to be incentivised by the land becoming as profit making as investing in industry might. In addition the agricultural labourer and his family would have to be released from the drudgery and squalor of working the land into the freedom and mobility of working in the non-agricultural sectors of the economy.[1]

All this required radical thinking – turning a smaller agricultural force into a more efficient means of production and eliminating the feudal ownership and paternalistic attitudes of the old landlords and aristocratic estate owners.

The first step, as we have seen, was the abolition by means of the Enclosures Acts of the remaining areas of community owned fields, pastures and woodlands. These passed into the hands of landlord farmers. Secondly the attachment of agricultural workers to their places of work had to be broken so that they could be released into industrial work. However, food production would be even more important as industrialisation increased in the towns and cities, so agriculture must be made more efficient by mechanisation and improvements to animal production. This, whilst good in principle, did not bode well for the future of the world. The eventual results of this mechanisation has resulted in the fact that in 1820 it took ten minutes of human labour to produce 1kg of wheat but by the 2020s it takes less than two seconds to produce the same quantity. However, the downside of this efficiency requires a massive use of fossil fuels- it takes 100ml of diesel to produce that 1kg of wheat.[2]

Throughout Europe the conquering French armies during the Napoleonic period preached 'the abolition of tithes, feudality and seigneurial rights' – thus spreading the word throughout northern France, north and central Italy, the low countries, Switzerland and west Germany. Catholicism and the influence of the church slowed the land revolution in Spain and southern parts of Italy.[3]

In Britain the Speenhamland System may have disincentivised workers and the passing of the Poor Law Amendment Act in 1834 did not solve the problems of low wages and an inadequate relief system. In 1846 there were still a million paupers in Britain.

Mr Benett was probably not a great deal more concerned with his own interests than other landowners at the time. Many in the upper echelons were concerned mainly with their own cultural pleasures, certainly not with ensuring that everyone had equal opportunities or rights. Such thoughts did not enter the heads of those who made political or financial policy in the early 19th century. The 18th century had been known as the age of elegance,

'*A Memento of the Great Public Question of Reform, 1832*', mezzotint

a balance being kept between a controlled monarchy, a Parliament which dispensed comparatively sensible laws and a church which was powerful but still respected. The advent of the 19th century with its rapid industrialisation, mechanisation and religious nonconformism brought changed attitudes.

The elegance of former country life with its cultivated estates, rich farmlands and apparently contented peasantry became disturbed, with increasing undercurrents of discontent bubbling up – initially well controlled – but gradually becoming more apparent, more unmanageable by the elite. Poor people, both in the countryside and in the newly industrialised towns and cities started to become aware that by getting together to put forward a claim for higher wages or improvements, they were more likely to succeed. 'Combining' then became the new bête noire for the ruling class, as it could be seen that such a strategy might well undermine the status quo.

Roger Wells in his article 'Social protest, class, conflict and consciousness in the English countryside' argues that between 1790 and 1834 the agricultural labourers in the south became the victims of an aggressive agrarian capitalism, which destroyed the old paternalistic social order.[4] This gave rise to an awareness of the disparities in the social system just as industrialisation did in the larger towns and cities of England at that time. The new Poor Law exacerbated the discontent, since the larger landowners tended to become guardians of the new poor law unions, thus putting the control of any benefits into the hands of the very people who employed and paid them. Wells argues that this change in rural society, growing over the years following the Napoleonic Wars, resulted in the Swing Riots and the unrest which followed the changes in the Poor Laws.

There was concern amongst the gentry that the agricultural rioting was led by political agitators. The assistant poor law commissioner, Charles A'court wrote in 1834 that he could:

> state with confidence that not distress... but political excitement, was the sole cause of the disturbances... the poor labourers were led away by designing individuals in situations far above want, whose only object appeared to be the division, if not the destruction of property.[5]

Thus Benett's concern about what he deemed to be a revolutionary sash worn by the young Charles Jerrard. However it would seem that the majority of the rioters genuinely thought that they had a right to try to get higher wages and that lower rents and tithes would enable the farmers to offer these higher wages. They did not feel that they were in any way breaking the law. Indeed they thought that the farmers were on their side, as Col. Mair wrote in a report to the Home Office on 26th November 1830: 'The small farmers if they do not aid are evidently glad to see the labourers at work fancying it will tend to their benefits, lowering of tythes etc.'.

Larger farmers were also keen to see the lowering of rents and tithes, agreeing that these concessions would enable them to raise wages. It was a balance of power game. Farmers in the Salisbury area did indeed to some extent sympathise and understand the labourers' needs – in Whiteparish 'Squire Bristowe' was reported to have sent beer to the 100 strong mob and that Richard Webb, another local farmer had given permission for his machine to be damaged and that this was done in the presence of both Squire Bristowe and his guest 'Squire Wynne'. In Salisbury market farmers were requested to assist the yeomanry, but refused to do so.

In Tisbury itself some of the rioters were initially led by a local farmer, Alford, a tenant of Lord Arundell. This followed his proposal to the vestry for a wage rise in the area. In the end the proposed meeting was held at Alford's farmhouse and was attended by some of the major Arundell tenant farmers and two parish overseers. They discussed 'what proposals they should make to the labourers the following day as to increase of wages'.

Details of this meeting are in an undated letter from Alford to Lord Arundell, which Arundell then sent on to the Home Secretary on 6th December 1830.[6]

Another local large farmer, Turner, who was also a parish overseer, told Alford that the mob was destroying his threshing machine with his permission. The labourers in both Fonthill and Tisbury told *The Times* correspondent that 'the farmers expressed no objection'.

It was further reported in *The Times* that 'the farmers were at the bottom of the riots – they gave them beer and urged them to excess'.[7]

Was this because the farmers themselves wanted and needed rent reductions? If rent and tithe reductions could be achieved, wages could rise and farmers' contributions towards poor relief would be reduced. Non-Anglicans in particular resented the tithe and poor relief contributions demanded and administered by the Anglican-dominated vestry. Arundell himself was a Catholic and many of the farmers in the area were either Catholic or nonconformist. So there were differences between Arundell and his tenant farmers on the one hand and Benett on the other – Benett saw the riots as a direct political and economic threat, but Arundell and his tenant farmers were more kindly disposed towards the labourers' distress and demands. The letter expressed the old paternalistic view of society and Benett epitomised the new thrusting changes in agricultural economy.

Benett became even more unpopular after the Poor Law Amendment Act was passed, which established the local unions and the implementation of new laws. This act affected the management of poor relief and in particular

Painting by George Hayter (1792-1871) commemorating the passing of the Great Reform Act of 1832

those who had been left to deal with their family disaster of transportation of the family bread winner.

In the Tisbury area the transition period between the passing of the act and the setting up of the new union caused problems. The then rector of Fonthill Gifford, the Rev. John Hill wrote in January 1835 that, 'the magistrates have ceased to order relief and the assistant commissioners have not yet begun to act in this district'.

In May of the same year the assistant overseer of East Tisbury reported that the parish was no longer providing employment on the roads and the poor, 'are now either roaming about the country in fruitless search of work or idling in the streets – and as can be expected very dissatisfied.'[8]

Whilst the old workhouse in Church Street was still in use, Benett, who had opposed the Poor Law Amendment Act during its passage through the parliamentary system, refused to co-operate with the assistant commissioner and would not sell any of his land to provide space for the erection of a new workhouse. Nor could the assistant commissioner find any other member of the gentry prepared to help in this regard.

The Tisbury guardians carried on without Benett's help and had to offer asylum in the old workhouse to many who were well disposed and industrious, but poverty stricken and unable to help themselves, although they did not want to be admitted. By 1837 the guardians were taking in one or two children from labouring families who had work, but could not manage on their wages. During the following winter the distress became worse, and when Benett finally attended a meeting of the guardians he proposed that Semley and West Tisbury should levy a 'private rate', inviting the inhabitants to 'give in proportion to their several rates' . The ratepayers agreed to this and afterwards all large families were relieved at the rate of 1s 6d per child after the third child. This system was extended to Fonthill Gifford. This was in opposition to the new law although Benett denied this and felt he had triumphed over the poor law commissioners. He welcomed the publicity it brought and said 'this system has been followed in secret in other places I am well assured, but I prefer publicity, for if the plan be good it will find imitators'.[9]

Benett's control in Tisbury area is said to have been a tyranny, although sometimes a benevolent one. He had a long held sense of responsibility for his employees and provided some out-relief, but he allowed no challenges to his authority. At least he did not propose, as did Lord Radnor in Alderbury, that large scale forced migration should be instigated to solve the unemployment and chronic pauper problem.[10]

It was not until 1868 that the new union workhouse in Monmouth Road, Tisbury, was completed.

The riots did have some effect upon parliamentary reform. Dissenters and the middle classes were turning against the aristocracy and a vote taken in Parliament in 1831 voted 302 for reform against 301 against. In March 1832 the Great Reform Act was passed. It did not really do much for the working population – the aim was to get better and more honest Members of Parliament, give the vote to property owners whose properties were valued at £10 per annum, drive out non-local MPs, get rid of corruption in the form of rotten and pocket boroughs, provide more polling stations, provide MPs in the new industrial towns and restore public confidence in Parliamentary authority. Voter registration was to be administered by the overseers of the poor in each parish.

The franchise was extended, but in the south Wiltshire area it did not extend the right to vote to many people. In Tisbury at the time the population was about 2259, having increased from 1961 in 1801. The number of people who now had the right to vote for the Southern Division of the county of Wiltshire 1832 in Tisbury amounted to 75 names, i.e. about 3.32% of the total population. Twenty-four of the names on the list are farmers, most of them as occupiers with rentals of over £50 per year payable. There are a couple of publicans including a James Macey at the Boot Inn, the organist at Wardour Chapel and of course John Benett at Pyt House. There were 36 freehold property owners, and a very few leasehold owners with the right to vote.[11] Even allowing for the fact that the population must have included a large number of children, the percentage of voters is still abysmally low. Nationally one in seven of adult males were enabled to vote. This was an increase from 1% of the population to 7%.

In Fonthill Bishop only eight men had the right to vote, of which two were publicans, and two farmers.[12]

The economist Lord King had already recommended the abolition of the Corn Laws, and as stated before, this suggestion had been the subject of derision by the then Whig government – Lord Grey declaring that this would 'lead to the destruction of the country' and Melbourne describing the suggestion as 'the wildest and maddest scheme that has ever entered into the imagination of man to conceive'.

It was therefore not until 1846 that repeal occurred, when Richard Cobden had founded the Anti Corn-Laws League and with the appalling famine in Ireland in 1846 due primarily to potato blight, even the then Tory government under Sir Robert Peel agreed, with the support of the Whigs, that matters had to change. The result split the Tory party.

The suppression of the Swing Riots did not stop the men in Wiltshire from protesting. Agrarian unrest continued – particularly following the introduction of the new Poor Law in 1834. In 1831 a strike in Ramsbury caused the authorities to call out the yeomanry to disperse the gathering. West Lavington workers went on strike to try to achieve a rise in wages. This was unsuccessful. But the labourers were not put off, they continued to protest; in Wroughton in 1834 the proposal to alter the workhouse rules caused the poor to collectively show their resistance by marching out of church one Sunday to smoke in the churchyard. This was repeated the following Sunday by 150 people. Around Devizes more demonstrations occurred and also some further away in Sussex at Ardingly, in Surrey at Chertsey and on the Norfolk/Suffolk border there were 'many meetings and occasional strikes'. Back in Wiltshire in 1834 in Compton Basset men were charged with intimidation for seeking to draw parish labourers into a strike.

An outbreak of incendiarism and poaching followed – almost revengeful on the part of the rick burners and poachers – gamekeepers often being the target, a few being attacked and even killed.

But the conditions for the ill-educated, poverty-stricken labourers were not improving. It would take other, outside influences to shift entrenched views. A just cause was simply not enough for employers or politicians to take notice or to act.

One factor which did help was that nonconformity to the established church was spreading. Primitive Methodism was becoming an alternative to attending Anglican services. Preachers for the new nonconformist religions were charismatic, the message simple. By 1830 Methodism had developed five 'circuits' for preachers in the Swing areas of the south of England – Wiltshire, Oxfordshire, Berkshire, Somerset, Gloucester, Dorset and Hampshire. By 1837 there were 11 of these 'circuits' operating, of which five were in Wiltshire. Independents, Wesleyans and Baptists too contributed to the collecting together, initially for peaceful, religious gatherings but also to disseminate education, information and the belief in 'combining' to improve themselves.

In Dorset the wages had been poor for hundreds of years. When the men of Dorset saw that in Hampshire there had been a wage rise following a demonstration, in Tolpuddle the labourers held several meetings and a spokesman was chosen to meet their local farmer employers. Dr Warren, the vicar of Tolpuddle, acted as chairman of the meeting and when the farmers agreed to a wage rise to 10s a week, Dr Warren told the labourers:

> I am a witness between you men and your masters that if you will go quietly to your work you shall receive for your labour as much as any man in the district, and if your masters should attempt to run from their word, I will undertake to see you righted, so help me God.[13]

The local farmers then went back on their word and reduced their commitment to 9s a week and then again to only 8s a week. The labourers, believing that justice and certainly Justice in the form of the word of God given by Dr Warren, was on their side, took their case to be heard before the bench which consisted of local Justices of the Peace. Now the vicar denied having given any pledge and the Justices agreed that the men must work for what the farmers were willing to pay them. The threat of a further reduction was to 7s and then back to 6s a week.

The men had a fearless and outspoken leader – George Loveless, a Methodist lay preacher of 37, married with three small children. He talked to the men about forming a friendly society. This was agreed and two delegates from a trade society visited Tolpuddle to give advice.

The Grand National Consolidated Trades union, inspired by Robert Owen, by now had nearly a million members. The two delegates from London helped the Tolpuddle men to start the Tolpuddle Lodge of the Friendly Society of Agricultural Labourers. The delegates insisted that there was to be a formal, swearing in ceremony, including the wearing of regalia and the taking of an oath of loyalty to the union. The new members were not keen on the oath taking but finally agreed to this, which was, for some of them, a complete disaster. It was the oath swearing which formed the basis for the accusations of 'administering and being bound by secret and unlawful oaths' under an act passed in 1797 to deal with a Naval mutiny at that time. It was not the combining to benefit a trade that was illegal, it was the oath swearing which enabled the local magistrates, the Member of Parliament, the landowners and the church to prosecute the workers. Spies had been planted amongst the 40 or so members who had joined in October 1833.

At dawn on 24th February 1834 six of the leaders of the group were arrested and taken to Dorchester gaol. Five were practising nonconformists – Wesleyans – and five amongst them were related to each other. George Loveless, his brother James, Thomas Standfield, his son John, and James Hammett were the nonconformists and only James Brine was a non-Methodist. James Hammett had not even been at the meeting – he was mistaken for his brother John, who was not arrested. James remained silent throughout the whole proceedings and indeed right through his transportation years, taking the blame on behalf of his brother.

As with the Swing rioters, Lord Melbourne was desperate to get the whole matter dealt with as quickly as possible. The government was still in fear of a real revolution, having been badly frightened by the 1830 French uprising. The men from Tolpuddle were put on trial very quickly, found guilty and sentenced to seven years transportation each. By the 6th March they had been taken to the prison hulks at Portsmouth and transferred rapidly on the convict ship *Eleanor*, bound for New South Wales. Except for George Loveless, who had been ill. He left for Portsmouth on 5th April and was transported to Van Diemen's Land, separated from his friends and relations.

Parliament was lobbied for pardons for them and in March 1836 a free pardon and passage back to England was granted, although the government employed many delaying tactics to stop their return. It was not until June 1837 that George Loveless returned, four more of them returned in 1838 and poor James Hammett did not manage to get back to England until 1839.

Trade unions raised a fund for them and all except James Hammett went to live and farm in Canada. James arrived home to Tolpuddle and remained there until he became blind in old age, and then opted to enter the workhouse so that he would not be a burden to his family. He died in the workhouse in 1891.[14]

Unlike the Swing rioters or the Pythouse rioters, these Dorset men are remembered and honoured. They became symbols of the right to combine, an example of the unjust society of the time and, known as the Tolpuddle Martyrs, an icon for the Labour and trade union movements. They were dignified throughout, calm and God fearing, as were many of the labourers involved in the agrarian radical movement of the period.

Now capitalism became all powerful – money was there to be made and enjoyed and workers to be exploited – it was said that they were regarded as machines. Of course, the newly released masses who went to work in industry were not released from poverty and illness – indeed, in many towns their lives were as impoverished and squalid as they had been in the countryside. The work was dominated by the factory owner's rules, his punishments system and fines and even the food they were able to eat was provided in lieu of wages i.e. by the 'truck' system. Houses were poor, cramped and overcrowded, insanitary and disease ridden. New diseases developed as a result of machine working, particularly lung problems. Children suffered dreadfully – they were cheap to employ. The rich remained rich, although the actual people who were rich were different from the aristocratic landowners of 50 years earlier, and the poor certainly remained poor, whether in the industrial towns or in the countryside.

Thus the evolution of the labour movement began. The trade unions, the mutual and co-operative societies, the working-class educational and leisure institute, the availability of newspapers, the spread of the nonconformists religious sects, all contributed to an idea of a free society. Combining, solidarity (in the form of non strike breaking), collective responsibility and if necessary, striking, rioting and machine breaking.

However, it took another 40 years before Joseph Arch formed the National Agricultural Labourers' Union and wages reflected this – they remained low. At the turn of the 20th century wages in Wiltshire were still only 11s.6d per week, some of the lowest in the land – Suffolk being worse at 10s 6d. per week. The highest wages were paid in the industrialised north of England – 17s in Northumberland and Westmorland, 18s in Durham and 19s in Lancashire.[15]

In the countryside the labourers were rarely able to be progressive about improving their conditions – they were always fighting on the back foot, defensively hanging on to insecure, badly paid jobs because there were no alternatives. In many rural areas there was no spare money to pay union dues even if they could get to a union meeting, and a lack of education would make it difficult for them to begin to understand that joining one would help. There were too many workers, not enough proper employment – most of it was casual – and to add to the misery, the more children they had, the more jobs would be needed for them.

What might help was a labour shortage. But there would never be a labour shortage in the countryside all the time families were so large. Indeed, how could they not have large families? There was no birth control available and many women were constantly pregnant – this was considered quite normal. Indeed, the more children that are born, the more likelihood for the parents of some sort of security in old age, so restricting the size of your family was not considered a good idea. This is still the case in some parts of the developing countries. Industrialisation eventually took some of these children into the growing towns and cities, but many were condemned to continue the lives of poverty, permanent hunger and hard physical labour on the land suffered by their parents, grandparents and even further back. It was a vicious circle.

In the south at least, the Swing Riots halted the progress of the threshing machine. Farmers were reluctant to introduce or reintroduce these machines because of the fear that the expensive machines would be broken. The economics of using them was also suspect – it was cheaper to use the plentiful but badly paid workforce than to invest in an expensive threshing machine.[15]

The one area in which the rural villagers did combine for their own benefit was in the establishment of friendly societies, such as the Oddfellows, the Foresters or smaller, local societies like the Slate Club or the Pig Club. These helped because they occurred spontaneously and taught the poorly educated working men how to organise and run a society for their own benefit.[16] From there it would be an easier step forward to joining a trade union and to reform society.

It did not happen quickly but gradually the labourers in the fields and the workers in the factories acquired knowledge, resilience and the skills needed to combine successfully and negotiate for everyone's benefit. This was not a revolution as Europe knew revolution, it was a persistent belief in their right to live freely, a determination to earn enough to keep themselves and their families in some degree of comfort, to educate their children and eventually provide some sort of care for the ill and elderly other than the workhouse. So even if the yeomanry was employed to strike them down and keep things under control, they would be up and running again. Not a revolution then, but a permanent resistance nurtured by radical thinkers and hardy workers.

Was the rioting in 1830, and for the purposes of this book, the Pythouse riots in particular, successful? For those involved in the actual events of that year it cannot be said to have been successful on a personal level and their immediate generation saw virtually no change. For the generations which followed it contributed to the eventual establishment of a fairer society, where more workers would be able to take advantage of education, become literate, influence political thinking and decision making and to live a less squalid life. There would be less exploitation and finally a recognition that labourers contribute as much to a stable, prosperous civilisation as do the cultured, richer elite classes.

Notes and References

Chapter 1 – November 1830
1. Hobsbawm, Eric and Rudé, George, 1969, *Captain Swing*, p 125
2. Ibid. p 123
3. *Hansard*, 8.2.1831 *Special Commission Debate (Mr J. Benett)* p 279
4. *House of Commons Journals* Vol. 86
5. Chambers, Jill, 1993, *Wiltshire Machine Breakers vol. 2 The Rioters*, pp 162 and 137
6. Ibid. Vol 1 p 309
7. PRO: *Letter from Lord Arundell 6 Dec 1830* Folios 162-8
8. Chambers, Jill, 1993, *Wiltshire Machine Breakers, vol. 1 The Riots & Trials*, p 67
9. Ibid. p 68
10. Ibid. p 311
11. Ibid. p 311
12. Ibid. p 104

Chapter 2 – The birth of Captain Swing
1. Griffin, Carl J, 2012, *The Rural War* Manchester University Press p 9
2. Hammond, J L and Barbara, 1995, *The Village Labourer 1760-1832*, p 39
3. Ibid. p 37
4. Ibid. pp 43-45
5. Ibid. p 58
6. Reed, Francis, 1991, *On Common Ground* Working Press p 14
7. Ibid. p 14
8. Ibid. p 15
9. Hoskins, W. G, 1971, *The Making of the English Landscape* pp 178-180 Pelican Books
10. Hammond, *The Village Labourer*, p 7
11. Hoskins, *The Making of the English Landscape*, pp 202-3
12. Thompson, E P, 1988, *The Making of the English Working Class*, p 221
13. Bunyan, Katharine, 2014, William Daniell The Bishop of Warminster Common, *Wilts OPC Project*
14. *Morning Advertiser* 7 October 1826

Chapter 3 – The Village Labourer
1. Hammond, *The Village Labourer*, p 173
2. Ibid. pp 240-1

3   Ibid. pp 196-7
4   Ibid. p 163
5   Ibid. p 321
6   Griffin, *The Rural War*, p 204
7   Ibid. p 162

Chapter 4 – 'pull down your messhines'
1   Marlow, Sylvia, 1991, *Winifred: A Wiltshire Working Girl*, Ex Libris Press, p 49
2   Moreau, R, 1968, *The Departed Village*, Oxford University Press, pp 69-71
3   Thompson, *Making of the English Working Class*, p 235
4   Griffin, *The Rural War*, p 52
5   Ibid. p 67
6   Ibid. p 87
7   Ibid. p 90
8   Thompson, *Making of the English Working Class*, p 250
9   Hobsbawm and Rudé, 1969, p 330

Chapter 5 – November 1830 (2)
1   Newman, Ruth, 1985, The 'Swing Riots' : Agricultural Revolt in 1830, in Hatcher Review, vol. 2 (19), p 441
2   Harfield, A G, 1964, Captain William Wyndham of the Hindon Troop, Royal Wiltshire Yeomanry, in *Journal of the Society for Army Historical Research*, vol. 42 (no. 169)
3   Information given to the author by the current owners of the adjacent Cools Farm
4   Hammond, *The Village Labourer*, p 262
5   Chambers, *Wiltshire Machine Breakers*, vol. 1, p 311
6   Ibid. p 312
7   Ereira, Alan, 1981, *The People's England*
8   Chambers, *Wiltshire Machine Breakers*, vol. 1, p 287
9   Hammond, *The Village Labourer*, p 278
10 Ibid. p 284
11 Chambers, *Wiltshire Machine Breakers*, vol. 2, p 265
12 TNA Census Returns

Chapter 6 – The Full Panoply
1   Escott, Margaret, Tumult, Riot & Disturbances, in Poole, Steve and Spicer, Andrew, 2010, *Captain Swing Reconsidered, Southern History*, vol. 32 p 150
2   Ibid. p 157
3   *Salisbury & Winchester Journal*, 31.12.1830
4   Chambers, *Wiltshire Machine Breakers*, vol. 1, p 99
5   Ibid. pp 99-102
6   Ibid. p 104
7   Ibid. p 107
8   Escott, Margaret, 2010 Tumult, Riot & Disturbances, pp 152-3
9   Chambers, *Wiltshire Machine Breakers*, vol. 1, p 108
10 Ibid. p 110

Chapter 7 – The Visitations of Providence
1. Chambers, *Wiltshire Machine Breakers*, vol. 1, p 119-21
2. Ibid. pp 124-6
3. Ibid. p 127
4. Ibid. p 184
5. Ibid. p 198
6. Ibid. p 162
7. Ibid. pp 215-20
8. Ibid. pp 224-225
9. Ibid. p 229

Chapter 8 – Setting an example
1. Hobsbawm and Rudé, 1969, p 111
2. Ibid. pp 304-5
3. Escott, Margaret; Tumult Riot & Disturbances, p 141
4. Newman, Ruth, 1985, The 'Swing Riots', p 438
5. Hammond, *The Village Labourer*, pp 267-8
6. Ibid. p 269
7. Hobsbawm and Rudé, 1969, p 257-8
8. Ibid. p 257
9. Ibid. p 127
10. Hammond, *The Village Labourer*, p 276
11. Ibid. p 291
12. Wallis, Rose Madeleine, 'We do not come here'; Captain Swing Reconsidered p 174
13. Hobsbawm and Rudé, 1969, *p 258-9*
14. Hammond, *The Village Labourer*, p 275
15. Ibid. p 278
16. Hobsbawm and Rudé, 1969, p 261
17. Ibid. p 262

Chapter 9 - Overspill
1. Chandler, John, 1983, *Endless Street*, pp 217-8
2. *Salisbury & Wiltshire Journal* 28.2.1785
3. Hughes, Robert, 2003, *The Fatal Shore*, Vintage, p 41
4. Williams, Lucy, 2018 *Convicts in the Colonies,* Pen & Sword, p 19
5. Hughes, 2003, *The Fatal Shore*, p 64
6. Williams, 2018, *Convicts in the Colonies*, p 26
7. Hughes, 2003, *The Fatal Shore*, pp 141-2
8. Williams, 2018, *Convicts in the Colonies*, p 21
9. Chambers, *Wiltshire Machine Breakers*, vol. 2, p 270
10. Williams, 2018, *Convicts in the Colonies*, p 41-2
11. Ibid. pp 48-9
12. Willetts, Jen, www.freesettlersorfelons Convict Ship Eliza in *Convict & Colonial History*

13 Ibid.
14 Chambers, *Wiltshire Machine Breakers*, vol. 1, *p 324*

Chapter 10 – Local Heroes
1 *Hansard,* 29 November 1830 pp 687-91
2 *Hansard,* 8 February 1831 *Special Commissions Amnesty Debate* p 269
3 Moody, Robert, 2003, *John Benett of Pythouse,* p 119
4 Hawkins, Desmond Ed., *The Grove Diaries 1809-1925,* p 170
5 Chambers, *Wiltshire Machine Breakers,* vol. 1, p 129
6 Edward Doran (ed.), 1912, *Notes by the 12th Lord Arundell of Wardour on the Family History,* pp 801-7
7 Ibid.
8 Dakers, Caroline, 2018, *Fonthill Recovered* UCL Press p 106
9 Cowan, Michael (ed.), 1994, The Peniston Letters 1823-30, *Wiltshire Record Society* vol. 50 nos. 1626-8
10 Ibid. no. 1636
11 Ibid. no. 1641
12 Newman, Ruth, 1985, The 'Swing Riots', p 443
13 Chambers, *Wiltshire Machine Breakers,* vol. 1, pp 328-9

Chapter 11 – Influencers and bloggers
1 Cobbett, William, 1983, *Rural Rides,* p 320
2 Ibid. p 296
3 Thompson, *Making of the English Working Class,* p 253
4 Hammond, *The Village Labourer,* pp 316-7
5 Thompson, *Making of the English Working Class,* p 795
6 Ibid. p 789
7 Ibid. p 792
8 Hobsbawm and Rudé, 1969, p 117

Chapter 12 - An Organiser and a windbag
1 Chambers, *Wiltshire Machine Breakers,* vol. 1, p 78
2 Moody, Robert, 2005, *Mr Benett of Wiltshire,* pp 189-90
3 Poole, Steve and Spicer, Andrew, 2010, *Captain Swing Reconsidered, Southern History,* vol. 32, p 49
4 Chambers, *Wiltshire Machine Breakers,* vol. 1, pp 285-8
5 Ibid. p 79
6 Ibid. p 282
7 Moody, 2003, *John Benett of Pythouse,* p 29-31
8 Thompson, *Making of the English Working Class,* pp 508-10
9 Ibid. p 681
10 Ibid. p 689
11 Hobsbawm and Rudé, 1969, p 117-118
12 Hammond, *The Village Labourer,* p 262
13 Ibid. p 315
14 Hobsbawm, Eric; *The Age of Revolution 1789-1848,* p 114

Chapter 13 – An Anti-Hero
1. Moody, 2005, *Mr Benett of Wiltshire*, p 33
2. Ibid. p 42
3. Moody, 2003, *John Benett of Pythouse*, p 161-2
4. Moody, 2005, *Mr Benett of Wiltshire*, p 77
5. Ibid. p 148
6. Ibid. p 156
7. Ibid. p 157
8. Ibid. p 176
9. Ibid. p 203
10. Ibid. p 204
11. Ibid. p 257-8
12. Ibid. p 260-1
13. Moody, 2003, *John Benett of Pythouse*, p 200
14. Ibid. p 198

Chapter 14 – Planned or Spontaneous?
1. Chambers, *Wiltshire Machine Breakers*, vol. 1, p 71
2. *Hansard*, 8 February 1831
3. Wilson, Ben, 2007, *Decency and Disorder 1789-1832*, p 75

Chapter 15 - The Garden of Eden?
1. *Hobart Town Courier*, 4 June 1831
2. Boyce, James, 2010, *Van Diemen's Land*, pp 21-3
3. Ibid. pp 25-6
4. Brown, Bruce W, 2004, *The Machine Breaker Convicts from the Proteus and the Eliza*, MA Dissertation, University of Tasmania, p51
5. Boyce, 2010, *Van Diemen's Land*, p 48
6. Ibid. pp 74-5
7. Ibid. p 59
8. Shakespeare, Nicholas, 2005, *In Tasmania*, p 96
9. Boyce, 2010, *Van Diemen's Land*, p 168
10. Ibid. pp 173-4
11. Ibid. p 231

Chapter 16 – Servants of the Crown
1. Brown, 2004 *The Machine Breaker Convicts from the Proteus and the Eliza*, p 82
2. Hughes, 2003, *The Fatal Shore*, p 384-385
3. Hobsbawm and Rudé, 1969, p 269
4. Brown, 2004 *The Machine Breaker Convicts from the Proteus and the Eliza*, p 92
5. Chambers, *Wiltshire Machine Breakers*, vol. 2, p 55
6. ourtasmania.com.au/Launceston/ross-bridge pp 2- 21
7. Chambers, *Wiltshire Machine Breakers*, vol. 2, pp 13-14
8. Ibid. p 254
9. *Colonial Times* 2 September 1845
10. Brown, 2004 *The Machine Breaker Convicts from the Proteus and the Eliza*,

appendix p 130
11 TNA Census Returns 1841, 1851, 1861

Chapter 17 – Roped to the Plough
1 Hughes, 2003, *The Fatal Shore*, p 368
2 Boyce, 2010, *Van Diemen's Land,* pp 152-3
3 Ibid. pp 149-50
4 Ibid. p 157
5 Ibid. p 176
6 Ibid. p 184

Chapter 18 – To plough Van Diemen's Land
1 Barnard, Simon, 2014, *A-Z of Convicts in Van Diemen's Land*, pp 74-5
2 Read, K. L, 1966, William Gunn in the *Australian Dictionary of Biography* Vol 1, p1-2
3 Chambers, *Wiltshire Machine Breakers*, vol. 2, p148
4 Barlett, Anne, The Brumbys of Norfolk Plains, in *Tasmanian Ancestry* pp 188-90
5 Chambers, *Wiltshire Machine Breakers*, vol. 2, pp 20-2
6 Ibid. p 252
7 Bignell, John, 1988, The Restoration of Thorpe Watermill, Boswell, Tasmania, in *Australian Historical Archaeology*, 6
8 TNA Census Returns 1841 and 1851
9 Chambers, *Wiltshire Machine Breakers*, vol. 2, p 254
10 TNA Census Returns 1851 and 1861

Chapter 19 – 'gallant poachers'
1 McAulay, Ida, 1966 John Bisdee, in *Australian Dictionary of Biography Vol.1*
2 Chambers, *Wiltshire Machine Breakers*, vol. 2, p 216
3 Simpson, Raymond, 2021, Research into Agricultural Riots in the Tisbury Area
4 TNA Census Return 1851 and Parish Records
5 Ibid.
6 Chambers, *Wiltshire Machine Breakers*, vol. 1, p 105
7 TNA Criminal Records
8 Obituary in TROVE.nla.gov.au. 1877 Archdeacon Dr W H Browne
9 Chambers, *Wiltshire Machine Breakers*, vol. 2, p 45
10 TNA Census Returns
11 *Former TIMES* Issue No. 6 June 2014 p 1
12 TNA Census Returns and Parish Records
13 Dyer, Alan, 2019, Francis von Bibra and his family Part 1, in *Early Pioneer Settlers on the Plains*
14 TNA Census Returns and Parish Records

Chapter 20 – the intrepid Jerrards
1 Richard, Christina, 2018, *The Grotto Makers*, p 118
2 Chambers, *Wiltshire Machine Breakers*, vol. 1, p 68
3 Ibid. p 107

4 Willets, Jen, www.freesettlersorfelons Convict Ship Eliza in *Convict & Colonial History*
5 Walsh, G P 1966, Thomas Barker in *Australian Dictionary of Biography*
6 Casey & Lowe 2002, The History of Barker's Mill, Darling Harbour extracted from *Cross City Archaeological Assessment*
7 Chambers, *Wiltshire Machine Breakers*, vol. 2, p 112
8 TNA Census Returns and Parish Records
9 Chambers, *Wiltshire Machine Breakers*, vol. 1, p 310
10 Willets, Jen, www.freesettlersorfelons Convict Ship Eliza in *Convict & Colonial History*
11 Mrs Auriol Biddle: information given about the Jerrard family

Chapter 21 – successful settlers

1 Chambers, *Wiltshire Machine Breakers*, vol. 1, pp 104-7
2 Green, F. C, 1967 Josiah Spode, in *Australian Dictionary of Biography Vol. 2*
3 Chambers, *Wiltshire Machine Breakers*, vol. 2, pp 245-8
4 Ibid. vol. 1, p 310
5 TNA Census Returns
6 Brown, 2004 *The Machine Breaker Convicts from the Proteus and the Eliza*, p 45
7 Sherman, Geoffrey B, 1998, Swing Rioters' Descendants' Meeting: Their Ancestors came by Eleanor, Eliza, Proteus et al in *Journal of the Genealogical Society of Tasmania Vo. 18 no. 4*
8 Chambers, *Wiltshire Machine Breakers*, vol. 2, p 259
9 Simpson, Ray: *Agricultural Riots in the Tisbury Area* p 15
10 Chambers, *Wiltshire Machine Breakers*, vol. 1, p 328
11 TAS.gov.au 1866 *in Parliament*
12 Anstey, Thomas 1966 in *Australian Dictionary of Biography*, vol. 1 (ed. Douglas Pike)
13 Simpson, Ray: *Agricultural Riots in the Tisbury Area* pp 15-22

Chapter 22 – Habitat

1 Boyce, 2010, *Van Diemen's Land*, p 122
2 Theoldfoodie.com., 2016, *Convict Chain Gang Rations in Van Diemen's Land, 1834*
3 The Cook and the Curator, 2017, *Convict Diet*, Museums of History NSW
4 Howeler-Coy, J, 1966, An Account of Food and Drink in Tasmania, 1800-1900, in *Papers and Proceedings of the Royal Society of Tasmania*, vol.100
5 Boyce, 2010, *Van Diemen's Land*, p 137
6 Shakespeare, 2005, *In Tasmania*, pp 39 and 62
7 Bourke, J. F, and Lucadou-Wells, R , Colonial Education; progression from cottage industry roots, in *Macquarie Journal of Business Law*, vol. 8, p 178
8 Boyce, 2010, *Van Diemen's Land*, p 184

Chapter 23 - Red Herrings and Loose Ends

1 Ratcliff, Eric, 2018, Fonthill and the Colonial Imagination, in *The Beckford Journal*, vol. 24

2 Ibid. p 45
3 Evans, K. Jane, 1991, Tabart of Fonthill: From England to Van Diemen's Land; Weston-super-Mare pp 48-54
4 Dakers, 2018, *Fonthill Recovered*, pp 138-9
5 Barsham, Elizabeth, 2011,Tasmanian Gothic Stuff no. 4 in *Tasmanian-gothic.blogspot.com*
6 TNA Census Return 1851
7 Gregg, Peter: August 2011
8 Longley-st-lukes anglican-church in Churchesoftasmania.com no. 134
9 A-tale-of-two-malahides 2022 in Tintean.or.au

Chapter 24 – Aftermath
1 TNA Census Returns and Parish Records
2 Naverage.co.uk
3 Dalton, Mary: The Pyt House Riot and the Tisbury-Tasmania Connection, *Hatcher Review*, vol. 3 (no. 30)
4 Moody, 2005, *Mr Benett of Wiltshire*, p 214
5 Ibid. p 234
6 Ibid. pp. 260-1
7 Waterson, Jill , 2008 , Fonthill Gifford in the mid nineteenth century, *History-pieces.co.uk*

Chapter 25 – Changing Society
1 Hobsbawm, *Age of Revolution*, p 150
2 *The Times* 30 July 2022 Rhys Blakely
3 Hobsbawm, *Age of Revolution*, p 155
4 Randall, Adrian, and Newman, Edwina, 1995, Protest, Proletarians and Paternalists: Social Conflict in Rural Wiltshire, 1830-1850, in *Rural History*, vol 6 (no. 2), 205-277
5 *British Parliamentary Papers*, 1834 (44) XXX1V 577e
6 TNA HO 52/11
7 *The Times*, 3 December and 10 December 1830
8 TNA John Hill to PLC 13 January 1834 and Assistant Overseer of East Tisbury to PLC 18 May 1835
9 TNA Benett to A'Court 19 December 1838
10 Randall and Newman, 1995, Protest, Proletarians and Paternalists, p 222
11 Maureen Withe , 2018, in *Wiltshire OPC Project*
12 Ibid.
13 Groves, Reg, 1949, *Sharpen the Sickle The history of the Farmworkers' Union*, p 17
14 Ibid. pp 20-1
15 Ibid. p 111
16 *Journey-book of England. Berkshire: including a full description of Windsor Castle London*, 1840, p 16

Bibliography

Books

Barnard, Simon, 2014, *A-Z of Convicts in Van Diemen's Land*, Text Publishing Co. Melbourne

Bennett, H S, 1987, *Life on the English Manor*, Alan Sutton

Bettey, J H, 1987, *Rural Life in Wessex 1500-1900*, Alan Sutton

Boyce, James, 2010, *Van Diemen's Land*, Black Inc.

Brown, Martyn, 1988, *Australia Bound!* Ex Libris Press

Chambers, Jill, 1993, *Wiltshire Machine Breakers, vol. 1 The Riots & Trials*, pub Jill Chambers

Chambers, Jill, 1993, *Wiltshire Machine Breakers vol. 2 The Rioters*, pub Jill Chambers

Chandler, John, 1983, *Endless Street*, Hobnob Press

Cobbett, William, 1983, *Rural Rides*, Penguin

Cowan, Michael (ed.), 1994, *The Peniston Letters 1823-30*, Wiltshire Record Society vol. 50

Dakers, Caroline, 2018, *Fonthill Recovered*, UCL Press

Daniell, William, 1850, *Warminster Common*, Vardy

Drury, Jill and Peter, 1980, *A Tisbury History*, Element Books

Ereira, Alan, 1981, *The People's England*, Routledge Kegan Paul

Graham, Henry, 1886, *Annals of the Yeomanry Cavalry of Wiltshire*, vol. 1, Liverpool Press

Griffin, Carl J, 2012, *The Rural War*, Manchester University Press

Groves, Reg, 1949, *Sharpen the Sickle: The History of the Farmworkers' Union*, Merlin Press

Hammond, J L and Barbara, 1995, *The Village Labourer 1760-1832*, Alan Sutton Publishing

Hawkins, Desmond (ed.), 1988, *The Grove Diaries 1809-1925*, The Dovecote Press

Hayes, Nick, 2020, *The Book of Trespass*, Bloomsbury Publishing plc

Hobsbawm, Eric and Rudé, George, 1969, *Captain Swing*, Phoenix Press

Hobsbawm, Eric, 2005, *The Age of Revolution 1789-1848*, Abacus

Hoskins, W G, 1971, *The Making of the English Landscape*, Pelican Books

Hudson, W H, 1978, *A Shepherd's Life*, Compton Press

Hughes, Robert, 2003, *The Fatal Shore*, Vintage

Journey-book of England. Berkshire: including a full description of Windsor Castle London, 1840, Charles Knight & Co.

Kneale, Matthew, 2001, *English Passengers*, Penguin

Marlow, Sylvia, 1991, *A Wiltshire Working Girl*, Ex Libris Press

Miles, Mrs E, *Tisbury Past and Present*
Moody, Robert, 2005, *Mr Benett of Wiltshire*, Hobnob Press
Moody, Robert, 2003, *John Benett of Pythouse*, pub Robert Moody
Moreau, R E, 1968, *The Departed Village*, Oxford University Press
Morris, Christopher, 1984, *William Cobbett's Illustrated Rural Rides 1821-32*, Fraser Stewart Books
Parker, Rowland, 1976, *The Common Stream*, Paladin
Reed, Francis, 1991, *On Common Ground*, Working Press
Richard, Christina, 2018, *The Grotto Makers*, Hobnob Press
Rowley, Trevor, 1987, *Villages in the Landscape*, Alan Sutton
Shakespeare, Nicholas, 2005, *In Tasmania*, Vintage
Thompson, E P, 1988, *The Making of the English Working Class*, Pelican Books
Webb, Edward Doran (ed.), 1912, *Notes by the 12th Lord Arundell of Wardour on the Family History*, Longmans
Williams, Lucy, 2018, *Convicts in the Colonies*, Pen & Sword
Wilson, Ben, 2007, *Decency and Disorder 1789-1837*, Faber & Faber

Papers
Anstey, Thomas, 1966, in *Australian Dictionary of Biography*, vol. 1
Barsham, Elizabeth, 2011, Tasmanian Gothic Stuff No. 4, in *Tasmanian-gothic.blogspot.com*
Bignell, John, 1988, The Restoration of Thorpe Watermill, Boswell, Tasmania, in *Australian Historical Archaeology 6*
Bourke, J F and Lucadou-Wells, R 2011, Colonial Education; progression from cottage industry roots, in *Macquarie Journal of business law Vol. 8 p. 178*
Brown, Bruce W, 2004, *The Machine Breaker Convicts from the Proteus and the Eliza*, MA Dissertation, University of Tasmania
Bunyan, Katharine, 2014, William Daniell 'Bishop of Warminster', *Wilts OPC Project*
Casey & Lowe, 2002, History of Barker's Mill, Darling Harbour, extracted from *Cross City Tunnel Archaeological Assessment*
Dalton, Mary: The Pyt House Riot and the Tisbury-Tasmania Connection, *Hatcher Review* vol. 3 (no. 30)
Devizes & Wilts Gazette, 17 February 1831, 'The Late Riots'
Dyer, Alan, 2019, Francis von Bibra and his family, part 1, in *Early Pioneer Settlers on the Plains*
Escott, Margaret, Tumult, Riot & Disturbances, in *Captain Swing Reconsidered*
Green, F C, 1967, Josiah Spode, in *Australian Dictionary of Biography*, vol.2
Hansard, 8 February 1831: Special Commissions
Harfield, A G, 1964, Captain William Wyndham of the Hindon Troop, Royal Wiltshire Yeomanry, in *Journal of the Society for Army Historical Research*, vol. 42 (no. 169)
Hobart Town Courier, 4 June 1831
Howeler-Coy J F, 1966, An Account of Food and Drink in Tasmania 1800-1900, in *Papers and Proceedings of the Royal Society of Tasmania*, vol.100
McAulay, Ida, 1966, John Bisdee, in *Australian Dictionary of Biography*, vol 1

Navickas, Katrina, Rural Resistance and the Swing Riots, in *Protest and the Politics of Space and Place*

Newman, Ruth, 1985, The 'Swing' Riots: Agricultural Revolt in 1830 in *Hatcher Review*, vol. 2 (no. 19)

ourtasmania.com.au/Launceston/ross-bridge

Poole, Steve and Spicer, Andrew, 2010, Captain Swing Reconsidered, *Southern History*, vol. 32

Randall, Adrian, 2009 ' Captain Swing: a Retrospect' in *International Review of Social History*, vol. 54, pp. 419-427

Randall, Adrian, and Newman, Edwina, 1995, Protest, Proletarians and Paternalists: Social Conflict in Rural Wiltshire, 1830-1850, in *Rural History*, vol 6 (no. 2), 205-277

Ratcliff, Eric, 2018 'Fonthill and the Colonial Imagination' in *The Beckford Journal* Vol. 24

Read, K L, 1966, William Gunn, in *Australian Dictionary of Biography*, vol. 1

Sherman, Geoffrey B, 1998, Swing Rioter Descendants' Meeting: Their Ancestors came by Eleanor, Eliza, Proteus *et al*, in *Tasmanian Ancestry*

Simpson, Raymond 2002, *Agricultural Riots in the Tisbury Area*

Theoldfoodie, 2016, Convict Chain Gang Rations in Van Diemen's Land 1834

TROVE.nla.gov.au., Obituary 1877, of archdeacon W H Browne

Wallis, Rose Madeleine, 2016, The Relationship Between Magistrates and their Communities in the Age of Crisis: social protest c. 1790-1834, PhD thesis, University of the West of England

Walsh, G P, 1966, Thomas Barker, in *Australian Dictionary of Biography*

Waterson, Jill, 2008, Fonthill Gifford in the mid nineteenth century, in *History-pieces.co.uk*

Willetts, Jen, www.freesettlersorfelons.com Convict Ship Eliza, in *Convict and Colonial History*

Williamson, Barry, 1997, *Lord Arundell's Park at Wardour*, Barry Williamson

Williamson, Barry, 1997, *Wardour and the Arundells Not So Long Ago*, Barry Williamson

Withey, Maureen, *Wiltshire OPC Project*

Young, Mary Blamire, 1957, *Village History, Fonthill Bishop, Berwick St Leonard, Fonthill Gifford*

Index of Names and Places

NOTE:, VDL, =, Van Diemens' Land

ABREE, Mary, 243
ABREE, (Abery, Albury, Abrey), Thomas, 52, 64-6, 73, 105-6, 163, 165-6, 199, 213, 228, 236
A'COURT, Colonel Charles, 246-7, 250
ADEY, Superintendent Stephen, 155
AFRICA, 87-8
AILESBURY, Marquis of, 127
ALDERBURY, Wiltshire, 43, 255
ALDERSON, Mr Justice Edward Hall, 51, 56, 57, 64, 66, 69, 82, 214
ALDGATE, London, 226
ALFORD, Joseph, 142, 245
ALFORD, Samuel/Richard, 6, 7, 123, 139, 142, 143, 144, 205, 251, 253
ALRESFORD, Hampshire, 125
AMERICA, 87, 88, 114
AMESBURY, Wiltshire, 1, 96
ANDERSON, William, 94, 146, 158
ANDOVER, Hampshire, 4, 267, 39, 123, 139
ANDREWS, George, 244
ANSTEY, Thomas, 216, 217
ANSTEY BARTON, VDL, 216
ANSTEY PARK, VDL, 216, 217
ANSTY, Wiltshire, 6, 101, 198, 205
ANTROBUS, Sir E, 58
ARCH, Joseph, 259
ARCHER, John Lee, 163
ARDINGLY, Sussex, 256
ARGYLE, Scotland, 161
ARTHUR, George, Lt., Gov., VDL, 153-5, 159-61, 164, 169-70, 172-4, 210, 217, 229
ARUNDEL, Sussex, 75
ARUNDELL, James Everard, 10th Earl of, 29, 93, 100-6, 116-17, 127, 131, 143, 163, 205, 215, 251, 253
ARUNDELL, John Tennant, 11th Baron Talbot of Malahide, 239-40
ASHCOMBE, Wiltshire, 103
ASIA, 89
ASSIGNMENTS, Pythouse Rioters, 180

ASTLEY, Sir John D, MP, 58, 63, 65, 135
ATHENAEUM CLUB, London, 132
ATLANTIC OCEAN, 87
AUSTRALIA, 87-9, 147, 167, 182, 197, 199, 202
AVON VALLEY, Wiltshire, 109
AXFORD, Thomas, 185
AYLESBURY, Buckinghamshire, 83

BACKHOUSE, James, 159
BAKER'S FARM, (Down Farm), 5, 191
BAKEWELL, Robert, 15, 16
BALL, Thomas, 60, 97
BAMFORD, Samuel, 119
BANSTONE, Thomas, 177
BANSTONE, Thomas (Macey), 52, 59, 60, 61, 73, 105, 177-80, 182, 199, 245, 247
BARFORD ST MARTIN, Wiltshire, 3
BARKER, James, 203
BARKER, Thomas, 202-4
BARRETT, Andrew, 204, 242
BARRETT, Edward, 185, 205
BARRETT, Eliza (Mould), 185, 187, 242
BARRETT, John, 59, 60, 61, 64, 99, 182, 184-7, 199, 213, 242, 245
BARRETT, Samuel, 52, 59, 73, 165, 184-7, 195, 199, 213
BARRETT, Sarah, (Jerrard), and Martha, 186
BARRETT family, Henry, & Elizabeth, Lucy, and Frank, 204, 206,
BARRETT family, John, William, Charles, James, Martha, Lucy, Henry, 186-7, 244
BARSHAM, Elizabeth, 236
BARTON STACEY, Hampshire, 28
BASKERVILLE, T B M, 58
BATH, Marquis of, 77, 104, 135
BATHURST, Lord, 229
BATT, Thomas, 96
BAUDIN, Nicolas, 147
BEARSTED, Kent, 75
BEAUFORT, Francis, 231
BECKFORD, William, 3, 54, 106, 132-3, 161, 233-4, 236
BECKFORD ARMS, Fonthill Gifford,

Wiltshire, 5, 8, 67, 235
BELFAST, Victoria, Australia, 189
BELL, Andrew, 233
BELL, Thomas, 94
BENETT, Etheldred, 136
BENETT, Fanny, 136-7
BENETT, John, MP, 1-10, 45-7, 49, 58-60, 63-4, 80, 96, 100-1, 105-6, 115, 118, 122,124, 126-138, 143, 161-2, 181-2, 189, 191, 196, 198-9, 208, 213-14, 236, 246-8, 250, 253-5
BENETT, John (son of above), 127, 136
BENETT, Lucy, (daughter of above), 136
BENETT, Lucy, (Lambert), 127, 136
BENETT, Thomas and Catherine, 126
BENETT, Thomas Edmund, 127
BERE REGIS, Dorset, 80
BERKSHIRE, 1, 75, 80, 83, 199, 257
BERWICK ST JOHN, Wiltshire, 101
BEVIS, Mr and Mrs, 244
BIBRA, Von, family, 196-7
BIGGS, Harry, 58
BILLINGSLEY, John, 13
BIRT (Burt), Ann, 242
BIRT (Burt), Anna, Maria, Thomas, and Emma, 242
BIRT (Burt), John, and Sarah, 242
BIRT (Burt, Burke), Thomas, 53, 59-63, 73, 105, 161-2, 165, 167, 236, 242
BISDEE, Edward, 188
BISDEE, John, 188
BISHOP, Thomas, 68
BISHOPDOWN, Salisbury, Wiltshire, 42
BISHOPSTONE, Salisbury, Wiltshire, 70
BISHTON, Rev., 183
BLACKMANS BAY, VDL, 147
BLANDFORD, James, 9, 52, 59-61, 65, 69, 73, 191-4, 213
BLANDFORD family, Mary, William, and Samuel, 191, 194
BLANDFORD FORUM, Dorset, 80
BOGNOR, Sussex, 275
BOND STREET, London, 216
BOOTH, Sir Edward, 58
BOTHWELL, VDL, 185
BOWEN, John, 147-8
BOYES, G W T, 161
BOYTON, Wiltshire, 135
BRACHER, James, 207-8
BRACHER, John, 128
BRADLEY, Michael, 5, 66-8
BRADY, Matthew, 154, 179
BRANDON, Norfolk, 36
BRASHER, John, 2, 43, 64
BRASHER, Samuel, 43

BRICKELL (Brickle), John, 8, 9, 47, 50, 59, 208
BRINE, James, 158
BRISTOL, 119
BRISTOW, Henry, 66
BRISTOWE, Squire, 250
BROAD CHALKE, Wiltshire, 3, 42, 70, 83
BROOK'S CLUB, St James's Street, London, 132
BROTHERTON, Col., 80, 114
BROUGHAM, Lord Chancellor, 111
BROWNE, Rev. Dr., 192-3
BRUCE, G W F H, 135
BRUMBY family, Robert, and James, 182, 184
BUCKINGHAMSHIRE, 80, 83
BULLINGTON, Hampshire, 51
BULPITT Brothers, 200
BURCOMBE, Wiltshire, 3
BURDETT, Francis, 118
BURN, David, 172
BURN, William, 236
BURT, Thomas (Birt), father Thomas, 167-8, son John, daughter Mary, grandchild Margaret, 168
BURTON, John, 6, 49, 70, 73
BUTTERMERE, Wiltshire, 41
BUXTON, Thomas, 177, 195

CALCUTTA, 92, 199
CAMPBELL TOWN, VDL, 192
CANADA, 258
CANARY ISLANDS, 93
CANDY, Mr, Stop Farm, 8
CANTERBURY, Kent, 37-8
CAPE BARREN, VDL, 175
CAPE GRIM, VDL, 155
CARLILE, Richard, 111-13, 120
CAROLINA, USA, 220
CHAMBERLEN, Mrs H J, 186
CHATHAM, Kent, 88
CHERTSEY, Surrey, 256
CHESHIRE, 77
CHEVERILL, Charlotte, 242
CHEVERILL, James, 4, 67, 213, 245
CHICHESTER, Sussex, 75
CHILMARK, Wiltshire, 4, 48, 66, 124, 131-2, 245
CHIPPENHAM, Wiltshire, 104
CIRCULAR HEAD, VDL, 155
CITY HOTEL, OATLANDS, 217
COBBETT, William, MP, 25, 27, 28, 39, 106, 123, 129, 134, 137
COBDEN, Richard, 256
COBURG, Cressy, VDL, 196-7

COCK, Captain Robert, 199, 200
COCKBURN, James, 9
COLBECK, James, 163
COLDBATH FIELDS PRISON, 119
COLLINGBOURNE DUCIS, Wiltshire, 41
COLLINS, David, 147-8, 151
COLLONS, Charles, 181
COLLONS, William, 181
COLT HOARE, Sir Richard, 127
COMBES, Joseph, 181
COMBES, William, 181
COOMBES, James, 6
COOMBES, Matthew, 66, 214
COOTE, Eyre, 104
COPENHAGEN, Denmark, 114
CORK, Ireland, 192
CORTON, Wiltshire, 64
COXE, William, Archdeacon, 128
CRAVEN, Fulwer, 58
CRAWFORD, Judith, 227
CRESSY, VDL, 182, 184
CRIPPS, Mr, 160
CUFF, James, 63
CUMBERLAND, 77
CURR, Edward, 155

DALLY, Mr, Ridge Farm, 4, 67-8
DALRYMPLE, Alexander, 89
DALTON, Dr Mary, 245
DANIELL, Rev., William, 19, 50
DARLING HARBOUR, Sydney, NSW, 202-3
DAS VOLTAS BAY, Namibia, 89
DAVEY, Thomas, Lt., Gov., VDL, 151-2, 174, 227
DAVIS, Thomas, 200
DEDDINGTON, VDL, 170
DENHOLME, Alexander, 218
DENMAN, Sir Thomas, 110-11, 124
DEPTFORD, London, 88, 206
DERWENT RIVER, VDL, 146-7, 209
DESPARD, Col., Edmund, 119
DEVIZES, Wiltshire, 43, 51, 83, 104, 116, 127, 130-1, 244, 256
DEWSBURY, West Yorkshire, 163
DICKENS, Charles, 241
DIDEROT, Denis, 18
DILLINGHAM, Richard, 175
DISS, Norfolk, 36
DOGGRELL, James, 9, 61, 96, 208
DOGGRELL, Noah, 9, 61, 96
DOMENICA, 117
DONHEAD ST ANDREW, Wiltshire, 207
DORCHESTER, Dorset, 70, 72
DORSET, 77, 80, 83, 113, 199, 257

DOWDING, William, 68
DOWN FARM, Fonthill Bishop (Baker's Farm), 4, 66, 69
DOWNES, Rev., Richard, 101
DOWNTON, Wiltshire, 1, 41
DUKE, John, 61
DULOT, Elizabeth (Tabart), 232
DULVERTON, Somerset, 216
DUNCOMBE, T, 247
DUNDAS, Charles, 26
DURHAM, 259
DURNFORD, Wiltshire, 242

EAST INDIA COMPANY, 26
EAST KNOYLE, Wiltshire, 46, 50
EAST STOUR, Wiltshire, 80
EBBESBOURNE WAKE, Wiltshire, 3, 42
EDINBURGH, Scotland, 210, 216
EDWARD IV, King, 238
ELEANOR, SS, 199, 200, 258
ELIZA, SS, 92, 96, 146, 160, 161, 167, 170, 175, 192, 199, 208, 215
ELY, Cambridgeshire, 108
ENFORD, Wiltshire, 41, 93, 118, 126-7, 129
ENGLAND, 92, 222
ESTCOURT, T G B, 57, 64
EVANS, K., Jane, 236
EXETER, Devon, 4, 25, 123
EYRE, George, 58
EYRES, John, 93
EYRES, Samuel, 52, 59, 61, 69, 73, 244

FANE, Arthur, 136
FARNHAM, Surrey, 4, 107
FARQUHAR, John, 3, 9, 132-3, 161, 234
FELPHAM, Sussex, 75
FENTON, M, 165
FIFIELD BAVANT, Wiltshire, 42, 127
FIGES, Mr., 42
FIGHELDEAN, Wiltshire, 1, 39, 41, 96
FISHERTON GAOL, Salisbury, Wiltshire, 63, 69, 74, 80-1, 85, 116, 199, 214
FLEET STREET, London, 113
FONTHILL, Wiltshire, 3, 21, 76, 132, 161, 197, 251
FONTHILL BISHOP, Wiltshire, 4, 47, 106, 132-3, 139, 144, 189, 211, 256
FONTHILL GIFFORD, Wiltshire, 6, 7, 47, 59, 70, 105-6, 123, 132-3, 135, 139, 143-5, 167, 178-80, 192, 198, 242, 247-8
FONTHILL, VDL, 232, 234-6
FORD, Job, 181
FORD, John, 9, 65, 136, 181
FORT, George, 43
FORT, George Yalden, 43

FOSSEY, Joseph, 155
FOWLE, William, 58
FOYLE, James, 97
FRANCE, 108, 114, 119, 131, 150, 226, 249, 250
FRANKLAND, George, 190
FRANKLIN, Sir John, 234
FROME, Somerset, 68

GAST, John, 122
GEORGE I, II, III, IV, King, 249
GEORGETOWN, VDL, 192
GERMANY, 250
GIBRALTAR, 80, 117
GILBERT, William, 247
GILMAN, Louisa, 183
GILMAN, William, 183
GILMORE, John, 28
GLENORCHY, VDL, 166
GLOUCESTERSHIRE, 77, 257
GLOVER, John, 154, 161, 170
GODWIN, William, 113
GOLDIE, Alexander, 155
GOOD, Mr, Dissenting Minister, 73
GOODWOOD, Sussex, 39
GORDON, Robert, MP, 58, 127
GORDON family, 100
GOSPORT, Hampshire, 83, 88
GRAY, John, 66, 214
GRAY, William, 52
GREAT BEDWYN, Wiltshire., 41
GREECE, 114
GREELY, Rev., 73
GREEN, James, 61, 97
GREGG, Peter, 237
GREY, Earl, PM, 3, 39, 76, 99, 160, 256
GREY, John, 136
GRIFFITHS, John, 219
GROSVENOR, Richard, Earl of, 2nd Marquis of Westminster, 103, 136-7
GROVE family, Charlotte, 101, 106, Harriet, 101
GROVE, Thomas, F, 44, 100-1, 106, 127
GROVE, Thomas junior, 58, 102
GROVES, Captain John, 146, 160
GUILDFORD, Surrey, 4
GUNN, William, 177-82

HACKER, John, 247
HALLEN, Ambrose, 203
HAMBURG, Germany, 190
HAMILTON, VDL, 209
HAMMETT, James, 258
HAMPSHIRE, 70, 75-6, 80, 82, 84, 123, 158, 199, 231, 257

HANNINGTON, Mrs, Black Horse Inn, 104
HARBIN, Rev., 243
HARDING, John, 46, 49, 50, 123
HARVEY, James J, and Keith, 238
HAWKINS, Lt., 184
HAYTER, George, 254
HEATH, Henry, 37
HEDLEY, Ralph, 32
HELLYER, Henry, 155
HELYER family, 127
HERBERT, Daniel, 163
HEREFORDSHIRE, 77
HEYTESBURY, Wiltshire, 43, 50
HIGH WYCOMBE, 117
HIGHWORTH, Wiltshire, 43
HILL, Rev., John, 254
HINDON, Wiltshire, 3, 42, 44-5, 47, 50, 76, 80, 97, 116, 123-4, 131, 134, 185, 243, 246, 248
HOBART, VDL, 93, 96, 146, 147, 148, 151, 152, 153, 155, 158, 160, 163, 165, 172, 177, 178, 178, 185, 188, 192, 208, 209, 219, 226
HONE, William, 111, 112, 113, 144
HORNE, Benjamin, 190
HORTLE, James, 182
HOWICK, Viscount, 160, 172
HOXNE, Suffolk, 36
HUDSON, W H, 44
HUME, John, 124
HUNT, George, 96
HUNT, Henry, MP, 2, 8, 27, 39, 93, 99, 100, 112, 117-125, 129, 130, 133, 134, 137, 246
HUON, VDL, 237
HUSSEY, Charles, 58
HUTTON PARK, Jericho, VDL, 188
HYDE PARK CONVICT BARRACKS, Sydney, Australia, 201, 203, 206

IDMISTON, Wiltshire, 41
ILCHESTER GAOL, 120, 122
INDIA, 216
INGRAM, Ann (Topp), 189
IRELAND, 114, 148
ITALY, 250

JAY, James, 59, 60, 96
JAY, John, 60, 64, 96, 199, 208
JAY, Thomas, 60, 65, 97
JEFFREY, William, 63, 66, 73, 199
JENNINGS, John, 43
JERRARD family, Joshua, Eliza, William, Emma, Samuel, Ellen, Thom, Henry,

204, 205, 242, 243, 244
JERRARD, Ann, 204, 205, 206, 244
JERRARD, Charles senior, 143, 198, 204, 205, 244
JERRARD, Charles junior, 52, 60, 61, 73, 143, 198, 199, 200, 202, 206, 213, 215, 250
JERRARD, Robert (Jerrett), 245
JERRARD, William, 204, 243
JOLIFFE, Rev., 28
JORDAN, River, VDL, 216
JUKES, Francis, 56
JUKES, John, 9
JUKES, Thomas, 207,

KEMP, Anthony Fenn, 226, 227
KEMP, Emily, 226, 227
KEMPS LAKES, VDL, 228
KEMPTON, VDL, 228
KENT, 1, 2, 33, 75, 76, 80
KING, Augustine, 63
KING, Henry, Thomas, George, and David, 181
KING, Henry, 4, 67, 124, 131, 132, 144
KING, Lord, 256
KING, Philip, Gov., Gen., Australia, 147
KINGSCLERE, Hampshire, 126, 127
KINGSTON-UPON-THAMES, Surrey, 4
KINGSTON, West Stour, Dorset, 126
KITSON, Rev., 56
KNELLER family, 100, 127

LAMB, George, 124
LAMBERT, Henry, 192
LAMBERT, James, 63
LAMBERT, William, 66
LAMPARD, James, 8, 9, 191
LANCASHIRE, 77, 120, 159
LANE, Joseph, 198
LANSDOWNE, Marquis of, 127, 135
LAUNCESTON, VDL, 151, 160, 163, 166, 172, 173, 179, 190, 191, 192, 240
LEGGE, Arthur, 60
LEICESTER, 113
LEWES, Emma (Tabart), 232
LEWIN, Lt., 146
LEWIS, Joseph, 166
LIEGERS, George, 218
LINCOLNSHIRE, 113
LITTLE SWAN PORT, 184, 195
LIVERPOOL, 113
LLOYD, George Thomas, 173
LOGAN, Thomas, 158
LONDON, 3, 25, 107, 112, 113, 119, 122, 137, 184, 211

LONG-WELLESLEY, William, MP, 130
LONGFORD, VDL, 183, 192, 244
LONGLEAT, Wiltshire, 77
LONGLEY ARMS, VDL, 237
LORD, Edward, 172
LORYMER, Clement, 155
LOVELESS, George, 206, 257, 258
LOVELESS, James, 258
LOVETT, Charles, 178
LOVETT, Henry, 247
LUCAS, Sam, 196
LUDLOW, W H, 58
LUSH, James, 70, 71, 72, 73, 74, 83
LYMINGE, Kent, 38
LYNDHURST, Hampshire, 89

MACEY, Charlotte, 178, 179, 180, 242, 245
MACEY family, Henry, 179, 180, James, 247, 255, John, 180, Nicolas, 247, William, 245,
MACEY, Samuel, see Banstone
MACKRELL, Sgt., 105
McNAMARA, Francis, 226
MACQUARIE, Lachlan, Gov., NSW, Australia, 152
MACQUARIE PLAINS, VDL, 209
MAIR, Lt., Col., John Hastings, 48, 55, 80, 105, 114-117, 142, 215, 252
MALAHIDE, VDL, 237, 239, 240
MALAHIDE, Fingal, Ireland, 238
MALMESBURY, Wiltshire, 104
MANCHESTER, 112, 120, 121
MARLBOROUGH, Wiltshire, 43, 104, 116
MARSH, James, 73
MARTIN, Charles, 53, 66, 67, 186, 207, 208, 211, 243
MARTIN, Elizabeth, 166, 184, 186, 207, 208, 211, 213, 242, 243
MARTIN, James, 243
MASON, Joseph, 28, 51, 200
MASON, Robert, 28, 51, 200
MATCHAM, George, 58
MEIKLE, Andrew, 20
MELBOURNE, William Lamb, 2nd Viscount, 51, 76, 77, 78, 80, 93, 106, 114, 116, 256, 258, MELBOURNE, Australia, 189
MELKSHAM, Wiltshire, 104
MEREDITH, George, 172
METHUEN, Paul, MP, 58,130
MICHELDEVER, Hampshire, 28, 39
MIDDLE WALLOP, Hampshire, 133
MILDENHALL, Suffolk, 36
MILES, Philip, 136
MONKLAND, George, 58

MONTESQUIEU, 18
MOORE, Captain, 146
MORRISON, James, 106, 133
MORTIMER, George, 54, 103, 234, 236
MOULD, George, 53, 70
MOULD, James (Hatch), 59, 60, 63, 73, 105, 177, 180, 181, 199, 242
MOULD, James (Tisbury), 52, 59, 60, 64, 65, 66, 73, 105, 182, 196, 197, 199, 242
MOULD, Kathy, 197
MOULD family, Eliza, 180, 242, 243, Elizabeth, 180
MOULD, William, 197
MOUNT VERNON, VDL, 228
MOXHAM, Andrew, 9, 52, 59, 61, 62, 63, 70, 74, 244
MOXHAM, Eliza, 212
MOXHAM, Elizabeth (Mould), 197
MOXHAM, Morgan, 212
MULLINS, Eliza (Mould), 197
MULLINS, Thomas, 187,

NASH, William, 64
NEIL, Samuel, 249
NETHERAVON, Wiltshire, 1, 39, 41, 96
NEW BRUNSWICK, Canada, 107
NEW NORFOLK, VDL, 211, 212
NEW SOUTH WALES, Australia, 150, 154, 172, 212, 226, 258
NEWCASTLE, 4th Duke of, 54
NEWCASTLE-on-TYNE, 83
NEWGATE GAOL, 108
NEWTON TONEY, Wiltshire, 41
NORFOLK, 76, 77, 80, 256
NORFOLK, VDL, 160
NORFOLK ISLAND, 88., 89
NORTH, Lord, 88,
NORTHUMBERLAND, 259
NORTON BAVANT, Wiltshire, 126, 127, 135, 137
NOTTINGHAMSHIRE, 77

OATLANDS, VDL, 166, 216, 217, 219
OBOURNE, Harriet (Martin), 245
OBOURNE, Henry, (Osbourne), 53, 69, 70, 74
OBOURNE, James, 244
OBOURNE, Robert, 66, 67, 74, 207, 211, 245
ODSTOCK, Salisbury, Wiltshire, 1
OLD BEACH, VDL, 180
OLDHAM, Lancashire, 108
OSMOND, Edwin, 237
OSMOND, Emily (Tabor), 237
OVERTON, Hampshire, 26, 28, 39, 122

OWEN, Robert, 257
OWLPEN MANOR, Glos., 236
OXFORDSHIRE, 257
OYSTER BAY, VDL, 172, 184

PAINE, James, 103
PAINE, Thomas, 111
PALMER, Samuel, 33
PANTON ESTATE, London, 103
PARHAM, Mary, 237
PARHAM PARK, Sussex, 125
PARKE, Mr Justice, J., 51, 56, 57, 58, 69, 82, 102
PARKER, Rev., R., 104
PARSONS, Mr, 165
PARSONS family, Sandy Bay, Tasmania, 212
PATTERSON, Lt., Col., 182, 227
PEARCE, Mr., VDL, Co., 160
PEDDER, Chief Justice, VDL, 171, 173
PEEL, Sir Robert, 256
PEMBROKE, Earl of, 127, 130
PENISTON, John, 42, 101, 104, 115, 133
PENNY, John, 66, 74
PENRUDDOCKE, J H, 44
PETERLOO MASSACRE, 111, 120, 125
PEWSEY, Wiltshire, 134
PHILLIP, Captain Arthur, 89
PHILLIPS, Thomas, 9
PIGGOTT, Thomas, 96
PITMAN family, Thomas, Richard, 191
PITMAN, Mary, 190, 191
PITMAN, Richard, 49, 52, 59, 61, 62, 64, 65, 73, 190, 199
PITT, William, MP, 88
PLACE, Francis, 118
PLYMOUTH, 88, 153
PORT ARTHUR, VDL, 154
PORT DALRYMPLE, VDL, 182
PORT JACKSON, NSW, 200, 227
PORT PHILIP, Australia, 148, 189
PORTSMOUTH, Hampshire, 73, 74, 83, 86, 87, 88, 89, 93, 158, 199, 258
PORTUGAL, 114
POTTER, William, 227
POWELL, Alex, 58
PRESTON, Lancashire, 122
PREVOST, Rev., Thomas, 128, 131, 132
PRIEST, William, 217
PROTEUS, 158, 161, 170, 175
PUDDLETOWN, Dorset, 80
PYTHOUSE, 10, 21, 100, 101, 105, 115, 123, 126-138, 144, 208, 245, 260
PYTHOUSE FARM, 8, 9, 45

QUIDHAMPTON, Wiltshire, 64

RADNOR, Lord, 43, 57, 106, 127, 255
RAMSBURY, Wiltshire, 41, 256
RATCLIFFE, Eric, 233
RAWLINGS family, 242
READING, Berkshire, 83
REBBECK, Richard, 198
RIDGE, 4
RINGWOOD, Hampshire, 139
RIO DE JANIERO, 93
RIXON family, Anna, Marie, Elizabeth, William, James, 195, 195, 196, 242, 243, 245
RIXON, (Rixen), Thomas, 52, 59, 61, 63, 73, 105, 194, 199, 213, 242, 245
ROBERTS, Mary (Abree), 165, 166
ROBINSON, Mr, Derwent River, VDL, 154
ROCKBOURNE, Hampshire, 104
ROCKLEY, Hampshire, 70, 83
ROMSEY, Hampshire, 83
ROSS, VDL, 240
ROSS BRIDGE, VDL, 163, 164, 170,
ROUSSEAU, JJ, 18
RUMBOLD, Henry, 43,

ST MARY BOURNE, Hampshire, 39
SALISBURY, Marquis of, 99
SALISBURY, Wiltshire, 1,3, 6, 39, 41, 44, 47, 51, 69-70, 72-3, 80, 82-3, 85-6, 114-15, 128, 130-1, 139, 144, 189, 191, 215, 251
SANGER, James, 181
SANGER, William, 52, 99
SCOTT, William, 4, 52, 66, 74, 245
SCROPE, George, P, 58
SEABRIGHT, Sir Thomas, 216
SELF (Selfe), Henry, 4, 66, 67, 69, 144, 189, 191, 192
SELYAR family, 100
SHAFTESBURY, 68, 83
SHEERNESS, 88
SHERGOLD family, 200,
SHERRINGTON, Wiltshire, 135
SHOOTER'S HILL, New Norfolk, VDL, 209
SINGAPORE, 160
SMITH, George, 200
SMITH, Mary (White), 217
SNOOK, Charles, and Anna, 184, 187,
SNOOK, Henry and Lavinia, 182, 183, 184, 243
SNOOK, John, 245
SNOOK, William, 6, 9, 49, 52, 59, 60, 62, 63, 73, 182, 183, 184
SNOOK family in VDL, William, James & Thomas, 183, Lavinia, 184, William, 184, 244

SNOOK, William junior, Mary, Maria, and Martha, 242
SNOW, James, 9, 61, 66, 208
SNOW, Mrs., 165
SOMERSET, 80, 99, 257
SORRELL, Julia, 228
SORRELL, William, Lt., Gov., VDL, 152, 153, 155, 179, 228
SOUTH AFRICA, 93
SOUTH LITCHFIELD, 126, 127
SPAIN, 93
SPEENHAMLAND, Newbury, Berkshire, 25, 109
SPODE, Josiah, 159, 160, 208, 209, 210
SPODE family, in Stoke on Trent, 208
STANFIELD, John, 258
STANFIELD, Thomas, 258
STAPLEFORD, Wiltshire, 64
STEED, Mr, 68
STEPHENSON, John, 199, 200
STEVENS, Ann, 163
STEVENS, Charles, 244
STEVENS, Sara, 210
STINGEMAN (Stingiman, Stingimore), Thomas, 53
STOUTS HILL, Glos., 234, 236
STUART, Lt., 4th Regt., 199
SUFFOLK, 1, 256, 259
SURREY and HAMPSHIRE HILLS, VDL, 155
SUSSEX, 1, 80
SUTTON SCOTNEY, Hampshire, 27, 39
SUTTON VENY, Wiltshire, 126
SWALLOWCLIFFE, Wiltshire, 198
SWIFT, Jonathan, 107
SWINDON, 104
SWING, Captain, 80
SWING RIOTS /, RIOTERS, 109, 111, 122, 123, 157, 160, 174, 199, 200, 201, 202, 212, 213, 220, 241, 256, 259, 2360
SWITZERLAND, 148, 220, 250,
SYDNEY, Australia, 152, 160, 201, 212
SYDNEY, Lord, 88

TABART, Francis Gerard, 231, 233, 234, 235, 236
TABOR, Aaron, 236, 237
TABOR, Emily Alice (Osmond), 237
TABOR, John, 237, 245
TABOR, William, 236
TALBOT family, 238, 239
TALBOT, Margaret, 238
TALBOT, Milo, Lord Talbot, 239, 240
TALBOT, Richard, 240
TALBOT, Richard de, 238

TALBOT, Richard Gilbert, 240
TALBOT, Rose, 239, 240
TALBOT, Samuel, 240
TALLENTS, William Edward, 54, 55, 116
TARGETT family, 244
TARGETT, James, 5, 9, 62
TARGETT, John, 59, 61, 66, 67, 69, 74, 244
TARGETT, Thomas, 53
TASKERS, Andover, Hampshire, 36, 39, 123
TASMAN, Abel, 147
TASMANIA, 164, 209, 220, 228
TASMANIAN ANCESTRY SOCIETY, 212
TAUNTON, Somerset, 123
TEFFONT MAGNA, Wiltshire, 48
TENTERDEN, Chief Justice, 110
THELWALL, John, 27
THOMPSON, E P, 121
THOMPSON, William, 218
THORPE MILL, VDL, 186
TISBURY, Wiltshire, 3, 4, 6, 7, 21, 48, 67, 68, 70, 86, 89, 92, 96, 99, 101, 102, 105, 106, 109, 115, 123, 131, 132, 134, 136, 137, 139, 142, 143, 161, 167, 182, 211, 212, 230, 243, 245, 246, 247, 251, 255

TISBURY AREA
  Beckford Arms, 234, 236, 237, 245
  Berwick St Leonard, 127
  Boot inn, 255
  Browns Lane, 198
  Chicklade, 126
  Church Street, 6, 9, 244, 247, 254
  Cuffs Lane, 212
  Donheads (St Mary and St Andrew), 102
  Duck Street, 191, 194
  Fonthill Abbey, 135, 136, 161, 233, 234, 236
  Fonthill Estate, 236,
  Fonthill Gifford Farm, 97
  Fonthill Splendens, 133
  Hatch, 46, 50, 101, 135, 139, 185, 197
  Hatch Farm, 61, 181
  Hibberds, High Street, 244
  High Street, 186
  Hook Manor, Donhead, 238
  Jobbers Lane, 206
  Knapp, 244
  Lawn Farm, 8, 9, 70, 191
  Lawn Lodge, 235, 236
  Linley Farms, 45, 63, 64, l96, 127, 131, 133, 191, 214
  Newtown, 8, 47, 137, 236
  Pythouse Farm, 8, 9, 60, 61, 65, 71, 105, 199
  Quarry, The, 186, 205, 245
  Ridge, 4, 137
  Semley, 102, 126, 127, 134, 255
  Tisbury Lodge, 236
  Tisbury Row, 185, 186, 198, 206
  Tisbury Union Workhouse, 190, 247, 254, 255
  Totterdale, 198
  Totterdale Cross, 198, 205, 244
  Vicarage Road, 244
  Wardour, 100, 101, 102, 105, 115, 139
  Wardour, Banqueting House, 234, 236
  Wardour Castle, 233, 234
  West Tisbury, 255
  Withyslade Farm, 6, 139
  Zion Hill Independent Church, 244

TOPP, Mary, 243
TOPP, Thomas, 59, 60, 61, 66, 67, 69, 70, 73, 188, 189, 190, 199, 243
TOWNSEND, 'Turnip', 15
TRIM, Joseph, 61, 96, 208
TRIMBY, James, 190, 243
TROBDIGE, John, 181
TULL, Jethro, 15, 31
TURNER, Alexander, 181
TURNER, Ellen, 194
TURNER, George, 61
TURNER, Henry, 181
TURNER, Thomas, 181
TURNER, William, 6, 9, 53, 60, 96, 243, 245,

ULEY, Glos., 231
UPAVON, Wiltshire, 118
UPHILL, John, 60, 97, 105, 162, 191, 208,
UPTHORPE, Berkshire, 186
USA, 108,

VAN DIEMEN'S LAND, 85, 92, 111, 117, 124, 135, 146, 147, 148, 149, 150, 153, 156, 160, 167, 169, 171, 176, 181, 192, 199, 206, 208, 217, 221, 225, 227, 237, 258
VAUGHAN, Baron, 51, 56, 57, 63, 39, 72
VERNHAM DEAN, Hampshire, 39
VICTORIA, Queen, 249
VICTORIA, Australia, 212
VINCENT, Jonathan, 53
VINEN (Viney, Vining), family, 207, William, Sarah (Singleton), 207, James, Elizabeth, 204, Harriet (Obourne), 245, Elizabeth (Martin), Mary Vinen, Joseph, Isaac, Thomas, Henry, Jean, (Moxham), 207, 211, 212, 241
VINEN (Viney, Vining), Henry, 53

VINEN (Vining), Thomas, 9, 52, 59, 60, 61, 62, 73, 166, 184, 186, 199, 207, 208, 210, 211, 212, 213, 237, 244
VINEY, James, 243
VOLTAIRE, 18

WALES, 220
WALLACE, Hamilton, 171,
WALPOLE, Sir Robert, 18
WARDOUR CASTLE INN, Oatlands, VDL, 217, 218, 228
WAREHAM, Dorset, 80
WARMINSTER, 50, 80, 104, 114, 123, 126, 130
WARREN, Dr, 257
WARRENER, E, 58
WARWICKSHIRE, 76
WATSON, Mary(, Topp), 189
WEBB, Richard, 251
WELLINGTON, Duke of, PM, 2, 3, 39, 76, 130
WELLS, Roger, 250
WENTWORTH, Captain D'arcy, 165
WEST, Uriah, 70
WEST AFRICA, 89, 93
WEST DEAN, Wiltshire, 1, 41
WEST GRIMSTEAD, Wiltshire, 66
WEST INDIES, 87, 100
WEST LAVINGTON, Wiltshire, 256
WESTMINSTER, 97
WESTMINSTER, Marquis of, 236
WESTMORLAND, 259
WEYHILL, Hampshire, 39
WHITCHURCH, Hampshire, 83
WHITE, Edmund, 59, 61, 63, 64, 65, 66, 73, 97, 105, 199, 213, 214, 215, 216, 217, 219, 222, 228, 244
WHITE HORSE INN, Lake Tiberias, VDL, 217
WHITE, Mary (Smith), 218

WHITE, John, 213, 244,
WHITEFOORDE, Mr, 219
WHITEPARISH, Wiltshire, 1, 41, 251
WILDE, Mr Serjeant, 51, 56, 59, 64, 67
WILKINS, Charles, 65, 96, 192
WILKINS, John, 9, 61, 63, 97, 207
WILLIAM IV, King, 249
WILLIAMS, Mr., 66, 67
WILLIAMS, John, 66
WILLIAMSON, William, 171, 172
WILTON, Wiltshire, 1, 3, 43, 64, 86, 96, 139
WILTSHIRE, 1, 70, 75, 76, 77, 80, 82, 83, 84, 92, 93, 99, 119, 122, 123, 131, 147, 158, 190, 199, 225, 231, 246, 256, 257, 259
WILTSHIRE YEOMANRY CAVALRY, 6, 10, 248
WINCHESTER, 83, 84
WINKWORTH, William, 51
WINTERSLOW, Wiltshire, 41
WITHERS, Peter, 70, 71, 72, 73, 74, 83
WOLLSTONECRAFT, Mary, 113
WOODS, Thomas, 181
WOODS, William, 9, 61, 65, 96, 181, 191
WOOLLOOMOOLO, Sydney, NSW, 2023, 204
WOOLWICH, London, 88
WORTHING, Sussex, 39
WROUGHTON, G W, 58
WROUGHTON, Wiltshire, 256
WYNDHAM, Charles, 58
WYNDHAM, Charlotte, 215
WYNDHAM, George, 215
WYNDHAM, Wadham, 58
WYNDHAM, Captain William, 42, 45, 46, 48, 49, 104
WYNDHAM, William, 42, 44, 58

YAPTON, 39, 75
YORKSHIRE, 77, 120
YOUNG, George, 53

Milton Keynes UK
Ingram Content Group UK Ltd.
UKHW020157241023
431186UK00003B/18